Supporting
Young Learners

A collection of articles from Extensions,
the newsletter of the High/Scope Curriculum.

Edited by
Nancy Altman Brickman and Lynn Spencer Taylor

Supporting
Young Learners...

Ideas for
Preschool and Day Care Providers

High/Scope® Press
Ypsilanti, Michigan

Published by

HIGH/SCOPE® PRESS
A division of the
High/Scope Educational Research Foundation
600 North River Street
Ypsilanti, Michigan 48198

313/485-2000, FAX 313/485-0704

Cover and text design: Linda Eckel

Photography: Gregory Fox

Library of Congress Catalog-in-Publication Data Number:
91-21317

ISBN 0-929816-34-X

Printed in the United States of America

10 9 8 7 6 5 4 3 2

C·O·N·T·E·N·T·S

v

Chapter Three: The Daily Routine   113

Chapter Four: Environments for Active Learning   149

P·R·E·F·A·C·E

The articles presented here originally appeared in *Extensions: The Newsletter of the High/Scope Curriculum*, a bi-monthly publication of the High/Scope Press. This collection spans the period from the inception of the newsletter in fall 1986 through spring 1991. *Extensions* is designed to inform staff of early childhood programs—who may be teachers, aides, day care providers, special educators, administrators, trainers, or curriculum specialists—about ideas from the High/Scope Curriculum for preschool and kindergarten. The topics covered include strategies for working with young children, suggestions for designing the physical setting and daily routine to promote learning, ideas for team planning and staff development, and news on curriculum advances. The information presented is intended for those who are familiar with High/Scope's approach as well as those wishing to learn more about it. For more detailed treatment of either curriculum issues or related High/Scope research, readers may wish to consult the High/Scope Press publications and audiovisual productions listed on page 297.

The High/Scope Curriculum, a developmentally based approach to early childhood education, was originally designed in the 1960s by David Weikart and colleagues in the Ypsilanti, Michigan, Public Schools. The development of the curriculum—which Weikart still directs—has continued since 1970 under the auspices of the High/Scope Educational Research Foundation. The "open framework" curriculum model can be adapted to serve many different populations of children in a wide variety of education and care settings. This approach is in use at thousands of programs worldwide, including public and private preschools, Head Start programs, day care centers, home-based programs, and K–3 programs. Training in the model is usually necessary for those who wish to implement it, and High/Scope offers a wide range of training and consulting services both at Foundation headquarters and on-site throughout the U.S. and overseas.

The High/Scope approach is continuously evolving, and one of the primary purposes of the *Extensions* newsletter has been to inform veteran curriculum users about new developments. In editing this collection, we have updated some of the original articles to conform to the curriculum as it stands today. We have made few major content changes, since the basic principles of the High/Scope approach have remained constant over the years, but have made numerous minor changes in the articles. Also, in a few cases, we have consolidated short articles to provide a fuller treatment of curriculum issues.

We would like to thank all those who have contributed over the years to the newsletter and thus to the production of this book. In addition to writing their own articles for *Extensions*, the authors—most of whom are past and present members of High/Scope's Program Department—have made many useful suggestions for improving the overall content of this publication. David Weikart also carefully reviewed and commented on each issue of the newsletter, always finding time for it despite a demanding work and travel schedule. We also extend our appreciation to the "unsung" contributors to this publication—the many participants in High/Scope training workshops and programs. These "front-line" early childhood staff were often the original sources of the practical strategies or cogent examples reported by the authors. Finally, we would like to acknowledge those who helped to produce the newsletter and this book: graphic artists Linda Eckel, Margaret Fitzgerald, and Jane DeLancey (who designed the original newsletter); Diana Knepp, who formatted the book for typesetting; and Marge Senninger, who provided many helpful "third opinions" on editorial issues.

Supporting
Young Learners

C·H·A·P·T·E·R O·N·E

Supporting Active Learning

· ·

Active Learning: Making It Happen in Your Program —
Mark Tompkins

Social Development in the High/Scope Approach —
Mary Hohmann

Be Responsive — Amy Powell

Helping Children Manage Themselves —
Michelle Graves and Ruth Strubank

Dealing With a Difficult Child — Michelle Graves

Multicultural Education: What It Is, How to Do It —
Bonnie Lash Freeman and Marilyn Adams Jacobson

"Special" Children: Building on Their Strengths — Mark Tompkins

The term *curriculum* leads most educators to expect a set of structured and sequenced tasks that provide the basic content for an educational program. Instead of such "packaged" activities, however, the High/Scope Curriculum offers a general *framework* that adults use to develop a specific program well suited to their particular group of children. Although the curriculum's guidelines are concrete and practical, they do not in themselves determine the day-to-day program: the necessary details of materials, scheduling, and daily activities are worked out, individually, by staff of each program. Since program staff take such an active role in planning their High/Scope educational program, it is vitally important that they understand the philosophy behind it. The articles collected in this first chapter discuss some of the guiding principles and assumptions underlying the High/Scope philosophy of early childhood education.

Two themes recur throughout this chapter. The first is the view that learning experiences for young children should be active: that is, such experiences should enable children to construct their own knowledge by working directly with people, materials, and ideas. The second is that the adult's role is not to direct or control this learning process but to *support* it. The opening article by Mark Tompkins offers an "anatomy" of the active learning process, comparing two typical learning activities from early childhood programs on the basis of key "ingredients" of active learning. Subsequent selections by Mary Hohmann, Amy Powell, Michelle Graves, and Ruth Strubank define in more detail what we mean by "adult support." These authors identify some key ways adults can encourage children's learning and problem solving without directing it. They stress a variety of strategies for working with children including the following: careful planning of the environment; sharing control of the learning experience with children; building on children's strengths; following children's interests, intentions, and plans; supporting children's enjoyment of materials and people; and recognizing and promoting developmentally appropriate activities and processes.

The last three selections in the chapter discuss the validity of this general approach for supporting the development of *all* young children. In her article, Michelle Graves discusses how staff of the High/Scope Demonstration Preschool successfully used the curriculum's child management strategies with one particularly difficult child; next, Marilyn Adams Jacobson and Bonnie Lash Freeman discuss multicultural awareness as a key learning goal for all groups of children and describe how adults can use the active learning framework to support multicultural learning. In the last article, Mark Tompkins discusses the effectiveness of a developmental approach for working with children with special needs.

Active Learning: Making It Happen in Your Program

T he following scenarios describe two
small-group experiences that occurred
in typical early childhood programs. Encouraging children's active learning was an important
goal of the adults in both examples. How well
did each activity meet this goal?

by
Mark Tompkins

*Example 1: It is mid-December, and
the children's interest in the winter holidays is
in "high gear." Natalie and the other teacher in
the classroom notice that several children have
used newsprint to wrap presents they made in
the art area. To build on this experience, the
teachers decide to gather additional newsprint,
assorted boxes, ribbon, and extra tape. They
then plan a small-group activity in which children can explore these materials. Natalie begins
her small-group time by holding up and talking
briefly about the objects other children have recently "wrapped" in the art area. She then
shows the group the materials she has collected
and encourages them to use these (and other
materials, if needed, from the art area) to create
presents and/or wrap them.*

*The children are busy instantly: several
children begin to wrap up boxes with paper and
large amounts of yarn; others make "presents"
to put in shoe boxes; others work at decorating
the newsprint wrapping paper with crayons and
markers. Natalie moves around the table interacting with individual children and small
groups of children. She imitates their actions, re-
peats their language, and converses with them
about what they are doing, occasionally asking
questions. By the end of small-group time, each
child has made something unique. Children have
enjoyed the activity so much that the teachers de-*

cide to create a new "wrapping shelf" in the art area with similar materials, so that the children can continue this play during future work times.

...

Example 2: Hilary's small group is making Thanksgiving turkeys. Hilary gives each child a shoebox containing scissors, string, pre-cut black and orange construction paper, a piece of aluminum foil, and some paste. "Now," Hilary begins, "I want each of you to choose something from your box that is black . . . . Good, Clarice, you got the black paper . . . . Good, Timmy . . . . No, Denise, the scissors are not black, they are silver. Put them back and find something black." After each child has removed the black paper, Hilary has them "choose something long and pointy." Once each child has found the scissors, Hilary shows everyone how to cut out feet, where to put the orange paper for feathers, where to draw the beak and eyes, and how to attach a string to hang the turkey up. "Good!" says Hilary, praising the children, "Your turkeys all have eyes, feathers, beaks, and legs."

A fundamental goal of the High/Scope Curriculum is for children to engage in **active learning.** Most early childhood educators would agree that children learn most when they are encouraged to explore, to interact with their peers, to be creative, to follow their interests, and to play. Yet many well-meaning teachers find themselves leading activities, like that in the second example, that fly in the face of this theory. A close look at the **ingredients of active learning** will reveal why the two activities differed greatly in the amount of active learning they encouraged in children.

Children are most engaged by learning activities that they choose themselves.

The Ingredients of Active Learning

Let's consider the two activities to pinpoint the necessary ingredients of active learning. Both Natalie and Hilary hold a common belief that when children are handling and manipulating materials, they are engaging in active learning. But, as shown in the wrapping activity, Natalie believes that children also need to make choices, to have access to a range of stimulating materials, to manipulate them according to their interests, and to work and communicate with peers during their play. Natalie's activity and her style of supporting children's efforts offered children more possibilities for active involvement than did Hilary's activity; Natalie utilized all the ingredients of active learning listed next:

• **Choice**—The child chooses what to do.

• **Materials**—There are abundant materials that children can use in a variety of ways.

• **Manipulation**—The child can manipulate objects freely.

• **Language**—The child describes what he or she is doing.

• **Support**—Adults and peers recognize and encourage the child's problem solving and creativity.

Below we'll discuss each of these ingredients in terms of our two examples. We'll also suggest ways to transform Hilary's activity into a truly active learning experience!

Choice. In the first activity, Natalie gave the children many choices. She based her plans for this small-group activity on children's recent interests and then allowed the children to make and/or wrap things in ways that suited them. She did not show children a model of a desired end product or plan the procedure she wanted children to follow—instead, she encouraged the children to make choices and decisions about what to do and how to do it.

Hilary, on the other hand, gave the children very few choices. She decided what they would make, the materials they would use, and the procedures they would follow. The children followed her instructions. Even within the framework of a defined activity like turkey-making, many more choices were possible: Hilary could have encouraged the children to decide what kind of turkey they would make, what materials they would use, and how they would go about the task.

Materials. The materials used by the children in Natalie's group were plentiful, open-ended, and in some cases chosen by the children as their individual projects progressed. Natalie

During active learning experiences, children talk about what they are doing with adults and their peers. Adults support children by listening and responding to them, not by bombarding them with questions.

did not have a definitive plan for how the children would use the materials.

By contrast, Hilary provided children with identical sets of materials designed for a specific purpose. It would have been better to provide a range of different materials from which the children could make choices. Open-ended materials, which can be used in a variety of ways, promote more learning than materials that are designed for a particular use, such as pre-cut shapes. Hilary could have said, "So, you are going to make a turkey. What can you use to make a turkey?" A child might have answered, "I want to use paper, crayons, and cotton." To which Hilary could have replied, "Okay, where can you get those things? . . . Yes, over on the art area shelf is a good place to look."

Manipulation. In the first activity, the children manipulated the materials in a variety of ways. They were very involved in the activity because they were given freedom to create the things they were interested in. By contrast, though the turkey-making "lesson" was a hands-on activity, Hilary limited what children could learn by telling them exactly what to do. Preschoolers can learn a lot by working with their hands: they discover the properties of materials (*heavy, bouncy, sticky, smooth*); they learn useful skills (*cutting, pasting, folding*); and most important, perhaps, they discover basic concepts and relationships (*rough/smooth, above/below, same/different*). But children can't make these kinds of discoveries unless they are allowed to explore and experiment.

Instead of providing a rigid set of instructions, Hilary could have made comments and asked questions that encouraged children to manipulate materials more actively, for example, "I see you are using pipe cleaners to make feathers, Brendan . . . . How do the feathers feel? . . . What happened when you squeezed them? . . . Can anybody else tell us about their feathers?"

Language. Children's conversation dominated Natalie's small-group time. They talked to one another and to the teacher about what they were doing and how they were doing it and, in some cases, discussed totally unrelated topics.

In the other small-group activity, Hilary did most of the talking. The children said very little and instead had to concentrate on following her instructions. Some of the children found that doing it "right" was too difficult a task, and they became distracted and impatient, while others quickly made their turkeys without saying a word to anyone.

If Hilary had allowed the children to make choices in making their turkeys, they would have had ample reason to communicate, both with her and with the other children. They would have been very much involved in the activity, and she could easily have asked such open-ended questions as "How did you make that? . . . That's one way. Are there any others?" or "What can you tell me about it?" This style of communication encourages children to make considered responses and to choose their own words.

Support. Natalie's goal was to get the children actively involved in the wrapping-paper play. She did this by allowing them many choices and by becoming a partner in their play. She used the materials in some of the same ways they did, she talked with them in the context of their play, and she spent time listening to the children and watching them work. Because children were actively involved in the activity, they engaged in many key experiences—in language, representation, classification, social development, and movement—as they worked with the materials. Natalie did not "teach" these key experiences to the children, but rather, recognized and supported them as they occurred.

Hilary took a very different approach with her group of children. She was not so much supporting children's efforts as she was instructing and testing them. Instead of giving children the freedom to discover things on their own, she told them exactly what to do. But she could have used more "partner language" (e.g., "You're squeezing the glue container, putting the glue on the paper"). This type of feedback gives the child a natural cue to continue talking about what he or she is doing. Hilary could also have repeated what a child had just told her (e.g., "It's a turkey with lots of feathers and long legs?") By repeating the child's statement, Hilary would have

On Active Learning — A Trainer's Perspective:

"It has struck me that it is not just young children in action, but adult trainers in action, like me. I need experience with this curriculum: living with it, doing it, working it out with people. That's action. Although I need to experience more of this work, I am understanding it, and I can use what I know effectively.

"I suppose this sense of 'Yes, I can!' is an important part of growing into, understanding, and putting into practice the High/Scope approach. I still have plenty of unresolved questions: What will the 'I-Can-Problem-Solve' small-group times look like? How can we best involve parents? What about High/Scope on home visits? But I'm confident that with experience, these questions can be answered. They will be worked out *in action*."

—Paul Niemiec, Clinical Supervisor, Westmoreland Human Opportunities Head Start, Greensburg, PA ∎

Even when adults set out particular materials for a group activity, they should encourage children to choose how they will use the materials.

acknowledged what the child had said and shown that she was interested in hearing more. Another support strategy Hilary could have used would have been to encourage children to help each other out. For example, instead of solving children's problems for them, Hilary could have directed one child to another by saying something like "Mary, Timmy would like to know where we keep the brown paper. Can you show him?"

It's clear that active learning is much, much more than children handling materials. It's an approach to early childhood education that allows children to make full use of their emerging skills and abilities. Also, teachers can learn more about each child in an active learning situation; in activities that are totally teacher-directed, all adults learn about children is how well they follow instructions.

Here are a few other benefits of active learning:

• **Giving children choices guarantees their interest.** When children are interested in something, they are more likely to learn new things and to remain involved in the task.

• **Children gain self-confidence.** They discover that they can plan and complete things and that there are no right ways and wrong ways, just problems to be solved.

• **Children develop independence as they become decision makers and problem solvers.** They learn not to rely too much on others to tell them how, when, or why. ■

Social Development in the High/Scope Approach

by
Mary Hohmann

One of the most frequently asked questions about the High/Scope Curriculum is how social development fits within our educational framework. Actually, the goal of supporting social development is a key assumption behind all the recommendations we make to teachers and caregivers; it is an integral part of our educational philosophy.

We believe that our general approach to teaching and learning promotes the development of both social and cognitive abilities. In our approach, social learning, like other kinds of learning, takes place through direct experience—through observation, modeling, trial-and-error, and problem solving—rather than through didactic lectures, drills, or elaborate systems of reward and punishment. In this article, we describe some of the key social and emotional capacities that are strengthened in young children when we approach learning in this way. We also discuss the elements of a program environment that encourage social development.

Our approach to social support is organized around five key capacities identified in child development literature as building blocks of children's social and emotional health. These capacities for **trust, autonomy, initiative, empathy,** and **self-esteem** provide the foundation for much of the social learning that occurs as the child grows to adulthood. These capacities develop in the order presented here; each must be established before the next can take root.

Briefly then, here's how we define and think about these five building blocks of children's personalities.

Learning to trust a new set of people outside the family is an important step forward for the preschooler.

Five Building Blocks of Social Development

Trust. Trust is the confident belief in others that allows a young child to venture forth into action knowing that the people on whom she or he depends will provide needed support and encouragement. Adults working with young children recognize that trust is primary—children must trust first, before they are comfortable exploring and learning.

The development of trust begins at birth as parents and caregivers respond to their infant's needs—feeding, changing, cuddling, playing—making their baby feel secure. By toddlerhood, the child's sense of trust has developed to the point that he or she can explore in the next room out of the adult's sight. But the toddler still

Two-Way Learning

When adults and children share control, both are learners and both are teachers:

Mrs. Rogers spends all evening learning how to operate a computer's joystick so that she can introduce Stickybear Town Builder, *a new computer program, to her group of 3- and 4-year-olds. The next day, with great trepidation, she shows a group of children how to use the joystick to drive a car around the town pictured on the computer screen.*

"Let me do that," says Jason, reaching for the joystick. In a few minutes, he masters the technique that had taken Mrs. Rogers all evening to learn. As she watches Jason deftly manipulating the joystick to get the results he wants on the computer screen, she decides to try to approach the next new computer program with the same eagerness and lack of worry she sees in Jason. ∎

needs to check back often to see that the significant adult is still there. Three- and 4-year-olds, bolstered by trust, can leave home for hours at a time to play with friends or to be involved in a high quality care setting. Learning to trust a new set of people outside the family is an important step forward for this age group. In a supportive environment, young children will extend the range of their trusting relationships, first to new adults, then to their peers.

Autonomy. Autonomy is the capacity for independence and exploration that prompts a child to say things like "I wonder what's around the corner" and "Let me do it." While children need to be strongly attached to their parents or primary caregivers, they also need to develop a sense of themselves as distinctly separate people who can make their own choices and do things for themselves. Saying no indiscriminately is one way toddlers test their emerging sense of autonomy.

By the preschool years, children no longer need to say no constantly to prove their independence. They can do many things without adult help, and should be encouraged to do so, even when the adult could do it better by taking over. When children dress themselves, pour their own juice, or make their own telephone calls to their friends, they are having valuable experiences that enhance their sense of autonomy.

Initiative. Initiative is children's ability to begin and then to follow through on a task—to take stock of a situation and act upon what they understand. Initiative emerges in infancy as children signal and act on their intentions—by pointing to and reaching for a toy they want, for example.

By the preschool years, children's intentions have become much more ambitious ("I'm gonna make a big fort with lots of windows"), but children often need adult assistance to help them think through such intentions and carry them out. Adults can support preschool children's capacity for initiative by encouraging them to imagine and describe their intentions and to solve problems that arise as they pursue their plans.

Empathy. Empathy is the capacity that allows children to understand the feelings of others by relating them to feelings that they themselves have had. Empathy helps children form friendships and a sense of belonging. By the preschool years, children still show more egocentrism than empathy, but adults who observe young children carefully will notice glimmerings of empathy. A preschooler might offer a pat for comfort when a special friend cries, for example. Adults help strengthen this capacity for empathy when they respond to and label children's feelings and when they encourage children to do the same.

Self-esteem. Self-esteem—the belief in one's own ability to contribute positively to other people and situations, a core of inner pride—is an attitude that can sustain children through the difficulties and strife in their lives. Self-esteem develops when trust, autonomy, initiative, and empathy are firmly rooted and when children have opportunities to experience success.

Ironically, many potentially negative experiences are the best opportunities to build self-esteem, if adults have the patience to look at the experience from the child's point of view and to encourage problem solving. For example, consider the 4-year-old who has new "basketball shoes" and is so enthusiastic about "shooting baskets" that he doesn't come in when it starts to rain. Then he slips and falls on the wet pavement. Instead of responding with a punitive lecture, the adult might calmly suggest that the child check the pavement for wetness and try

Reciprocity

In an environment where control is shared, there is reciprocity—give and take—between children and adults:

An infant lies on her back looking up at her mother and making clicking noises with her tongue. When she stops, the mother answers by making clicking noises with her tongue. Now it's the baby's turn again. The dialogue continues until the baby turns away, focusing her attention on a little green rattle she can just reach with her hand.

...

Manuel, a toddler, wants to help with a grown-up task—carrying water to the water table. "Me do it," he says, tugging at the full water bucket his teacher is carrying. She puts the bucket down but it's too heavy for Manuel to budge. His eyes fill with tears.

"Manuel," the teacher says, "what about the wagon? You can pull the bucket in the wagon."

Manuel's face brightens. He gets the wagon, they lift the bucket in, and Manuel pulls it to the water table. Together they empty the bucket. "Again," he says, heading back to the sink with his wagon and the bucket. ∎

again when it is dry. By pointing out ways children can solve their own problems, adults lay the groundwork for experiences that build a feeling of competence.

Who's in Control? — Contrasting Environments for Children

Children develop the capacities for trust, autonomy, initiative, empathy, and self-esteem in supportive environments. The qualities of a supportive environment are better understood when seen in contrast with two other popular approaches to teaching and learning that we would characterize as **laissez-faire** and **directive.** Many early childhood environments are characterized by one of these two approaches or by a mixture of the two.

A **laissez-faire environment** is largely controlled by the children themselves. In these settings, adults purposely leave children on their own to interact with one another and the materials provided, intervening only upon request, for informational purposes, and to restore order. This approach works well for some strong, independent children who take a leadership role with their peers and who are able to commandeer adult help when they need it. Because of the lack of structure and adult involvement in this kind of setting, however, some children can get very frustrated. They often have difficulty finding something to do; they may give up or fall apart in the face of problems; or they may feel anxious, confused, or out of control.

In contrast to the freedom children have in **laissez-faire** environments, a **directive** environment is created when adults take control. Adults talk; children listen and follow directions. Ideally, children remain still, quiet, and attentive while adults show and tell them what they need to know according to a set of skill-based objectives. Then children drill and practice until they know the facts well enough to pass a test or score well on an assessment instrument. Children who do not conform to demands for stillness and silence are publicly shamed and removed from the class.

This approach works well for those children who are good at sitting still and following directions. They experience the sense of success that comes from meeting adult expectations. But the range of acceptable behaviors in such an environment is so narrow that most young children will require large doses of criticism, shaming, and punishment to keep them on track.

In contrast to these two popular approaches to child care and education, a **supportive** approach is characterized by **sharing of control** between children and adults. When control is shared, there is a balance between freedom and structure. Adults create an orderly setting and daily routine, within which children can take initiative and follow through on their own interests. In a supportive environment, children and adults alike are initiators. While some activities, such as group times, are often set in motion by adults, the children participating in the activities also make their own decisions about what materials to use, how to use them, and how to extend the activity. Throughout the day, even during routine activities like eating, sleeping, and toileting, adults plan ways to share control with children.

In their interactions with children, adults in a supportive setting do not take a "leave them on their own" approach. Instead, they are consistently present. They are genuinely interested in and committed to watching, listening to, and conversing with children; they encourage them and assist them as they solve problems that arise throughout the day. When difficulties and conflicts arise because of children's immaturity, adults withhold judgement, instead modeling and engaging children in social problem-solving.

We've outlined three common approaches to interacting with children that can be observed in early childhood settings. It is also important to

. . . .

Contrasting Environments for Children

Laissez-Faire Environment

Children are in control most of the time. Adults are bystanders who provide supervision.

• Adults intervene only to respond to requests, offer information, restore order.

• Curriculum content comes from materials and peers.

• Play is the primary activity.

• Various approaches to child management are used.

Advantages: This approach offers plenty of freedom for children and respects their need for play as a primary activity. It mirrors the conditions of adult life, therefore preparing children to cope with the "real world" and develop survival skills. This approach often works well for strong and independent children.

Disadvantages: Some children are confused, anxious, and out of control. Because there are few limits, children can become very disruptive when they don't know what to do or when they encounter a problem. Some children have difficulty finding something to do or someone to play with. Children may give up or fall apart in the face of problems.

Directive Environment

• Adults are in control.

• Adults talk and give directions.

• Curriculum content comes from adult objectives.

• Drill/practice/testing are primary activities; play is not valued or is used as a reward *after* adult-directed tasks are completed.

• Criticism, punishment, and shaming are the predominant strategies for child management.

Advantages: This kind of approach is initially easy for adults to implement because curriculum content is based on clear-cut adult objectives, and the teaching style resembles the educational experiences of most adults. Directive environments often foster a sense of competence in those children who are good at meeting adult expectations.

Disadvantages: Most of the behaviors that are most natural to young children are not acceptable in this environment, thus creating a need for heavy doses of punishment, criticism, and shaming to enforce adult expectations. These are negative experiences that will not enhance most children's capabilities for trust, autonomy, initiative, empathy, and self-esteem.*

Supportive Environment

• Children and adults share control.

• Adults observe children closely, focus on strengths, provide consistent support for children's activities.

• Content comes from materials, children's initiatives, and dialogue with peers and adults.

• Purposeful play and problem solving are the primary activities.

• Adults take a problem-solving approach to child management.

Advantages: This approach offers a consistent, balanced environment in which children's personal initiative, strengths, and interests are valued and in which children are supported as they learn how to communicate with and get along with others. These experiences support the development of children's capacities for trust, autonomy, initiative, empathy, and self-esteem.

Disadvantages: The supportive approach is difficult to implement, especially at first. Special training, administrative support, and a cohesive team effort are usually needed for successful implementation. ■

*High/Scope research comparing the long-term effects of three curriculum models supports the view that the directive approach is not as supportive of social development as those curriculum approaches in which children have a greater degree of control over their learning activities. In High/Scope's longitudinal Curriculum Comparison Study, teenagers who attended a direct instruction program as preschoolers fared less well on measures of delinquency and other indicators of social competence than youths who attended two other programs that encouraged children to initiate many of their own activities. (For more information, see page 116, "Research Results: Long-Term Impact of Child-Initiated Learning.")

note here that while many programs primarily use either a laissez-faire or directive approach, it is also common for settings to shift between these approaches at different points in their daily routines. In many programs for example, so-called "free play" times—in which adults are relatively uninvolved in children's play except when they intervene to resolve disputes or help with special problems—are juxtaposed with highly structured "group times" in which adults teach children academic or preacademic skills in a highly directive way (see "Shifting Environments for Children" on page 23). Note, too, that within any early childhood setting, regardless of the stated approach to adult-child interaction, there are usually adults whose prevailing style of working with children is more or less laissez-faire, supportive, or directive.

Building on Children's Strengths

Greg's teachers have noticed that he plays constantly with trucks, so much so that they're tempted to divert him to another activity. Observing carefully, however, they discover that his truck play is increasingly complex and challenging. Greg enjoys mimicking a wide range of truck sounds, including the sounds of the engine as the truck goes up a steep hill, and the sounds of the five gears shifting. To capitalize on Greg's strong interest in sounds, the teachers decide to add some simple musical instruments to their day care center. Greg immediately starts making up his own songs on the xylophone, often about trucks and "long hauls." ▪

We believe that a supportive environment, in which adults and children **share control**, is the best setting for fostering children's basic capacities for trust, autonomy, initiative, empathy, and self-esteem. Next, we describe some specific ways adults can provide the consistent support children need to thrive in such an environment.

Key Ways to Support Children

Above, we discussed **shared control** as the overriding element of environments that foster children's social development. **Consistent adult support** of children's activities is an another key element of such environments. Let's look at some strategies adults can use to provide this type of support.

Focusing on strengths through child observation is often the starting point for efforts to support children. Children, like adults, exhibit both negative and positive behaviors, but it is important to attend to, concentrate on, and value what children do well. When adults observe carefully to see what children *can* do, they can capitalize on children's natural desire to learn about things that particularly interest them. In the example of Greg in the side column, adults help him extend the range of his learning by focusing on his strong interest in trucks and his facility for imitating sounds. By contrast, when adults focus on what they see as children's weak areas, children often feel defensive and shrink from trying new things.

The example of Greg also underlines another key principle for adult support: **a commitment to play.** Play—with things, people, language, and ideas—is the way normally developing children interact with the world. Adults value, appreciate, and encourage children's play because play is what engages children, and it is only when children are engaged that they will learn.

In addition to providing play materials for Greg that relate to his interests, the adults also showed their support for his play by engaging in truck-related play alongside him, and sometimes, by joining in his play.

Creating honest relationships between children and adults is another key principle of providing support to children. Supportive adults relate to children in a direct, matter-of-fact way. They share their **genuine interest** in what children are saying and doing, and conduct

. . . .

Shifting Environments for Children

In many early childhood centers the locus of control shifts back and forth between adults and children. In these centers, a **laissez-faire approach** is used at some parts of the daily routine and a highly **directive approach** is used at others. At still other times, **shared control** may be the prevailing approach. For example, here's a summary of the morning's activities at the Tall Timbers Center. Look at each activity to see whether it is primarily controlled by adults, children, or adults and children together.

The day begins with greeting time. The children cluster around Miss Beale and Miss Lee, eagerly sharing their tales about what they did at home, special outings, surprising occurrences, their pets, their siblings, and so forth. The teachers announce the special events for the day.

Next it's time for "free play." The children play with the materials and with one another while Miss Beale and Miss Lee work at record keeping and prepare for the daily lesson. They take turns reminding the children to use their indoor voices and walking feet, and they inter-

vene to restrain Max and Billy from kicking, biting, and throwing blocks.

At one point, Miss Beale summons five children over to a small table for the letter lesson of the day. Since she really values this as her true teaching time with the children, she runs this session like a "real" school. She expects children to watch and listen as she explains and demonstrates how to print the letter G. Next she passes out worksheets and pencils so that they can practice filling the whole page with G's. When Miss Beale is done with her lesson, she supervises the whole group at free play, while Miss Lee conducts a lesson on colors for five of the younger children.

Outside play is the last activity of the morning. While most of the children play outside, Miss Lee gets the children's lunches out, assisted by two children who are the "lunch helpers" for the day. The children pour milk while Miss Lee arranges the chairs and lunch sacks. Meanwhile, Miss Beale supervises free play outside, spending most of her time keeping track of whose turn it is to ride the two "big wheels" and making sure children don't throw sand out of the sandbox. ∎

. . . .

Instead of praising children mechanically, supportive adults encourage children by showing genuine interest in what they are doing.

reciprocal dialogues with children in which each party takes turns talking and listening. They also ask **honest questions**—questions that they really don't know the answers to. For example, when 4-year-old Loretta brings in a shell to show her teacher, the teacher avoids bland praise (e.g, "That's nice, Loretta") and instead responds with an honest question: "I've never seen a shell like that, Loretta. Where did you find it?" This honest and matter-of-fact question leads to a dialogue in which both child and teacher share their beach experiences. Eventually, other children join in, and some make plans to bring in their beach treasures the next day.

Adults also support children by **taking a problem-solving approach to child management.** Adults approach children's negative behaviors—fighting, crying, teasing, aggression—calmly and directly, looking for ways to turn them into opportunities for teaching and learning. Rather than shame or punish children for immature behavior, adults encourage them to resolve the issues at hand. These principles are highlighted in the example, in the side column, of Rachel, Billy, and Brandon. The calm, supportive approach the teacher models here helps all three children involved get over their excitement and move toward a solution to the problem.

The matter-of-fact way this teacher handled a disruptive situation is just one example of the many possible strategies adults can use to support children. Many educators find it difficult to define such concrete strategies for encouraging social learning, because development in this area is often seen as less tangible than the development of cognitive abilities. In this article, we've tried to show that by using the principles of **shared control** and **adult support,** teachers and caregivers can develop a practical, down-to-earth approach to promoting social development that can be successfully applied in all kinds of early childhood programs. ∎

Encouraging Problem Solving

Rachel has spilled her paint on Billy's shoes, causing Brandon, excited, to shout: "Look at your shoes, Billy. Your mommy's gonna be mad." Both Rachel and Billy start to cry and crawl under the table.

Mrs. Williams, who has taken in the situation from across the room, walks over and hands Rachel a wet paper towel, saying calmly, "Rachel, give this to Billy so he can wipe the paint off his shoes before it dries." Rachel comes out from under the table and hands Billy the towel. He stops crying and starts to wipe off his shoes. "Now," Mrs. Williams says to Rachel and Brandon, "how shall we get this paint up off the floor so that you can get back to painting?" ∎

Be Responsive!

by
Amy Powell

Two principles are central to the High/Scope Curriculum. The first is that **children construct their understanding of the world from their own active involvement with people, materials, and ideas.** This principle is based on the constructivist theories of development of Jean Piaget and other developmental psychologists. It suggests that all children—whether they are infants, preschoolers, or second graders; children with mental retardation, learning disabilities, or above average intelligence—are *active learners*. They acquire knowledge by actively experiencing the world around them—choosing, exploring, manipulating, practicing, transforming, experimenting. The range and depth of children's understanding of the world is continually changing and expanding as a result of day-to-day transactions with people, materials, and ideas.

The second principle that is central to the High/Scope Curriculum is that **the role of adults who teach and care for children is to support children's construction of their own understanding of the world.** This principle implies that adults—whether they are teachers, parents, day care providers, administrators, or therapists—can most effectively foster children's acquisition of knowledge and understanding of the world by supporting their active involvement with people, materials, and ideas.

We ask adults who are beginning to implement the High/Scope Curriculum to adopt these principles and use them to guide their practices with children. This often requires dramatic changes on both programmatic and personal levels. Arranging spaces for children to work and play, establishing a daily routine and the

26 • *Supporting Young Learners*

plan-do-review process, understanding the key experiences, and using new methods for observation, planning, and assessment are important steps in implementing the High/Scope model.

Yet, many of us have observed that even when programs have some or all of these "structural" elements of the High/Scope Curriculum in place, they have not yet achieved a full implementation of the High/Scope model. This is because **the essence of the High/Scope approach**—the key element that makes a program uniquely "High/Scope"—**is the way adults *interact* with children.** By observing adult/child interaction styles in a program, we can often gain a sense of how far staff have progressed in adopting our approach and where further staff development is needed.

Interaction—A Dialogue

By *interaction*, we mean the verbal or non-verbal dialogue that is created when adults play or communicate with children. In the High/Scope approach, both children and adults contribute to this dialogue and there is a balance between adult and child contributions. Achieving this balance is perhaps the most difficult aspect of implementing the High/Scope Curriculum because it requires adults to make changes in their own styles of working with children. In their interactions with children, adults are often used to being "in control" and it may be difficult for them to learn to share control.

Why do we focus on adults' interactive style? Note that there are many ways that adults support learning that *do not* involve direct interaction—for example, an adult may add materials to the classroom or refer one child's problem to another. But when adults play or converse directly with a child, they are contributing to the

Supporting Children's Play at Different Levels

Supporting children of all ages as they play is an important way adults help children learn. Adults who are interacting with children recognize that the nature of play changes as children grow older. In the following examples, note how the child's developmental level affects the way children play with similar kinds of materials. Note also how the adults in these cases tailor their interaction strategies to the child's level.

Infant

A blanket is draped over a table. The child hides behind the blanket and pops out, smiling at a nearby adult. The adult joins the child's peek-a-boo game, responding with surprise and saying "Peek-a-boo" each time the child jumps out from the blanket, and eventually imitating by doing his own peek-a-boos with another blanket.

Preschooler

A blanket is draped over a table. A preschooler begins a pretending game: "Let's hide in the cave," she says, "the tiger is coming." She gathers up some stuffed animals and baby blankets and climbs under the table.

An adult picks up a stuffed bear and gently pokes the bear's head behind the blanket.

"Can we come in and hide, too?" The preschooler invites them in, and the adult joins the preschooler in her game of making a nest of blankets to hide the animals in.

"Where's the tiger now?" asks the adult.

"He's coming closer," says the child.

"How do you know he's closer?" asks the adult.

"I can hear his footsteps," says the preschooler. And he's growling, too."

Early Elementary Child

A blanket is draped over a table. A child gathers up some extra blankets and begins experimenting with enlarging the tent. She adds chairs as additional support for the blankets and begins trying out different ways of draping the blankets over the chairs.

"Can you help me make a big tent?" the child asks the adult. "I'm trying to make a tent with three rooms."

The adult joins the child and begins helping her drape the blankets in various ways. The child is frustrated because the blankets keep slipping off.

"I wonder what we could use to hold down the blankets," the adult says.

"Maybe we could tie the corners," the child says. The adult helps the child tie the corners of the blankets to the table legs.

"I wonder what else we could do," the adult says. Then the child remembers that the tents she has seen on family camping trips are held up in part by ropes. She gets a rope and, with the adult's help, anchors the rope on a chair. Then she drapes a blanket over it. The pair continue to work with the blankets, table, chairs, and rope until they succeed in building a large tent that satisfies the child. ∎

child's development in one of the most important ways they can.

Research indicates that the way adults interact with children in a variety of caregiving, play, and teaching situations plays a very important role in children's learning and development. Studies of infants and toddlers have examined the interactive styles of parents and other primary caregivers. These studies indicate that a child-oriented style in which parents are sensitive and responsive to children's cues, interests, actions, and communications is positively associated with quality of attachment, engagement, cognitive and language development, and other desirable outcomes.

Studies of the relationship between teachers' interactive styles and the development of older children also support the importance of a child-oriented interactive style. These studies demonstrate that in classrooms where teachers are responsive—guiding and supporting children's activities rather than directing or controlling them—children take initiative more often and are more likely to be actively involved and persistent in their work.

What is it about a child-oriented adult interactive style that supports children's active involvement with people, materials, and ideas? The literature on achievement motivation—children's internal striving to acquire knowledge and skills or to accomplish tasks—offers one explanation. Motivational theorists suggest that children (in fact, all learners!) are most likely to become actively involved or motivated in activities and interactions that are *enjoyable* and related to their current *needs* and *interests* and that allow them to experience feelings of *control* and *success*. These kinds of motivating experiences are most likely to happen when adults interact *responsively* with children.

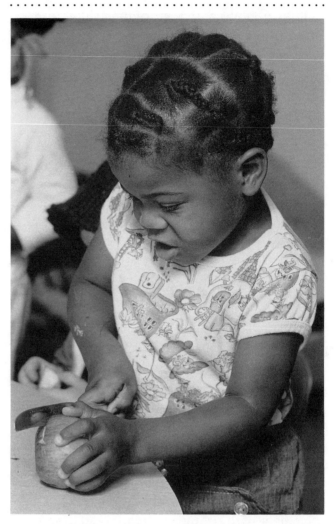

Research on achievement motivation suggests that children are most likely to be actively involved in activities that allow them to experience feelings of control and success.

Hallmarks of a Responsive Style

What do we mean by a responsive style? Regardless of the role of an adult who is working directly with a child—whether he or she is a parent, caregiver, teacher, or therapist—the following qualities of the adult's behavior seem to define this responsive style.

Responsive adults support children's enjoyment of people, materials, and ideas. Play is the activity that is most natural to children and adults encourage children's learning by supporting and participating in their play. Adults are often frustrated by the tendency of young children to play constantly, even during activities that, for adults, are likely to be more goal-directed, like getting dressed or walking up a staircase. However, adults who want to interact meaningfully with a child often find they must "slow themselves down" and adopt the child's playful attitude. In the long run, they find that children are more cooperative and more involved in what they are doing when they are having fun with adults than when they are pushed by adults to complete tasks.

Responsive adults follow children's interests. Adults often express surprise when children do not attend to or become involved with materials or activities that the adult has introduced. "But it was so interesting!" is a typical response. It is important in these situations to make a distinction between what is interesting to adults and what is interesting to the child. Sometimes the adult may not be comfortable with the interests children express—in TV characters for example—yet children are most likely to become actively involved in activities that are directly related to these interests or to other current needs, experiences, and interests. Responsive adults also recognize that young children's interests are reflected in their current activities and communications and may shift rapidly. By "tuning in" and responding to children's behavior, and by incorporating children's needs and experiences into activities and conversations, adults encourage children to pursue their interests. They convey to them the message: "Your interests are worthwhile and important to me."

Using a Developmental Framework

Responsive adults help children experience feelings of control and success by encouraging activities that are neither too easy nor too difficult for them. In promoting such activities, adults in High/Scope settings use the key experiences as a framework for understanding child development. The key experiences help adults recognize and promote activities that offer developmentally appropriate challenges to children. For example, consider the 4-year-old who comes into preschool one Wednesday very excited about an upcoming family event.

"It's almost my Dad's birthday," she says.

"It's on Saturday," her mother says. "She can't wait."

"Just three more days," the teacher says. "After this day, there's another school day, then another school day, and then a 'stay-at-home' day, and that's your father's birthday."

Another day, then another day, then another day," the child replies slowly and thoughtfully, "and then on that day I get to stay home and watch TV and it's my dad's birthday!"

The teacher in this example knows, from the key experiences in understanding time, that anticipating future events is a valuable developmental experience for preschoolers, so she tries to help the child gain a deeper understanding of when the event will occur. From her training in the key experiences, the teacher

Are there limits to the principle of following children's interests? Yes, being responsive to what a child is interested in does not mean the adult always does exactly what the child asks. In responding to a small girl's interest in watching a video about superheroes, for example, a day care provider would keep curriculum components like the key experiences and the ingredients of active learning in mind. Instead of encouraging the child to watch a video, she might offer to help the child make her own "pretend" video about superheroes or she might suggest they make accessories for superhero toys out of art materials.

Responsive adults share control with children. Adults encourage children to make meaningful choices. They follow the child's lead when talking with a child or entering his or her play activities. Conversations between adults and children are reciprocal exchanges: the adult does not dominate the exchange by asking didactic questions or lecturing. When adults and children play together, and the adult introduces something new, it is clearly relevant to the game or activity the child has established. Even in activities that are largely planned by adults, such as specific movement or music activities, adults share control by providing choices and encouraging children to work with the materials given in their own way.

Responsive adults approach the child at the child's level of understanding. This means that adults match the information they provide and the ways they provide it to the ways the child knows the world. Adults communicate in words or gestures that the child can understand and try to match the child's style of communication. They recognize that the child's methods of reasoning and problem solving are different from adult thinking skills and accept the child's incomplete or inaccurate explanations of events in the world.

Responsive adults encourage children to experience success. They promote activities that are neither too easy nor too difficult, allowing the child to be successful, yet providing real challenges. To encourage activities that meet these criteria, adults need an understanding of the important abilities children are developing at any given age. In the High/Scope approach, the key experiences provide a general framework adults can use to assess whether young children are likely to be both successful at and challenged by an activity. The adult then uses this knowledge of the *general* kinds of experiences that are appropriate for young children in conjunction with *specific* observations about the child to determine whether a given activity or concept is too easy or too difficult.

These general principles of being responsive to children apply to interactions with children of all ages. However, the specific strategies or curriculum practices adults use to apply these principles vary according to the child's age or developmental level. On page 28 we provide some examples of how children play at different levels and how the adults interacting with them support their play and language.

...

How can adults get started in developing a more responsive interaction style? Most of us who are implementing the High/Scope Curriculum are used to making concrete changes in our programs: rearranging the classroom or center, adding materials, incorporating planning and review times in the daily routine, and so forth. These kinds of changes are relatively easy to make. But changing our own styles of interacting with children is not so easy. Change in this area is highly personal and individual. Our own backgrounds, our knowledge of and training in child

also knows that terms like "Friday" or "end of the week" are too abstract for many preschoolers, but that they can often grasp concepts of time that are stated in terms of simple time sequences. Using this knowledge, she restates and amplifies what the child says in a way that is challenging, yet understandable, for the child.

When the child adopts some of the teacher's language in restating her prediction, she shows that she has taken on the challenge of adjusting her thinking about when the event will occur. Through this process of dialogue about a personally meaningful event, the child gains a sense that she can successfully predict the event with greater precision, and that she has some control over the future. ■

Responsive adults follow the child's lead in conversation and play.

development, what we have experienced in our own relationships, our own ideas about how children learn, and the ways we ourselves have been taught—all these factors influence our own styles of working with children. To change, we must first become aware of our particular interactive style by examining the ways we communicate and work with children. Next, we identify one aspect of our behavior that we can modify and choose one or two strategies that we believe will help us make a change.

As we try new ways of interacting with children, we document the process and outcomes, both for ourselves and for the children. Then the process begins again. It's up to us to continue to change and develop! ■

Helping Children Manage Themselves

"I don't understand why Vicky is terrible at sharing blocks during work time. When she can't have them all, she sits on the floor and cries."

...

"Christopher is always the last one finished with his materials at work time. He balks at putting away his toys when it's time to clean up."

...

"Mark flits from area to area. He can't seem to stay with anything for more than two minutes."

...

"Jessica doesn't have any respect for the classroom materials. The other day, before I could stop her, she took the scissors and cut the back of a doll's hair."

...

"The 15 minutes right before lunch is one of the worst times in our day. Most of the children are hungry and tired, and often there are fights while they wait in line for the bathroom."

by

Michelle Graves

and

Ruth Strubank

These are a few examples of the **child management** issues teachers face in working with young children. With the High/Scope Curriculum, we believe that many management problems are prevented because the classroom environment is carefully planned. Many other problems, of course, must be dealt with on the spot. Our ultimate goal in handling management issues is to help children become aware of their own actions, of how those actions affect the people and things in their environment, and of how the choices they make can help them resolve difficulties and conflicts. We also want children to learn that control comes from within, so we encourage adults to avoid using their positions of authority to impose control.

Preventive Management Strategies

Listed below are some basic prevention strategies.

Think about the principles of child development and how these relate to your children's abilities to understand what behavior is appropriate. If necessary, redesign your environment with their developmental limitations in mind. For example, it is difficult for many young children to understand the concept of sharing. A child who is engrossed in his play may not be developmentally ready to consider that there are others who also want to use the same play materials. When children refuse to share, we should be careful not to label this as "misbehavior." To reduce conflicts over sharing materials, provide enough of each material and plenty of attractive alternatives so that children won't always have to share.

Establish a consistent daily routine so children will be able to predict and plan for the things that are about to happen. Christopher, in the example, may be reluctant to put his toys away because he thinks he won't have a chance to play with the same materials again. Once he gets used to the routine and realizes that the same materials will be available during tomorrow's work time, he will be more willing to clean up.

Make your classroom or center an environment rich in opportunities for children to be independent and make choices. If we want children to develop into independent thinkers and decision-makers, we have to give them practice in working independently and making choices. If we continually limit their opportunities to

Giving children plenty of opportunities to do things independently helps them feel comfortable with taking risks and solving problems.

choose, how can we expect them to learn to make good choices? For example, saying to children "You cannot play with the blocks today because I didn't like the way you used them yesterday," or "I'm closing the sand table because you're dumping too much sand on the floor," does not give them the chance to think of and try out new ways to solve the problem. Children who feel comfortable taking risks because they are not continually threatened with failure will develop into adults who know the value of exploring alternatives in problem solving.

Design your space with areas and materials that are of interest and value to the population of children you serve. For a child like Mark in the opening example, we would recommend that classroom adults ask family members what the child's favorite home toys are and also observe closely at preschool to discover those things that the child enjoys working with most.

Ann: I've noticed that the transition from clean-up to washing hands is one of the most difficult for children—there's always a lot of dawdling and silliness. Maybe it would improve things if one of us helped move children into the bathroom while the other continued to work with children who are cleaning up.

Ruth: One of the things that seems to help children get moving is singing. Whoever helps the children to the bathroom could sing, "You wash your hands, and I'll wash my hands, and we'll wash hands together." I'll take part of the group and do that.

Ann: And I'll help the other children clean up. I'll watch to see who is finishing up or getting tired of clean-up—and I'll send them to you before problems start. I'll also help children who are done in the bathroom move to the recall table. ∎

Then they should make sure that materials reflecting these interests are available in the classroom, adding new materials if necessary.

Together with your team members, set reasonable limits and agree on the rationale you will use to explain these to the children. There are many issues children must sort out before they can interact smoothly with others and with their surroundings. This learning process will be easier if adults send them clear, consistent messages in certain areas. Some examples of limit-setting:

"No running in the classroom. You can run outside where there is more space and there are fewer sharp edges."

"I can't let you hit the children or throw things because someone might get hurt."

"The bus driver cannot start the bus until you are sitting in your seat. This will help to keep you safer if she has to stop suddenly."

Model ways of interacting with materials and people for children. Children learn by example. If you are respectful of their individual needs and the materials in your room, they are likely to imitate you. For instance, before leaving an area where you are working with children you could say, "I'm changing my plan to work in the block area but first I'm going to put the modeling dough back on the shelf."

Plan for transition times. Children learn best when they are actively involved. If they have long waits between activities, they are apt to be bored or frustrated and may fill in the gaps with troublesome behavior: fidgeting, fighting, teasing, or just staring off into space. Reassess your schedule to see if you can reduce the time spent in transitions. When a period of waiting is unavoidable, plan ways to keep the children active. For example, plan group fingerplays and songs and allow children to leave the group one or two at a time to wash their hands or to get their snack; give children responsibility for things they would otherwise have to wait for you to do, such as pouring the juice or passing out lunchboxes.

Respect and plan for the different abilities, interests, and pacing levels of each child. Children will quickly misbehave if they are always made to do the same thing, in the same way, at the same time. Talk with team members about the differing needs of each child in your classroom. How can you allow each of them to work in the ways that fit them best, within the curriculum framework?

Prevention techniques will reduce management difficulties in the classroom greatly, but will never totally eliminate them. You will still have to intervene often to help children use materials appropriately and resolve conflicts with other children. Below are some on-the-spot techniques to handle common management problems.

On-the-Spot Management Techniques

Intervene immediately to stop behavior that is unsafe or destructive. When children are fighting with others or destroying classroom materials, adults must immediately take action. If children are hitting one another, it may be necessary to physically separate them to calm them down. Intervening immediately sends a clear message that it is not all right to hurt others or destroy materials.

Use language to identify children's feelings and concerns. "Pia, I can see it upsets you when you want to use all the blocks and other children want to use them too." Sometimes a simple acknowledgment of a child's feelings is all that is needed to move him or her toward a resolution of a problem.

Which *On-the-spot* Strategies Is the Adult Using Here?

[Four-year-old Alicia is working at a letter matching game on the computer. Katie, another child, comes up behind her and starts to observe. Katie asks Alicia if she can join her, but Alicia refuses, saying it's *her* turn. Katie waits several minutes for a turn at the computer, and when Alicia goes off to the block area, Katie takes her place. After a few minutes, Alicia returns to the computer area and stands behind Katie, looking very distressed. A teacher approaches Alicia.]

Teacher: Alicia, you look very sad.

Alicia: I want to work on the computer again.

Teacher: You could ask Katie if you can work with her.

Alicia to Katie: Can I do the computer with you?

Katie: No!

Teacher to Alicia: It looks to me like you're not going to have a turn on the computer now. What else could you do?

Alicia: Read a book with you.

[The teacher and Alicia read together in the quiet area. Later, in their team meeting, the teachers discuss what happened between Katie and Alicia and plan to follow up.]

Teacher: Tommorrow, at planning time, why don't we remind Katie and Alicia of what happened? I can ask them if they might want to plan a way that they could work together at the computer. ■

Conflicts between children can be opportunities for learning and problem solving if adults encourage children to verbalize feelings and think of potential solutions.

Ask children to put their own feelings and desires into words. After calming children involved in a physical conflict, adults should encourage them to verbalize their concerns: "Keith, tell Bob it makes you angry when he knocks over your blocks."

Ask children to think of their own solutions to a perceived problem. "Christopher, I can tell you're excited about these small-group-time materials. Since clean-up time is very close, let's think of a way you can use them tomorrow."

Give children choices only when they are truly options. Saying to a child "In five minutes it will be time to clean-up, O.K.?" leaves you wide open for her to reply, "No, I'm not done playing yet." Instead, be clear in your expectations: "In five minutes, clean-up time will start. Then we can get ready for recall time."

Avoid language that passes judgment on a child. Telling Jessica, "It's not nice to cut the doll's hair. I can't trust you with the scissors" can lower her self-esteem and does not help her see what things she *can* cut.

When you stop behavior that is unacceptable, explain the reasons to children. In the previous example, you can instead say, "Jessica, I can see you want to cut. The doll's hair is not a choice for cutting because it won't grow back and tomorrow no one will be able to comb it. Let's look together in the art area for some things you *can* cut."

Before stepping into a situation, decide if children can settle things without your help. As children mature developmentally and gain more experience in resolving conflicts, they will begin to find their own solutions to problems. A recent example from our demonstration classroom occurred when two children were fighting over a purse. Another child stood in between them, put her hands on each of their shoulders and said, "Let me help you solve this problem."

Using the above strategies patiently and persistently will create a climate in which children develop inner controls and learn to approach conflicts with others with a problem-solving orientation. Having such a clearly defined framework for child management also helps teachers and caregivers gain distance and a sense of control as they handle conflict and disruption. ∎

Dealing With a Difficult Child

by
Michelle Graves

The High/Scope Curriculum recommends a preventive approach to child management in which team members work to avert management problems by creating a supportive classroom environment and an orderly daily routine. When prevention fails, we advise adults to help children resolve their own conflicts and frustrations through problem solving rather than through adult-imposed control or punishment. The goal of this approach is to help children become aware of how their own actions affect others and of how the choices they make can help them overcome difficulties and conflicts.

While this approach enables *most* children to function fairly smoothly in most early childhood settings, sometimes staff find themselves spending a disproportionate amount of time dealing with the problems created by one or two "difficult" children. When faced with one child's severe behavior problems, they often ask themselves whether they, as program staff, are the "real problem." They may first try to lessen the child's troublesome behavior by altering the environment, but when such efforts fail repeatedly, they may wonder whether the child needs an entirely different approach.

Each "difficult child" is a different individual, and we don't claim to have answers for every child; however, we have dealt successfully with such problems in the High/Scope Demonstration Preschool. Following is a description of one such difficult situation we experienced and the process the staff went through in coping with it.

Jeremy (the name is fictitious) was 3½ years old when he entered our program. We soon noticed that when Jeremy could not have exactly what he wanted, he would react violently: biting, kicking, screaming curses, throwing things, and occasionally making a "mad dash" out of our classroom space. These outbursts, which occurred once or twice each morning, were so severe and disruptive that it often took 10–45 minutes of a staff member's time to calm Jeremy down.

During the next few months of school, much of our time together as a team was spent in discussions about Jeremy. Here are some of the strategies we developed for dealing with him.

We took turns being the adult who stopped the behaviors when they occurred— spreading this difficult task around helped us be more patient with Jeremy. Even though we wanted Jeremy to develop inner controls, it was usually necessary at first to **physically supply the control that Jeremy lacked.** For example, we would separate Jeremy from the person being bitten or the object being thrown, and we would hold him inside the classroom when he tried to run out. As we held Jeremy, we would calmly and patiently explain why we could not let him do what he was doing, labeling the feelings that we thought were causing the behavior. In restraining Jeremy, we tried to avoid sending mixed messages. For example, if the adult spoke in a calm voice but her body was tense as she held him, Jeremy might not feel that we were confident that he would learn to control his own behavior.

We made an effort to spend time with Jeremy during his calmer moments, playing next to him or describing his behavior and the positive reactions he was getting from other children: "When you built together with Sally today, the house you made was big enough to fit three people inside."

We recorded our observations of Jeremy. We kept track of the frequency of his outbursts

- Take turns with other team members in dealing with child's problem behavior.

- When child's behavior gets out of control, stop the inappropriate behavior, physically supplying the control the child lacks while calmly explaining the reasons why the behavior is unacceptable. Describe and label the child's feelings if he/she is unable to describe them.

- Convey your confidence that the child will learn to control his/her behavior.

- During the child's calmer moments, play and talk with him or her.

- Record observations of the child, and look for patterns in his/her behavior.

- Use the daily routine as a vehicle for helping the child control his/her behavior

- Look for ways to encourage the child to take responsibility for his/her behavior

- Help other children in the classroom understand and label their reactions to the child who is disruptive.

- Involve the child's parents in the team's effort to find ways to deal with the child.

- Set a time limit: decide in advance when the team will re-evaluate the situation and how long they will endure the situation if there is no improvement.

- Look for help from outside agencies and community volunteers. ∎

and looked for patterns: Did the problems tend to occur at certain times of the day? Were they related to changes in the classroom routine? Much later in the year, with the help of his family, we kept track of how much he was sleeping and what kinds of foods he was eating.

We used the daily routine as a vehicle for helping Jeremy control his behavior. If Jeremy refused to do something that the group was doing (such as clean up after work time) we could remind him of the many choices that would be possible at other parts of the routine. "It's time to for you to clean up and get your jacket on, but when we get outside, you can decide what you want to play with there." When Jeremy understood the schedule better, he was sometimes able to cope more appropriately with frustration.

We tried to help the other children understand their own feelings about Jeremy in the classroom and the ways they could deal with his unpredictable behaviors: "I know it scares you when Jeremy comes close to you. Tell him: 'It hurts me when you try to bite. Stop it.'"

We looked for ways for Jeremy to take responsibility for his behavior. For example, when he pulled the arms out of a doll, we helped him find a way to repair it before he chose another activity.

We involved Jeremy's parents in the process of finding ways to deal with him. This was perhaps the most difficult part of dealing with this situation. We tried to balance our reports on Jeremy's problem behavior with some positive comments. It took several meetings and phone calls before the parents realized that we were not passing judgement on them. Once they trusted us, they were able to provide us with a great deal of support, both by continuing our classroom management strategies with Jeremy at home and by telling us about outside stresses that might be affecting Jeremy's behavior in preschool.

To avoid being overwhelmed by the problems created by a disruptive child, team members may plan to take turns dealing with the child. Another helpful strategy is to decide in advance when the team will re-evaluate the situation.

As a team, we talked about and set time limits (for example, "We'll try this for three weeks. If we don't see any improvement, we will. . .). Knowing that we wouldn't have to endure the situation indefinitely helped us over the rough spots with Jeremy. We anticipated that we might have to repeat our management strategies many more times with Jeremy than we have to with most children before we would see results. However, we didn't want to spend so much time and effort on Jeremy that the rest of the class suffered or that staff members got burned out. **When we felt stretched (along around week three) we looked to community resources for support.** We contacted a local Foster Grandparent Program and accepted volunteer workers in our classroom. They helped with the other children so staff members could spend more time dealing with Jeremy. We also asked a social worker from the local social services department to observe in the classroom. She gave us some much-needed encouragement by confirming that we were on the right track with Jeremy.

As it turned out, our patience and persistence with Jeremy were eventually rewarded. Slowly, Jeremy's development progressed; as he grew older, the techniques we were modeling gradually became a part of him instead of something that came from us. He hit others less often, used language more often to describe his anger, and he stopped running out of the classroom.

Reflecting on this experience, we realize that we used the same basic strategies with Jeremy that we use with most children, but we used them with more intensity, frequency, and patience. We're glad that we did not "throw in the towel" too early and we believe that the patience we displayed helped Jeremy find control within himself. We realize, however, that such efforts are not always successful. If we had felt that all involved were losing too much by continuing in the situation, our next step would have been to help Jeremy's parents find a more appropriate placement for him. ■

Multicultural Education: What It Is, How to Do It

by

Bonnie Lash Freeman

and

Marilyn Adams Jacobson

Traditionally, multicultural education has been considered most relevant for classrooms serving cultural and racial minority children. But we at High/Scope believe that a deepened awareness of culture is a valuable experience for all children, particularly those who live in markedly homogeneous or culturally isolated settings.

If multicultural education is for *all* children, then what is it? It is the adult's active awareness of opportunities to support and extend children's experiences as they participate in their own cultures and learn about the cultures of others. Our definition of culture is everything that makes up the lifeways of a people—their arts, beliefs, customs, values, and the products of their work and thought. Culture includes the past—the history and traditions of a people—but the present is just as important. Culture is dynamic and ever-changing.

Effective multicultural education is also developmentally appropriate: at the preschool level, it is not the study of exotic cultures, historical events, and artistic achievements far removed from the child's everyday experiences. Multicultural education is not a set of curriculum "add-ons"—special activities, or posters and artifacts arranged in an "ethnic corner" of the classroom, center, or home. Instead, it is a perspective that is embedded in everything we do. As with all activities in the High/Scope Curriculum, we recommend that adults encourage cultural learning by **starting with children's direct experience**—the people, ways of living, and physical surroundings of each child's home and commu-

A Multicultural Classroom

Here are some ideas for arranging and equipping a classroom, day care home, or center to reflect a multicultural perspective.

• **Consider the major themes of the culture of the community.** For example, a classroom in a farming community may contain several sets of toy farm animals, agricultural tools, and toy barns. In cultures where home life is central, the house area might be especially large; for example, in a New York classroom serving many children from Puerto Rican backgrounds, the house area included a bedroom, living room, and kitchen. In addition, because music was a central part of many of these children's home lives, the music area was incorporated in the house area.

• **Provide low wall space in each area for the display of children's art work, family photos, and pictures of various scenes from everyday life:** different kinds of homes, modes of transportation, work settings, child care settings, and family scenes. Such pictures can stimulate conversation and role play if they show things that are familiar or moderately novel.

• **Visit children's homes or talk with family members to see if your materials and role play props reflect the children's lives.** For example, a teaching team in California learned from home visits that many parents were professionals who traveled a great deal. The team decided to in-

nity. Our approach to culture has five broad goals:

1. To strengthen the child's positive sense of identity as a member of many different groups (family, class, culture, linguistic group, race, gender).

2. To develop the child's social competence (the ability to accept the points of view of others, express feelings appropriately, resolve conflicts with others, care for one's own needs, show concern for others, work cooperatively to meet a common goal).

3. To develop the child's ability to communicate in standard English and to maintain his or her home language or linguistic style; to develop the child's appreciation of linguistic differences.

4. To broaden the child's cultural experiences and to develop respect and appreciation for differences among people (speech patterns, appearance, lifestyle, and ideas).

5. To work toward effective and reciprocal relationships between home and school.

The following strategies for team planning and teaching will help you achieve these goals.

Team Planning for a Multicultural Program

Here are some ways team members can enhance their program's multicultural perspective:

• **Develop team members' own multicultural awareness and sensitivity.** Each team member can start by examining his or her personal background and attitudes and exchanging these insights with other team members. For example, the team might choose a theme, like religion, gift-giving, or personal achievement, and discuss how that theme is expressed in their families and in the communities in which they were raised.

Team members can develop their own multicultural awareness and sensitivity by examining their personal backgrounds and attitudes and sharing their insights with team members.

• **Study the children in your own classroom** to become aware of the various cultures and communities represented, and therefore the wide range of experiences your program should be supporting and extending. As you consider the children your program serves from a cultural perspective, avoid the one-dimensional view of culture that only looks at broad ethnic, linguistic, and religious groupings, ignoring the many other facets of people's lives that make up their cultures.

• **Take advantage of the unique backgrounds of team members as you plan for individual children.** For example, a team member who knows the home language of a new child can help to orient that child.

• **Examine the teaching team's division of labor to avoid cultural or gender stereotyping.** All team members—whether teachers or aides—should work directly with children. Many housekeeping tasks can be rotated among team members. Male team members should not be exempt from diaper-changing, just as female team

corporate a variety of suitcases in their house area. The suitcases sparked a great deal of role play based on the children's experiences with their parents' comings and goings.

• **Evaluate the books in the classroom for their multicultural content.** Do you have books that reflect children's immediate lifestyles? The ethnic make-up of their families and communities? Is there a balance between "make-believe" and contemporary stories of everyday life? Are men and women shown in a variety of roles? Are there some books written in the home languages of all your children, and if possible, some bilingual books that use English with each of the home languages?

• **Periodically reassess your materials** to accommodate new children and new themes in children's lives. ■

members should change light bulbs when needed.

• **View parents as team members and invite them to serve as volunteers and resources in the classroom.** For example, in one preschool, a mother whose hobby was spinning wool shared this with the children. The staff helped her plan ways to actively involve children in her demonstration, such as having them touch and smell the fleece and take turns pedaling the spinning wheel.

• **If in doubt about a cultural observance or ethnic term, ask a parent what is appropriate.** (To a Japanese parent: "Which term would you prefer we use to describe your family, *Oriental*, or *Asian*?")

• **When planning any holiday or birthday observances, make sure that your recognition of the occasion is acceptable to all families.** For example, send a note home with children to outline tentative plans for Easter egg dyeing and a special snack-time in which children will taste and discuss Passover foods. Ask parents for feedback and invite them to participate. It's important to inform parents about **all** such occasions. Some parents may even object to birthday parties.

Teaching Strategies: Providing Multicultural Experiences

When providing learning experiences that have a cultural dimension, we recommend using the same general teaching strategies that apply to any developmentally appropriate activity. **Start with a concrete experience** that grows from the child's own interests, **encourage the child to represent the experience, help the child build upon and extend the experience**, and **invite other children to share in or contribute to the activity.** In each stage of the process, **provide**

Learning about the immediate community and neighborhood of the program is a meaningful cultural experience for preschoolers.

choices so that each child can shape the activity to his or her personal interests. For example,

> *At small-group time, Christian carefully arranged his wooden cubes and tapped on them with two 4-inch cuisinaire rods as he sang "La Bamba." When the teacher questioned him, she found out that he was imitating something he did at home—playing his drum set along with the stereo. The teacher asked Christian to bring in one of his drums and his record to show the children at circle time the next day. She also brought in a collection of drums (bongos, a rubber-headed tin can drum, several oatmeal boxes, and an African pressure drum). After the children had experimented with them together, she set the drums out in the music area along with a cassette containing a variety of musical selections.*

Here are some other teaching strategies:

• **Encourage children to share information about their families and friends.** Select a general theme (family members, children's homes, holiday foods, parents' occupations, vacations, etc.) and ask children to share personal experiences in that area in some way (by discussing them; through photos or drawings; or by bringing in objects from home). Compile and display these items, if possible.

• **Approach holidays from the child's point of view.** In planning holiday activities ask yourself these questions: Am I starting from the child's perspective? Will children be actively involved and making choices? Am I focusing on the process or the product? For example, one teaching team planned a Christmas performance that required children to memorize lines and to wait for long periods of time while other children rehearsed their parts. When the children became bored, restless, and disruptive, the teaching team realized the activity was not developmentally appropriate.

• **Plan field trips in the immediate community and neighborhood of your program.** Remember, "good things come in small packages"—that is, meaningful experiences come through short walks rather than elaborate expeditions. Take children to a classmate's home to see a baby sister, to wash the doll clothes at a nearby laundromat, to a gas station, to the local deli.

Remember, at the preschool level, cultural experiences should **start with the familiar, or moderately novel,** and work from there. This philosophy not only will result in developmentally appropriate activities, it also will provide children with a deeper understanding of their own cultures, and those of their classmates, than can be presented in preachy speeches, glossy posters, or prepackaged lessons. ∎

"Special" Children: Building on Their Strengths

Nine children are playing with paper, different-sized bits of plastic foam, and glue during small-group time at the High/Scope Preschool. Observing carefully, the teacher notices that the children are all using the materials in different ways: four of the children are stacking the plastic foam pieces and then gluing them together to make an "apartment building"; others are gluing the pieces one by one on colored paper. One child who is clearly working at a different level is Stephen. He is playing with the glue bottle, squeezing it and turning it upside down. As the glue oozes out, Stephen touches it and spreads it on his hands.

by

Mark Tompkins

At the heart of the High/Scope Curriculum is the concept that educational activities should be attuned to each child's level of development. In the above example, children's different developmental levels are expressed in the variety of ways they use the same materials. Stephen, a 4-year-old with special needs, plays with the glue in a way that is usually typical of children two or three years younger.

Though Stephen came to the program with a diagnostic label—Down syndrome—this diagnosis is not the major factor guiding the teacher's responses to Stephen. She is more interested in *what Stephen can do* and *how he does it* than in what he can't do. She is constantly looking for ways to expand Stephen's experiences and support his development. She focuses on Stephen's strengths and interests rather than on his weaknesses.

We believe the High/Scope Curriculum is appropriate for children who, like Stephen, have

"Special" Children: Building on Their Strengths • 53

special needs. In this article, we'll use the example of Stephen to show how we apply our developmental approach with these "special" children.

Strengths of the Developmental Approach

Teachers and trainers who use the High/Scope Curriculum are frequently asked about the program's appropriateness for handicapped children. Such questions often stem from the belief that a curriculum emphasizing child-initiated activities may not provide special-needs children with the carefully monitored, structured experiences they need to compensate for their disabilities. In this compensatory approach, the teacher directs each child's experiences based on what the child *can't* do.

While a deficit-oriented approach may be successful in building skills in narrowly defined areas, we believe that it can also create problems. Skills learned through highly structured exercises may be "splinter skills" that the child can't apply in any meaningful way. For example, a child who is not really ready for reading may learn to read the word *stop* on a worksheet, if he is drilled on it repeatedly. However, he may then be unable to recognize the same word when he sees it on a stop sign. Another problem with the deficit-centered approach is its failure to accommodate the child's own interests. When children are repeatedly asked to perform tasks that seem arbitrary to them, they may lose interest in school or become passive and overly dependent on the teacher.

Years of experience working with handicapped children has shown that a developmental approach can prevent many of these problems and can create effective learning environments for many such children. When seen from a developmental perspective, many of the

Writing Meaningful IEPs

Federal law requires school staff working with special-needs children to develop an Individualized Educational Plan (IEP) that documents the goals and objectives for each child as agreed upon by teachers, health professionals, and parents. Writing an IEP can be a difficult task for developmentally oriented teachers, who tend to teach spontaneously, building upon the child's initiative rather than carrying out a structured lesson plan. If the task of IEP-writing is defined in terms of highly structured teaching tasks and rigid timetables, it becomes so incompatible with a developmental approach that it may seem like a meaningless formality.

Writing an IEP does not have to be a frustrating exercise in paper-shuffling, however. Here are some practical hints for making your IEPs easier to develop and more meaningful:

State your IEP objectives as broadly as possible to provide flexibility. Use the High/Scope key experiences as the basis for your objectives. For example:

Objective—David will investigate and describe the attributes of things.

Materials—Equipment and objects in each of the six areas of the room.

Compare this broad objective with such narrow goals as

Objective—David will sort and name shapes with 90% accuracy.

Materials—Attribute blocks, flash cards.

Integrate basic curriculum goals (for example, increased self-reliance and independent problem solving) **with specific goals for that child** (for example, improved coordination in

the right hand): *Jeremy will unzip and hang up his coat every morning without help.*

Tie your objectives into the normal routine of your day. Example: *Margarita will indicate a plan every day during planning time and will work on it for at least 5 minutes.* Remember, activities that require a range of skills and relate to a child's interests are more likely to result in learning that transfers to "real life" than drills focusing on narrow skills whose purpose the child does not understand.

Integrate activities prescribed by therapists within the natural context of your day. Example: *Ahmed will reach with his atrophied arm to a high shelf during work time. Adults will place materials he often chooses to use on the top part of the shelf so he will have to reach to get them.*

State objectives in terms of groups of materials, not in terms of specific sets of materials. For example, instead of *Monique will sort and match the attribute blocks by shape and color,* try *Monique will put away the materials she has just used, sorting the objects as needed by their functions, shapes, and sizes, and matching the objects to the labeled containers and shelves where they belong.* The important goal is to encourage Monique to put things away and in the process to classify, sort, and match objects. Limiting her learning experiences to a specific group of materials might be counterproductive— we want Monique to use her developing skills in a variety of settings.

The above suggestions are intended to help you develop IEPs that enable everyone—teachers, parents, health professionals, and child—to work together toward common goals. ∎

needs of a handicapped child are not so abnormal because they often reflect the normal needs of an earlier developmental period. Since the curriculum focuses on children's strengths, adapting to the needs of these special children is not a novel demand. Furthermore, there are some qualities shared by children at all levels—all children need choices, consistency, freedom to play, and opportunities for warm relationships with adults and other children. These universal needs are often neglected when teachers focus heavily on the "need to remediate."

For some teachers of special-needs children, a shift to the High/Scope approach may mean a rethinking of their teaching styles. The curriculum requires them to plan a rich environment that offers many choices, to observe carefully to discover children's strengths, to learn how to enter children's play without directing it, and to become aware of the learning that is occurring during these activities.

This approach to teaching may be difficult to learn—it is hard for teachers to give up the sense of control that comes from directing children's learning. However, many teachers working with special-needs children find that it is actually easier in the long run than directive teaching. When children are allowed to choose their own activities, it becomes easier to identify their developmental needs. In addition, management problems are reduced. And the greater confidence, competence, self-control, and independence that children develop in this approach makes the teacher's role more rewarding.

Stephen: How This Approach Worked for One Special-Needs Child

Now that we've outlined our philosophy for working with special-needs children, we'll

Rather than plan highly structured tasks to remediate this child's disability, the caregiver focuses on broad developmental needs—in this case, the child's need to use her expanding language abilities in the context of a game she enjoys.

show how this approach was applied by continuing with the example of Stephen, the child with Down's syndrome who was introduced earlier.

Stephen was 4½ years old when he entered the High/Scope Preschool. Before he started, one of the teachers visited his home and Stephen and his family visited the classroom. Together, Stephen's parents and the teachers decided on two major goals for Stephen: increasing his positive interactions with other children and adults and developing his language skills. It is important to note that the teachers did not see Stephen's verbal and social capacities as deficit areas, but rather as broad areas of development in which he was ready to make some advances.

In the early part of the year, Stephen spent much of his time freely exploring the different materials and areas in the classroom. He enjoyed playing with the materials, but rarely stuck with anything for very long—he tended to flit from

Room Arrangement Checklist for Special-Needs Children

Sometimes modifications in your room arrangement can help children with handicaps use the classroom more independently. Here are some suggestions:

☐ Keep boundaries between areas open enough so that children with wheelchairs or walkers are not obstructed as they move from area to area.

☐ Pad the edges and backs of shelves and tables so that children with mobility or visual impairments won't get hurt from frequent bumps.

☐ Accent the divisions between work areas by using different colored carpet in each area or by laying down tape boundaries.

☐ Provide a partially enclosed area where easily distracted children can go to play quietly or to calm down.

☐ Make sure that many of the spaces where materials are stored are labeled with real objects (a Lego taped to the outside of the appropriate container, for example) so that they are easily understood by children who are not able to use more abstract representations. Textured labels (made of sandpaper or felt, for example) can be helpful for children with visual impairments.

☐ Don't move things without explaining the change to children—or better yet, let them help you make the change. Consistency in the environment is very important if children are to use the materials effectively.

area to area, emptying the shelves of toys and materials as he moved through the classroom. When he was absorbed in what he was doing, he demanded little attention from the adults or his classmates. However, his lack of language and social skills made it difficult for him to play near other children who were using materials he was interested in playing with.

It soon became apparent to staff that they had to create situations in which Stephen would need to use language and would be motivated to play next to others. These two goals appeared to be closely related: the teachers had observed that as Stephen's ability to use language increased, so did his positive interactions with others. Following are some of the strategies they used:

• As Stephen worked with materials, the teachers described his activities for him. This enabled him to attach language to what he was experiencing without the pressure of answering questions.

• At planning time, Stephen did not at first indicate a plan, but would simply go to the area he wanted to work in. The teachers would follow him there and verbalize his plan for him by talking about some of the things he might want to do there. As the year progressed, he began to use one- or two-word phrases to describe what he wanted to do. The teachers would then repeat back what he said. Some other planning strategies that eventually were effective for Stephen included asking him to point to the area he planned to work in, asking him to bring something he was planning to play with to the teacher, or asking him to choose photos of materials he wanted to work with.

• The teachers made an effort to familiarize Stephen with the daily routine, as they did with all the children. They felt that if he understood the sequence of events, he could cope more easily with transitions and changes throughout the day. In the early part of the year, the teachers planned that one adult would always be near Stephen during a transition to help keep him on track. The adults frequently reminded Stephen of the order of events by showing him a chart that had pictures of each part of the routine in sequence.

• To help with the transitions from work time to clean-up time to recall time, the adults also capitalized on Stephen's involvement with materials. They encouraged Stephen to set materials he had worked with or things he had made in a special pile close to the table where he would be at recall time. At recall, he would show the materials to the other children and the teachers would help him describe or act out what he had done.

• The teachers helped Stephen "talk" to his classmates by speaking for him. For example, when Stephen grabbed for a strainer that another child was playing with, the teacher intervened, saying: "Stephen is trying to show you that he wants to play with your strainer."

The teachers talked with Stephen's parents daily about what was going on in school. Their familiarity with the program made it easier for Stephen's parents to talk with him about school experiences and to follow through on classroom strategies at home (for example, by establishing a consistent home routine and by labeling toy shelves so that he could put his own toys away).

Over time, the teachers noticed that Stephen used materials for longer periods of time, increased his language production, and was more and more interested in playing with other children. He learned the names of the materials and the areas, and spontaneously began to use phrases like "More juice, please" and "Play with markers." Increasingly, Stephen used language

☐ Consider removing small objects if you have children who might swallow them.

☐ Don't just put new materials on the shelf: introduce them in small-group experiences so that children can experience them first in a protected setting.

☐ Provide plenty of materials that children can manipulate over and over again: for example, plastic plumbing pipes or large nuts and bolts. Often such objects become favorites of the young handicapped child because they have seen them at home, they can be put together and rearranged in a variety of ways, and they are simple to use.

☐ As you do with all children in your group, observe the handicapped children carefully to see which materials are appropriate for and interesting to them. ■

to get the other children's attention, rather than grabbing, pushing, or otherwise using his body to get his way. As his social behavior became more appropriate, the other children accepted him as a playmate, often inviting him to play with them.

Clearly Stephen made significant advances toward the language and social goals the adults set early in the year. Stephen was able to make this progress because he found himself in an environment where his strengths were recognized, where his uniqueness as a child was supported, and where he was accepted as a friend by many children. ■

C·H·A·P·T·E·R   T·W·O

Key Experiences for Child Development

. . . .

Key Experiences: Keys to Supporting Preschool Children's Emerging Strengths and Abilities — Mary Hohmann

Communication: Why It's So Important in the High/Scope Curriculum — Bettye McDonald

Right! Young Children Can Write! — Jane Maehr

Math Learning: Making It Happen Naturally — Sam Hannibal

Movement Experiences: Needed, But Neglected — Phyllis S. Weikart

Music and Movement Throughout the Daily Routine — Ruth Strubank

If a set of beliefs about how children learn and how adults support learning form the *process* of the High/Scope approach, then the *content* is provided by the High/Scope **key experiences.** ✓ These experiences are not viewed as a set of specific topics and learning objectives; instead they are seen as generic *processes* that children experience repeatedly in the natural course of their daily lives. Together, the key experiences define the kinds of knowledge children in the preschool years are acquiring as they interact with materials, people, and ideas.

As Mary Hohmann explains in the opening article, the key experiences are activities that young children naturally engage in. The role of early childhood staff is to create an environment in which these developmentally important activities can occur and then to recognize, support, and build upon them when they do. The key experiences are divided into nine categories: social development, representation, language, classification, seriation, number, space, time, and physical development. The chapter does not cover the key experience categories comprehensively, but instead discusses a few key experience areas in depth. Addressing the early childhood field's ongoing concern about the foundations of academic learning, selections by Bettye McDonald and Jane Maehr explore the development of language and literacy, and an article by Sam Hannibal discusses the beginnings of mathematical thinking. The development of movement skills, one of the most active areas of curriculum development for High/Scope in recent years, is highlighted in the concluding pieces by Ruth Strubank and Phyllis Weikart.

Key Experiences:
Keys to Supporting Preschool Children's Emerging Strengths and Abilities

The key experiences are at the heart of the High/Scope Curriculum's understanding of young children. What are they? How can they influence adult behavior in early childhood settings?

by

Mary Hohmann

The key experiences (listed in the side columns on pages 64–68) are a series of statements describing the social, cognitive, and physical development of children from the ages of 2½ to 5 years. Each statement highlights an experience that is essential for the development of the fundamental abilities that emerge during the preschool years. Taken together, the key experiences provide a detailed picture of the typical actions of young children and the kinds of knowledge they are involved in constructing. Adults use the key experiences to guide them in observing, understanding, and supporting children's interests and emerging abilities.

How Are the Key Experiences Organized?

The key experiences are organized around (1) social development; (2) representation and language; (3) classification, seriation, number, space, and time; and (4) physical development.

Social development. Through these key experiences children develop a sense of initiative, confidence, and trust in themselves and others. These key experiences support children's intense desires to interact successfully within a social context: "I know what to do!" "I'll show you."

The High/Scope key experiences are central to young children's development. They occur most often in *active learning* situations in which children have opportunities to make choices and decisions, manipulate materials, use language in personally meaningful ways, and receive appropriate adult support and guidance.

Social development
• Making and expressing choices, plans, and decisions

• Recognizing and solving problems

• Expressing and understanding feelings

• Taking care of one's own needs

• Understanding routines and expectations

• Being sensitive to the feelings, interests, needs, and backgrounds of other persons

• Building relationships with children and adults

• Creating and experiencing collaborative play

• Developing strategies for dealing with social conflict

"Let's both have the paint, okay?" "That boy's sad 'cause he wants his mom."

Language and representation. The language key experiences encourage children to talk about what they are doing, what they feel, and what they want—in their own words. When children use their own words to describe their experiences and feelings, even if it is a struggle, they are more conscious of their discoveries and better able to apply them in future situations than if an adult speaks for them. The representation key experiences serve the same function as the language key experiences; representation helps children remember, re-enact, and apply what they know. In this set of key experiences, however, children recall and interpret their experiences through their pretend play, drawings, and paintings, and by making models out of blocks, clay, wood, etc.

Classification, seriation, number, space, and time. These key experiences provide children with hands-on opportunities to work with and understand the relationships among things in their world: how things are the same or different; how things compare to each other; where things are in space and time; how to use things to make other things happen. By finding out about the things in their world and how they work, children gain a sense of control over themselves and their environment.

Physical development. Through these key experiences, children move in a variety of ways, developing coordination, body awareness, and a sense of physical enjoyment, which in turn support their social and cognitive growth.

Careful observers of young children recognize where the key experiences originate—with the children themselves! This is why we say they are developmentally appropriate. Rather than impose adult-set goals on children, the key experiences identify the kinds of activities young chil-

As adults and children work together, their roles become interchangeable—both are teachers and both are learners!

Representation
• Recognizing objects by sound, touch, taste, and smell

• Imitating actions and sounds

• Relating pictures, photographs, and models to real places and things

• Role-playing, pretending

• Making models out of clay, blocks, etc.

• Drawing and painting

Language
• Talking with others about personally meaningful experiences

• Describing objects, events, and relationships

• Having fun with language: rhyming, making up stories, listening to poems and stories

• Writing in various ways (drawing, scribbling, letter-like forms, invented spelling, conventional forms)

• Having one's own language written down and read back

• Reading in various ways: recognizing letters and words, and reading storybooks and other printed materials

dren are naturally attracted to. This makes it easier for adults to support children's interests and to help children become more aware of what they are doing. As children become conscious of their interests, strengths, and abilities, they are more apt to draw upon them when trying new things. This, in turn, helps them grow.

How Do the Key Experiences Affect Teaching and Learning?

Once adults start using the key experiences to guide their observations of children, the roles of adults and children as teachers and learners take on new dimensions.

Classification
• Investigating and labeling the attributes of things

• Noticing and describing how things are the same and how they are different

• Sorting and matching

• Using and describing something in several different ways

• Distinguishing between "some" and "all"

• Holding more than one attribute in mind at a time

• Describing what characteristics something does not possess or what class it does not belong to

Seriation
• Comparing along a single dimension: longer/shorter, rougher/smoother, etc.

• Arranging several things in order along some dimension and describing the relationships: longest, shortest, etc.

• Fitting one ordered set of objects to another through trial and error

Number
• Comparing number and amount: more/less, more/fewer, same amount

• Arranging two sets of objects in one-to-one correspondence

• Counting objects, counting by rote

Blending teaching and learning. As adults and children work together, guided by the key experiences, the roles of teacher and learner become interchangeable. Adults learn about children's individual interests, strengths, and abilities by watching, listening, and conversing with them. Children learn about people and things from working in an environment that adults have planned and arranged for their learning. In this atmosphere of mutual respect and appreciation, people of all ages can learn by doing.

Sharing control. Since the key experiences come from the things young children actually want to do (for example, putting things together and taking them apart), rather than from adult notions of what they should be doing (for example, "cutting on a straight line"), they allow children and adults to share control over the learning environment. Adults set up an environment that offers a rich variety of materials children can work with in many ways. Within this framework, children are free to choose materials and decide what to do with them. During one work time, for example, 3-year-old Jacqui used scissors to cut paper fringes and modeling dough and carried these about in her purse as pretend money. Her teacher recognized these actions as the first part of the classification key experience, "using and describing something in several different ways."

Children and adults also share control over the learning environment through the language key experiences—adults listen patiently as children describe in their own words what they are doing, thinking, feeling, and observing: "Look it! Paint going down!" Adults also promote children's language by encouraging children to talk to each other—"Tell Josh what your paint's doing" and by asking occasional questions that encourage children to think out loud: Adult:

Careful observers of young children recognize where the key experiences originate—with the children themselves! In the natural course of building a model, this child is engaging in key experiences in representation, classification, and number.

Space
• Fitting things together and taking them apart

• Rearranging and reshaping objects (folding, twisting, stretching, stacking) and observing the changes

• Observing things and places from different spatial viewpoints

• Experiencing and describing relative positions, directions, and distances

• Experiencing and representing one's own body

• Learning to locate things in the classroom, school, and neighborhood

• Interpreting representations of spatial relations in drawings and pictures

• Distinguishing and describing shapes

Time
• Starting and stopping an action on signal

• Experiencing and describing different rates of movement

• Experiencing and comparing time intervals

• Experiencing and representing change

• Recalling events, anticipating events, and representing the order of events

• Using conventional time units, and observing that clocks and calendars mark the passage of time

"What's making your paint do that?" Child: "It's alive!"

What children say and do guides adults in adding new materials and experiences to the environment. In other words, children are in control of what they do, say, imagine, and understand, while adults are in control of deciding how they can most effectively support children's thinking and actions.

Sharpening observation skills. Adults using the key experiences become increasingly skilled observers. Instead of saying, for example, "Samantha played in the sandbox again today," an awareness of the key experiences (in this case, "using something in several different ways") enables adults to make more detailed observations:

"Samantha spent a long time at the sandbox figuring out different ways to fill and empty a baby bottle. First she used her hand as a scoop, then she used a measuring cup. After pouring

Movement, physical development

• Moving in locomotor ways

• Moving in non-locomotor ways

• Moving with objects

• Following movement directions

• Describing movement

• Expressing creativity in movement

• Feeling and expressing beat

• Moving with others to a common beat ■

all the sand out on her hand, she put the bottle on its side and pushed sand into it, and then she shoved the bottle into the sand to fill it. Next she tried filling the bottle with a fork, but the sand ran through the tines. Then she picked up the funnel and a big spoon. "Look it, look it," she said again and again. "I see," I said to her, "You are scooping up sand and putting it in the funnel and it's pouring out the bottom into the bottle."*

Building on strengths. The key experiences help adults support and be enthusiastic about what children are doing:

"Did you see how much painting Garvy was doing today?! First he painted lines using all the colors, then he covered the whole paper with red. He was really watching the paint drip down and using his fingers to stop some of the drips. When I asked him about the drips, he said the paint was alive, so I knew he was really thinking about what he was doing. He was exploring materials, discovering relations through direct experience, transforming and combining materials, and he was really involved for the whole work time."

The key experiences spotlight children's interests, strengths, and abilities for adults. This enables adults to convey their enthusiasm about all the things children are doing to fellow program staff, to parents, and to the children themselves. When children's actions are seen in such a positive light by so many persons, growth and learning flourish.

How Can Adults Learn the Key Experiences?

Mastering the key experiences needn't be an overwhelming task. Adults need to allow plenty of time, and start wherever they feel most comfortable. Here are some strategies we recommend to teaching teams. Team members:

• **Refer to** *Young Children in Action*, the High/Scope preschool manual, beginning with the chapter that interests the team most. Next, team members skim the accompanying chapter in *A Study Guide to Young Children in Action*, particularly the summary statement and the exercises in identifying the key experiences in real-life situations (see resource list, page 297).

• **Identify materials** that support specific key experiences. Adults can list, for example, all the materials currently available in their active learning environment on a daily basis that might encourage children to "make models of clay, blocks, etc." The next step is to brainstorm a list of all the materials that might be added to the center to encourage further model-making.

• **Share stories about** children's activities with classroom colleagues and decide which key experiences were occurring. For example, *"Ricky, Rocky, and Chris were excited about the three boxes we put in the block area. They began thinking of ways they could make a train. Finally they made one, using boxes taped together for cars and blocks for seats."*

• **Record anecdotes** about children classified by key experience category (social development, representation, language, classification, seriation, number, space, time, and physical development). Make a key experience chart for each child with a column for each category; write down the anecdote in the appropriate column. This makes it easier for staff to save stories (like the one above) to share with colleagues and parents and also to organize them around the key experiences that are most readily identifiable.

• **Use small-group time** as a learning laboratory. Adults provide a range of interesting materials for children to use. During the activity,

Cindy O'Brien, Fayette County Head Start, Reflects on the Key Experiences in Her Journal:

"The key experiences make order out of chaos. They focus attention on one element in a profusion of messages. Observation is important and must be used with the key experiences. The key experiences give you some way to put meaning into your observations of children's play." ▪

adults watch what children do and listen to what they say, using the key experiences as a framework for understanding their behavior. At the end of the day, they record on their key experience charts all the things they learned about each child at small-group time. When one adult gave children containers of stones and shells, she learned, for example, that Ronnette was intent on *investigating and labeling the attributes of things*. Here is the anecdote she entered, under classification: 2/17— Ronnette said, "This one gets all them pointy things right by the side."

• **Post the key experiences** where adults can see them during work time. As team members watch, listen to, and join children in their play, they note which key experiences are occurring. For example, if Jamie says "Look it! Look at my tunnel!", the adult might think of the key experience *observing things and places from different spatial viewpoints*. The adult could reply, "I see," and lie down on the floor to look through the tunnel. If Jamie joins her, he would be looking at his tunnel from another perspective.

As program staff continue to develop their understanding of the key experiences by using these strategies, they'll find them increasingly useful. Eventually, the process of using key experiences as a framework for observing and supporting children becomes second nature to adults in High/Scope programs. ▪

Communication: Why It's So Important in the High/Scope Curriculum

by

Bettye McDonald

In High/Scope classrooms, teachers and children communicate in many, many ways. **Natural communication between teacher and child and among peers is the key to strengthening and extending the young child's language development.** Some communication methods are common to all early childhood settings, but others are inherent to High/Scope's curriculum approach. We encourage teachers and children to work together to pose and solve problems, plan activities, choose materials, and clean up; asking and answering questions is a key aspect of these interactions. In this approach, **teachers' questioning styles and planning methods serve as catalysts for child exploration and self-discovery.**

In a classroom with 18 or 20 young children, teachers may find that children are at many different levels in language development. Some children need good speech models and lots of experience in labeling and describing their actions; others can't respond well to open-ended questions, but will benefit from having their statements expanded; still others will be challenged by open-ended questions that encourage higher-level thinking. We don't think these variations in students' developmental levels have to slow down or inhibit language experiences in the classroom. Working within High/Scope's daily routine, teachers can meet the needs of a variety of students by providing numerous opportunities for children to experience language in naturally occurring situations.

Normal communication between adults and children is one key to strengthening and extending language development.

Teachers Make the Difference!

High/Scope consultants have visited many, many early childhood classrooms and centers over the years, and have observed adults use many different approaches to encourage and support children's language development. In our view, some are much more successful than others. Consider these classrooms:

> *Classroom A: Teacher Janet A. is sitting at the art table with Jude and Herbert, who are putting scotch tape on red construction paper. Jude says, "Me went to the movies last night." Janet replies, "Jude, say, 'I went to the movies last night.'" Jude dutifully says, "Me went to the movies last night." Janet replies, "I went to the movies last night, Jude." Jude responds, "You did? I didn't see 'ya!"*

We can see that Janet is trying to correct Jude's language. It's equally obvious that Jude is doing what most preschoolers would do—he is taking Janet's comments *literally*.

Classroom B: Teacher Howard H. moves from one group of children to another, always making comments and asking questions. Approaching one child, he says, "Bobby, you are building a road for your car. Where are you going on your road?" Howard then moves to another child and says, "This is a truck you are using, Charley. The truck is red; it is a dump truck. This dump truck is bigger than the truck Zee is using." Then Howard approaches Gloria and says, "What color is your barn?" When Gloria replies that her barn is orange, Howard says, "No, it is brown," and moves on to work with another child.

Howard is bombarding the children with questions and statements for which he has predetermined the answers or for which there are no answers. He moves quickly from child to child, rarely pausing to elicit children's replies. He is unaware of the importance of employing a noncritical questioning and conversational style when talking with young children. When teachers answer questions for children and/or correct their responses abruptly, children become less willing to ask questions.

Classroom C: Teacher Roberta C. walks over to the housekeeping area where the children are playing "family" and knocks on an imaginary front door. Bebe answers the door, saying, "Com'on in, Teacher, we're playin' Momma." Roberta asks, "May I visit you for a short while?" Bebe replies, "Sit down and I'll git 'ya some coffee. Here." Roberta says, "Will you serve something else with this coffee?" Bebe thinks for a moment, then says, "Yeah. Here is a doughnut." (Bebe puts a pine cone on a plate and passes it to Roberta.)

Roberta is trying to provide an opportunity for Bebe to **talk with others about personally**

Language Key Experiences

• Talking with others about personally meaningful experiences

• Describing objects, events, and relationships

• Having fun with language: rhyming, making up stories, listening to poems and stories

• Writing in various ways (drawing, scribbling, letter-like forms, invented spelling, conventional forms)

• Having one's own language written down and read back

• Reading in various ways: recognizing letters and words, and reading storybooks and other printed materials. ■

Rather than bombard children with questions, adults support language development by first observing children closely and then using language that relates directly to their activities.

meaningful experiences and to allow Bebe to **describe objects, events, and relationships.** These are two of the six **key experiences in language** promoted in High/Scope classrooms. The key experiences are listed on page 73.

In their attempts to communicate, young children must comprehend an idea formulated by another person, express themselves within the context of the topic at hand, and integrate this information into a sequence of events and experiences that will expand their understanding of the world in which they live. In their attempts to respond to others, young children use language to represent their personal, egocentric perceptions of events and things. The process of moving beyond this egocentric stage of development is facilitated by children's consistent and meaningful verbal interactions with both peers and adults.

Communication Checklist

Consider the following suggestions as you encourage and support communication among the children in your classroom:

☐ Are you providing a warm, accepting environment with a variety of accessible materials that invite children to explore and manipulate and to talk about what they are doing?

☐ Are your comments, discussion, and questions appropriate to each child's level of understanding? Are you providing as much specificity, variety, and complexity as possible in the language you use with children?

☐ Are you choosing the right time to talk with children? It's not a good idea to interrupt their play abruptly. Instead, observe what they are doing for a while and wait for an opportune moment to initiate a conversation that will fit the situation.

☐ Are you listening to and observing children to find out what meanings they are giving to words and then helping them develop, clarify, and refine them? Are you focusing on what children say, not on how they say it?

☐ When children ask questions, are you helping them find the answers for themselves and then elaborating on these answers?

☐ Are you helping the children develop observational skills to broaden their experimental base?—"What did you see on the side of the building, Jasper? Did you notice anything on the front of the building?"

☐ Are you restating what a child has told you, modeling the correct pronunciation, grammar, and/or syntax, yet keeping your language at a level the child can understand? Maintaining eye contact? Speaking directly to the child and calling him or her by name? Allowing time for a response? Children will adopt your methods, consciously or unconsciously, and will benefit from them throughout their lives.

☐ Are you repeating the same idea in several different ways?

☐ Are you asking children open-ended questions? "What would you have done, Christy?" "What can you tell me about . . .?" "Why do you think that happened, Larry?"

If you have answered yes to most of these questions, you are conversing with children in a style that is likely to promote their active language learning. ■

Right! Young Children Can Write!

by

Jane Maehr

*"Whatever be the system of English Gram-
mar used in the schools, the object of it should be
the preparation of the children for writing and
speaking the language correctly. . . . All this we
do, and much more, before we require them to
write what are called set compositions. If they
get mechanical skills, and learn to spell, capitalize, punctuate. . ., they will begin to compose as
soon as they have any ideas. . . ."*

— Excerpt from *The Common School Journal and
Educational Reformer*, December 15, 1852

Although we've changed many educational practices since 1852, it's surprising how often we see writing in preschools and
kindergartens approached almost as it was in
Boston 140 years ago!

Many educators, and parents, continue to
assume that young children must progress
through a sequence of clearly defined skill areas
to acquire listening, speaking, reading, and, finally, writing facility. Thus, young children are
often not encouraged to write until after they
have learned how to read and have mastered the
mechanics of writing (grammar, capitalization,
punctuation).

However, recent studies in the area of *emergent literacy*—the early stages of learning to write
and read—have produced exciting findings on
how young children develop their literacy skills.

Now we know that young children compose before they know much about the conven-
tions of writing and reading or have the skill to
control the formation of letters. As young children gradually realize the usefulness of writing,

When to Use Dictation

When children describe a drawing they have made or a project they have completed, should we automatically transcribe their thoughts into conventional print? Current research suggests that in addition to taking dictation from children, it is also important to encourage them to "write in their own way" and then "read" their messages to us.

Children who often dictate their thoughts and stories rather than write them in their own way, or who don't even try to write because the puzzle of letters and symbols seems too complicated, should be encouraged to venture into writing on their own. If children are led to believe their efforts to write are unintelligible, they may decide the risks they have taken to communicate are too great to be taken again.

We're not suggesting there will never be occasions when children would dictate their thoughts to adults. Certainly we should record group experiences and events so there is a basis for shared enjoyment and frequent occasions for re-reading. Dictation also is an effective device for demonstrating the initial connection between oral and written language. It also may serve as a back-up resource for children's early attempts to recall activities and plans. And with early language users, dictation may well serve an empowering function, enabling children to bring us into their worlds by

Taking dictation is an effective device for demonstrating the connection between oral and written language. Adults should also encourage children who cannot yet write conventionally to "write in their own way."

even unconventional writing, they are encouraged to develop related literacy skills.

A Developmental Approach to Literacy

A **developmental approach** to literacy emphasizes the **gradual emergence of skills in all areas of language** rather than the **end results of this process:** formal skills in speaking, reading, and writing.

High/Scope curriculum developers and teaching adults recognize that preschoolers and kindergartners have plenty of ideas and that they enjoy composing, and even reading, what they've written—if they are encouraged to read and write *in their own way.*

In High/Scope preschool and kindergarten classrooms, centers, and homes, young children often write and read in unconventional forms (scribblings, drawings, letter-like marks) to relay their thoughts and describe their experiences. We don't view their attempts to communicate in this way as "mistakes." Instead we encourage young children to "write" without worrying about the mechanics of writing. Just as important, when children want to "write" or "read," we realize they have important things to tell us.

High/Scope teaching adults and parents, though supporting the naturalness of learning about reading and writing, don't adopt a "hands-off" or "laissez-faire" approach to literacy development. Instead they **enrich the total atmosphere** in which a child lives and learns so that authentic reasons for learning to write and read are readily apparent to the child. Also, they **provide young children with numerous opportunities to hear good literature and to use language** in many forms to accomplish tasks.

In High/Scope learning settings, adults **provide children with every possible opportunity to observe and use purposeful writing.** On the first day at the High/Scope Demonstration Preschool, for example, each child chooses an identification symbol that is used to label his or her cubby, artwork, and other belongings. Children's symbols are usually drawings of shapes of familiar objects (e.g., circle, star, boat, tree). Each child's symbol is displayed on an identification sign that also includes the child's printed name and photo. In addition to using their symbols daily, children have plenty of opportunities to observe the actual process of writing as adults involve children in writing messages, parent notes, and lists of things to do. Because the symbols and processes of writing are commonplace in High/Scope early learning environments, chil-

having us transcribe their thoughts and ideas.

Nevertheless, dictation is just one tool to use in the process of helping young children become literate; it is not the only one. ∎

Useful Resources

Clay, M. M. (1975). *What did I write? Beginning writing behavior.* Portsmouth, NH: Heinemann Educational Publishers.

Hiebert, E. H. (1988, Nov.). The role of literacy experiences in early childhood programs. *The Elementary School Journal.*

Kontos, S. (1986, Nov.). What preschool children know about reading and how they learn it. *Young Children.*

Pflaum, S. W. (1986). *The development of language and literacy in young children* (3rd. ed.). Columbus, OH: Charles E. Merrill Publishing Co.

Schickedanz, J. A. (1986). *More than the ABCs: The early stages of reading and writing.* Washington, DC: NAEYC.

Strickland, D. S., & Morrow, L. M. (Eds.). (1989). *Emerging literacy: Young children learn to read and write.* Newark, DE: International Reading Association.

Teale, W. H. (1988, Oct./Nov.). Writing in the early childhood classroom. *Reading Today.*

Teale, W. H., & Sulzby, E. (Eds.). (1986). *Emergent literacy: Writing and reading.* Norwood, NJ: Ablex.

Temple, C., Nathan, R., Burris, N., & Temple, F. (1988). *The beginnings of writing* (2nd ed.). Boston, MA: Allyn and Bacon, Inc.

dren have ample opportunities to observe the relationship between *spoken* and *written* language.

Moreover, High/Scope preschools, kindergartens, and day care homes or centers often have some type of "writing area" or "office center." In a preschool or day care program, for example, the writing area may simply be an informal arrangement, such as a table containing writing implements and materials; in a kindergarten, it may be a full-fledged activity area. Whatever the setting, the place where children are encouraged to "write" should be stocked with a variety of writing tools. Most important, it should be a place where children feel free to "write in their own way."

Children who respond in such a setting by saying "I can't write" or "I don't know how," or who assume that an adult will automatically write for them, will soon learn that adults believe they can write. Although they may write in unconventional forms, children learn that adults understand and value their messages. A comment from an adult such as, "You write it your way—I have you here to read it to me!" not only assures children that it's OK to write in their own way but also that they are capable of reading their messages. Gradually, as the pieces of the literacy puzzle fill in, children gain increasing skill in both writing and reading conventionally.

Conventional and Unconventional Writing

Even casual observers of young children's writing will see that they often combine conventional and unconventional print. Some preschoolers and many kindergartners know how to write their names conventionally. However, as we've noted earlier, most preschoolers are usually more comfortable scribbling their messages or at-

Learning to appreciate books is built into the opening of the day at the High/Scope Preschool, as adults and children read and explore books together as the children arrive.

tempting representational drawings than trying to write in conventional form. Occasionally, preschoolers will move on to forming letter-like units or even a letter or two found in their names. At the beginning of the school year, some kindergartners will be able to string nonphonetic letters together in imitation of print; as the year progresses, some will begin to invent the spelling of isolated words and compile lists of words they know.

It's important for adults to recognize that such experimentation at both the preschool and kindergarten levels allows children to use the

**Ways to Help
Children Help
Themselves
Develop as Readers
and Writers**

• **Encourage parents
to set aside time for
reading to and with chil-
dren,** to reward children
with extra reading time,
and to choose books for
special family occasions.

• **Support all at-
tempts by children to
write,** without insisting on
correct forms. Encourage
parents to do the same.

• **Encourage each
child to "read back"
what he or she has writ-
ten** (even if *you* can't read
it, its meaning to the child,
as writing, should be acknowledged). Encourage
parents to do the same.

• **Encourage children
to take risks in relating
sounds to letters** ("I wonder how you'd go about
writing that word"); then
accept their phonetic
spelling (*LFANT* for *ele-
phant*).

• **Encourage chil-
dren**—at school or at
home—**to use writing to
make things happen:**
(Making a "Keep Out"
sign for the door; writing
invitations).

• **Encourage children
to enjoy language and
literacy in all its forms:**
singing; chanting; telling
stories and jokes; reciting
poems; or just talking.

• **Be prepared to
read, read, and read
again children's favorite
books** and encourage
parents to do the same. ∎

more comfortable nonconventional forms of writing to express complex thoughts. By encouraging children to write in their own way, we assure
that the composition process, as a whole, does
not stand or fall on children's knowledge of or
skill in conventional writing.

Drawing, Writing, Reading — Understanding the Connections

When using the teaching techniques of the
emergent literacy approach, adults understand
the relationships between children's drawing,
writing, and reading. We realize that some children may consider their drawings to actually be
writing, and if asked to "read" their text, they
will respond with a clear message or story. Older
children may recognize that drawing is an
illustrative form, but still continue to use it as
writing. We can encourage children to use a
broader range of writing forms by providing
many opportunities for them to practice writing—not by stressing the "correct" form.

Sometimes well-meaning parents or other
concerned adults point out errors in children's
initial attempts to write. They may discourage
their children's early writing attempts by expecting them to produce accurate "adult" forms of
writing. These children may need additional encouragement from us to continue the literacy
learning process. We can also assure their concerned parents that the trial-and-error process
whereby children gradually gain an understanding of the rules that govern spelling will usually
produce conventional spellers.

It's very important that we **resist the pressure to introduce skill-and-drill practice in
children's early years.** Forcing young children to
practice writing out-of-context words they do
not understand and cannot read, suggesting that
they print letters so that they fit in lined spaces,

insisting that words always be spelled conventionally, and over-emphasizing practice involving discrete letter/sound relationships will not make children become better writers and readers. In fact, such demands may actually make it less likely that children will develop a pleasurable association between reading and writing.

Supporting Children's Writing

Instead of such overly structured activities, adults in **day care settings and preschools** can promote the continuing development of writing skills by offering numerous **informal opportunities** for children to observe, explore, and experiment with writing. When children observe that adults are writing to accomplish real tasks, they learn the value and function of this form of communication. For example, adults can involve the children in writing brief notes to parents, in listing foods to purchase for tomorrow's snack time, or in noting down the telephone number of a pet store they're planning to visit.

It's also a good idea to have a box of writing tools and materials available for children to use when they want to "write their own way." Or, the materials could be arranged on a special table set aside for this purpose. (The side column lists some suggested materials.)

Adults should respond warmly to all attempts children make to write, including random scribbles, letterlike marks, and drawings that children call "writing." For example, they can ask open-ended questions like "Tell me what you've written" or "That's interesting . . . what about this part?" When adults **respond positively to all such efforts at written language,** children learn that their decision to take a risk with writing was worthwhile.

At the **kindergarten** level, informal opportunities to write should continue, but it's also ap-

Materials for a Writing Center

For preschoolers—
Colored pens; markers; multicolored pencils; large and small crayons; erasers; stamp sets; unlined paper of all colors, sizes, and shapes; order pads; assorted stickers and stamps; folders and magazines; partially filled notebooks; official-looking memo pads; etc.

For kindergartners—
All of the above, plus: picture dictionaries; desk calendars; menus; maps; telephone directories; old checkbooks; carbon paper; donated "junk mail" for cutting and pasting; staplers, paper clips and other fasteners; printing sets; a sturdy typewriter, word processor, or computer; etc. ■

Adults who accept and encourage all *children's attempts at writing—even if they "write" in scribbles or other unconventional forms—are supporting their emergent literacy.*

propriate for adults to begin to provide **slightly more formal and organized opportunities for writing.** For example, teachers can set aside a special time of day for writing, and at that time ask children to work in an "office center" they have set up. (The office center can be also be available as an option for children at work time.) In the office center, children should easily find everything they need (see side column) to write names and lists, to design a sign for the block center, to send notes to friends or letters to Grandma, to record telephone numbers, to write about a new baby sister, or to make up a story.

Even though many kindergartners can recognize some letters and a few familiar words and phrases, kindergartners, like preschoolers, may revert to drawing or scribbling when encouraged to write a story. Adults should accept this as a valuable attempt at writing and avoid prodding children to write only in words.

In the course of the year, some kindergartners will experiment with phonetic spelling and may begin to move closer to conventional forms. Teachers should treat such new developments as part of the natural process of developing literacy. As in all stages of this process, attempts to use emerging skills should be warmly supported, not pushed or scrutinized for errors.

Both at the preschool and kindergarten levels, this developmental approach to writing emphasizes learning experiences that are meaningful to children, not drill and practice of isolated skills.

Young Writers—Two Examples

To illustrate the development of early literacy, we'll conclude with writing samples produced by two children. Each child is well along in the process of becoming literate, but each is at a different developmental stage. The writing of each attests to the fact that contrary to the assumptions of 1852, preschoolers and kindergartners do have "ideas." And not only do they have ideas but they are quite capable of composing the text that expresses those ideas—well before they have mastered the mechanical skills and conventional forms of writing and reading!

Alice, a four-year-old preschooler, composed her story left to right, with linear mock writing. Notice that Alice added dots and firmly positioned horizontal lines as though to underscore the effort expended to fill the lines with variations of the same forms.

Alice "read" her story as follows:

"Once upon a time a mama was doing work and Freddy Cougar came into her house and ate her all up. Pretty soon she came to life and her little girl was happy. The End."

Rebecca, a five-year-old kindergartner, illustrated her text with drawings. She formed most letters conventionally, but her capitalization was random and she didn't use any punctuation.

Rebecca's sample shows that she has made considerable progress in letter/sound understanding and clearly has begun to understand the rules of spacing and directionality. But more important, it's apparent that Rebecca sees herself as a "writer" and delights her audience with an detailed account of what happened one day when the class snake was fed in front of interested kindergartners. ■

Math Learning: Making It Happen Naturally

Michael is telling Mrs. Rodriguez that he will use the large blocks to make a garage. "How many blocks will you need, Michael?" she asks. "I am going to use all the big blocks to make a garage for my cars," Michael replies with a sweeping gesture and a smile.

...

Susan is cutting strips of construction paper to make a "gluing picture" of a house. First, she cuts two red strips, each about 10 inches long, and glues one strip on the left of the paper and another on the right. She then attempts to connect the two vertical red strips by gluing a blue strip horizontally at the top end of the right strip. But the blue strip isn't long enough to reach the left strip, so she cuts another blue strip and pastes it down as an extension. This strip extends beyond the left strip, but this doesn't bother her. Susan goes through the same process to make the bottom of the house. She then pastes down more strips to subdivide the house into eight rooms. She places a small plastic bear in each of the eight rooms. "Here's my bear house I made by gluing," Susan announces proudly.

...

In the house area, Jimmy and Roland are preparing a meal. Moving back and forth between a real sink in the art area and a toy stove in the house area, Jimmy fills a plastic glass with water from the sink and dumps it into a large pan on the toy stove. After he makes several trips to the sink for water, the pan is over half full, and he dumps in some bottle caps and chestnuts. Meanwhile, Roland sets the table. He gets four plates from the shelf and places them

by
Sam Hannibal

around the table. Next to each plate he puts a cup, spoon, fork, and knife. "What are we having for lunch today, Jimmy and Roland?" asks Mr. Lopha. "Soup," says Jimmy. "And crackers and juice," adds Roland.

Do you realize that in each of these classroom scenarios, children are confronting and responding to quantitative, or "pre-math," concepts? The mathematical content of these activities may not be immediately apparent to the casual observer, because the activities don't reflect commonly held notions of what math is all about. For example, none of these children is counting out loud, doing paper-and-pencil math problems, or measuring with a formal tool, such as a ruler or measuring cup. Yet, each scenario represents a **developmentally appropriate mathematical experience**—because these preschoolers are solving problems at their level of mathematical understanding, in activities they enjoy.

Children at the preschool level are beginning to understand and work with such mathematical skills as *estimating, comparing sizes and quantities, one-to-one matching, counting, and measuring.* In the High/Scope Curriculum, the basic reasoning skills that underlie these concepts are developed through active experiences with a wide variety of concrete materials, enhanced and extended through challenging interactions with adults.

Key Experiences That Prepare for Math

The **key experiences in number** (listed in the side column on the next page) provide guidelines for promoting young children's experiences with important math concepts. Other important reasoning skills that prepare children for math are developed through key experiences in *classification*, *seriation*, *spatial relations*, and *time*, curriculum areas that are discussed more fully in other High/Scope materials.

Because many preschoolers can memorize easily, teachers may be tempted to encourage children to recite addition or multiplication facts. This is premature, since computation is rarely understood at this age. However, young children do benefit from learning number names, so rote counting is included in the key experiences; it must be noted, though, that children will not count accurately until they have had many experiences with one-to-one correspondence.

Teachers should keep the High/Scope key experiences in mind while working with children in activities involving mathematical concepts and skills. The key experiences provide a basis for observing children to see which math or "pre-math" concepts can be introduced, interacting with children to help them put their ideas into their own words and to help them develop their ideas further, and planning additional activities to develop or practice math concepts and skills.

Recognizing Opportunities for Pre-Math Learning

Accurate observation of children is an important first step for adults who wish to encourage children's pre-math learning. Let's take another look at the classroom scenarios that open this article, to identify some of the math or pre-math concepts and skills that are arising in children's play.

• **Michael** answers the teacher's "how many" question with a rough estimate (*all*) rather than a specific number like 5 or 7. This is typical of how preschoolers' understanding of *quantity* develops. Typically, young children

Key Experiences in Number

• Comparing number and amount: more/less, same amount; more/fewer, same number.

• Arranging two sets of items in one-to-one correspondence. *Example: Are there as many crackers as there are children?*

• Counting objects, counting by rote. ■

In supporting mathematical learning in young children, adults do not promote premature experiences with paper-and-pencil exercises; instead they provide materials that encourage children to count, compare, and make visual estimates.

describe amounts and quantities in gross terms (*a lot, more than you, a little bit*) before they begin to judge quantities by counting. Practice making such gross estimates is in itself a valuable experience that prepares the child for an understanding of number. If Mrs. Rodriguez wishes to take Michael one step further, however, she could ask him to go to the block area and count all the big blocks there. But if Michael shows no interest in counting, she should continue working with him on visual estimating.

• **Susan** shows her understanding of *one-to-one correspondence* when she creates eight similar rooms and places a bear in each one. Her struggles with the paper strips indicate her developing understanding of *length measurement*. Susan solves the problem of making a vertical strip to span the distance between the two horizontal

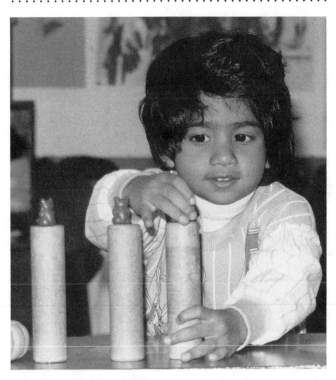

This child is developing her understanding of one-to-one correspondence as she places one bear on each pole.

strips by piecing the strips together. Though it would be easier and more accurate to use a single strip as a measuring unit, she relies on visual estimates of length, piecing the strips together until they "look right." Introducing a ruler at this point would be inappropriate; Susan must first develop the skill of using a whole object as a measuring unit before attacking the more abstract problem of measuring with a formal tool.

• **Jimmy** is working with the concepts of *quantity* and *volume* as he empties the water glass. He is also finding out with his whole body how many trips to the sink it takes to fill his cooking pan. **Roland,** in thinking about the number of people coming to eat and setting that many places at the table, is using *one-to-one* *correspondence* and appears to be *counting* with real understanding.

Children develop the foundations for more advanced math skills through these kinds of active experiences. Next we describe how adults can set the stage for such age-appropriate experiences and build upon them when they occur. We'll conclude with a scenario of a classroom math experience that arose spontaneously and was appropriately supported by an adult.

Mathematical Learning: The Adult's Role

Adults can help children discover and learn math concepts by **providing materials** that they can count, measure, put together and take apart, compare, fill, and empty. Providing a wide variety of appropriate materials, however, is not enough. Children also need time to explore the materials and to use them at their own pace, in ways that are of particular interest to them. Adults can provide this time by **establishing a routine that allows children to work on self-chosen activities.** Mathematical problems will arise naturally as children work on such activities—they will thus do math as it occurs rather than because the adult says it is "math time."

Even with appropriate materials and a routine that encourages child initiation, not all children will automatically increase their understanding of number, amount, measurement, and other math concepts and skills. Another necessary ingredient for math learning is the **support of adults** who encourage children to think about what they are doing and to put what they know into their own words.

Following is a scenario in which we show how an adult can enter a young child's play and encourage him to develop his mathematical thinking. Jimmy, at 4½, is an older preschooler.

[Mr. Reams meets Jimmy at the sink where Jimmy is using a plastic glass to fill a big baking pan with water.]

Jimmy: I'm going to make some soup for you and Mrs. Sims and Sally and Erin.

Mr. Reams: That's a good idea. I like soup. What kind of soup are you making?

Jimmy: Chicken soup. My mom made some yesterday.

[Jimmy walks to the stove in the housekeeping area, carefully empties the glass of water into the pan on the stove, and comes back to the sink to refill his glass.]

Mr. Reams: How much chicken soup are you going to make? How many glasses full of water have you put into your pan?

Jimmy: [Filling the glass again] I'm going to make lots of soup. I've put in three glasses of water already and this one will make four.

[Jimmy continues adding water to the pan in this manner until he has the amount he wants. Mr. Reams helps him keep track of the number of glasses of water he is using—a total of eight. On the last trip, Mr. Reams follows him to the stove.]

Mr. Reams: You know, Jimmy, I think I'll make some chicken soup just like yours and take it home. Is there another pan the same size as the one you're using?

Jimmy: Yes. It's right here.

Mr. Reams: Thanks, Jimmy. I'm going to fill my pan with the same amount of water as you needed. Would you help me mark on my pan where your water stopped?

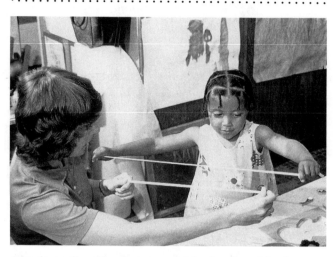

An understanding of length measurement develops through hands-on experiences in comparing lengths.

[Mr. Reams and Jimmy place the two pans side by side, one full and one empty. Jimmy marks the water level in his pan with a marker. Jimmy wants to help Mr. Reams fill his pan, so both he and Mr. Reams go to the sink, taking with them the pan and the plastic glass.]

Mr. Reams: What do we put in the water to make chicken soup, Jimmy?

Jimmy: Chicken.

Mr. Reams: OK, we'll put chicken in our pan [pretends to add chicken]. Jimmy, do you remember how many glasses full of water you used to fill your pan?

Jimmy: Eight. I think it was eight. Yes, it was eight.

Mr. Reams: Okay, eight. If we put eight full glasses of water in my pan, would it come up to this mark? What do you think?

Jimmy: It might, or it might go over that mark. It might even spill out over the side.

Mr. Reams: Why don't you put eight glasses full of water in the pan and see what happens.

[Jimmy puts eight glasses of water in the pan.]

Jimmy: Look! It's up to the mark. That's where my water was.

Mr. Reams: If we poured this water out and put in eight more glasses full, do you think it would be at this level again?

Jimmy: I'll do it again and see.

[Again Jimmy puts eight glasses of water in the pan, and again it comes to the same mark.]

Jimmy: It's at the same mark again. It's always at the same mark.

It is clear from this scenario that an adult can gently enter into a child's play and introduce an appropriate math focus. By asking open-ended, thought-provoking questions, by posing problems, and by listening as children explain things in their own words, adults will help children develop and extend their thinking about math concepts. ■

Movement Experiences: Needed, But Neglected

by
Phyllis S. Weikart

Physical movement is an important curriculum area that is often given short shrift in early childhood education and care programs. This is unfortunate, because positive movement experiences in the preschool and kindergarten years lay the foundations for health, fitness, and success in sports and music activities throughout life.

Movement experiences are important not only for children's physical development but also for strengthening their social and cognitive skills. For example, success in movement activities enhances the child's feelings of competence and self-esteem. In addition, movement activities offer valuable practice in attending, following directions, and linking language with movement—all skills that contribute to a child's academic performance.

In the past, basic movement skills developed almost automatically. Parents and older siblings transmitted these skills as they held, played with, and moved with their infants and toddlers, rocking and patting them to songs and chants, dancing and marching with them to music. Children built on these skills as they played actively with other young children: running, climbing, skipping, and galloping; playing games like tag, Red Light-Green Light, and hopscotch; chanting and singing while jumping rope.

Today, however, more and more children are entering primary school without the movement skills that children used to learn as a matter of course. Fewer and fewer kindergartners, for example, can move to the steady beat, can follow simple movement directions, can perform simple balancing tasks, or can move in unison with their classmates.

What Happened to Play?

Why are we observing this decline in movement skills? One explanation is that today's young children have fewer opportunities than those of previous generations for movement, play, and language interaction with adults and peers. There are several contributing factors:

• **First and foremost among the explanations is the U.S. child's excessive television viewing,** an activity that, according to one team of scholars, "consumes more time in a child's life than any other activity except sleeping." (See Tomlinson & Keasey in *Child Development*, Dorsey Press, Homewood, IL, 1985, page 26.) This passive activity takes time away from the activities that could develop a child's motor skills—skills that will be necessary throughout life—and contributes to the alarmingly low levels of fitness many researchers have documented in American children.

• **Today's smaller families are another contributing factor.** Young children have fewer siblings and often fewer neighborhood friends to play with informally, and this can adversely affect a child's motor skill development. Older children provide models for younger children. Young children who do not have older friends or siblings to play with lose many opportunities to engage informally and spontaneously in games and activities and to imitate the older child's actions.

• **Further, neighborhood play areas are often scarce these days, and where they do exist, they are difficult for adults to supervise indirectly.** There aren't many areas where children can run about and play freely and safely

Outdoor Movement Experiences

Mercedes Garcia, a teacher at the Broadoaks School, Whittier College, Whittier, California, reports that a variety of outdoor music and movement experiences are provided as part of their High/Scope Curriculum preschool and kindergarten programs. At work time, one option available on some days is for children to go outside and continue to work with movement and music materials, games, or activities that have been introduced at circle times. Sometimes, children choose to do these activities individually; at other times, a group of children may choose to repeat an activity they have enjoyed at another time.

Some of the activities that are most popular with children are moving with softballs, hoops, or streamers; action games and songs that involve singing or chanting; and moving to favorite musical selections.

When children are working individually outdoors with movement materials, the teacher's role is to observe, imitate, and facilitate, asking questions such as "How would *you* use the hoop?" "Could you make a different plan to use the hoop?" "What have you and Ryan been doing with the ball?" "Could you show Timmy how you moved your streamers?" "Did you move them high or did you move them low?" When children are moving to music, teachers encourage them to select their own way of marking the musical beat to help them develop beat awareness. ■

One reason for the decline observers have noted in children's movement skills and fitness is the scarcity of neighborhood play areas where children can run about and play freely and safely without adults present.

without adults present. If there is a neighborhood play space, it often is located on a corner lot instead of a backyard, and a responsible adult can't just glance out a window or door to see how things are going. This makes it difficult for the adults in charge, because they must be present to supervise the children. This is understandable, but an adult's obvious presence may stifle children's natural and inventive play.

• **Another trend that has adversely affected children's physical development is the increasing placement of children in day care and preschool programs.** In many of these programs, there is not enough space or adequate supervision for the kind of play that encourages gross-motor skill development. Also, in today's drive for formal learning, many preschool teachers and day care providers do not realize how important informal physical play is to a young child's overall development.

• **Finally, High/Scope's extensive experience providing training for early childhood** staff suggests that many adults who work with young children do not know what movement skills children of a given age can and should develop. They have never been trained in conducting movement activities and they lack guidelines and concrete ideas.

For all these reasons, and to help solve the related problems, High/Scope has developed **eight key experiences in movement for young children.** This set of experiences has grown out of our work with many populations of children and our training and conference experiences with staff from a wide range of education and care settings. These key experiences are designed to (1) help 3- to 5-year-olds develop and strengthen their motor coordination skills and (2) prepare them to be successful in future movement, music, and classroom experiences. The eight key experiences are given in the side columns. Since the space does not allow for a detailed discussion of all eight key experiences here, the focus of the rest of this article is on one: *feeling and expressing beat*. This key experience was selected because it lays the foundation for the easy acquisition of other physical skills; in addition, once understood, this key experience is easy to plan for and is a good starting point for teachers who want to enhance the movement activities in their classrooms.

Basic Timing: Feeling and Expressing Beat

A group of preschoolers are singing and doing "Pizza Hut" (an action song) at circle time. They are successfully performing the motions of the song in unison. Most of these children have had two years of action songs and beat-keeping activities.

...

Key Experiences in Movement

Following movement directions: Responding to spoken directions, visual demonstrations, or hands-on assistance

Describing movement: Using language to develop awareness of what the body is doing, to plan movements, and to recall movements

Moving in nonlocomotor ways: Moving in place, without transferring weight

Moving in locomotor ways: Moving from place to place (walking, jumping, skipping, etc.)

Moving with objects: Moving with balls, ribbons, paper plates, scarves, bean bags, etc.

Expressing creativity in movement: Using movement to solve problems, represent, fantasize

Feeling and expressing beat: Developing the ability to feel and walk to the steady beat of music or rhythmic language

Moving with others to a common beat: Performing sequences of movement to the beat in coordination with a partner or with the group ∎

Sure-Fire Beat Activities

Here are some suggestions for activities that help children develop beat competency.

• Have the children slowly pat different parts of the body with both hands simultaneously, while chanting the name of the body part as it is touched. For example, you and the children chant *chin, chin, chin, chin* while touching both hands to the chin as each word is spoken. Repeat this sequence with several different body parts, then ask children to take turns picking what part of the body the group will pat.

• Have children march in place or around the room to instrumental music. Children can take turns leading the group. Prepare the children for marching to the music by chanting *march, march, march, march* with them as they march with their feet in place. (Children do not chant as they march to the music, though the teacher may establish the steady beat by chanting *march, march, march, march* once or twice.)

• If you are sitting next to children during circle activities, pat the steady beat on children's backs or knees as rhymes and songs are sung or chanted. If a child hangs on to you or sits on your lap, move that child to the beat while chanting or singing.

• Chant children's names (or their favorite words) with children, as everyone pats themselves or takes steps to each beat of the chant. Allow children to choose which

Moving with various objects helps children develop many basic movement capacities.

As music plays on the tape recorder, a group of kindergarten children are marching around the classroom. The teacher notes that very few of the children, less than one fifth, are marching to the beat.

In the first example, young children are demonstrating motor skills that are easily attainable by children of this age group who have had appropriate movement experiences. By contrast, the children in the second example have not acquired a basic movement capacity—basic timing. *Basic timing* involves the acquisition of two skills: *beat awareness*, the ability to express the beat by moving the upper body (e.g., by patting both hands on knees, shoulders or other parts of the body), and *beat competency*, the ability to walk to the beat.

Basic timing is one of the most important skill acquisitions of early childhood because it is a foundation for so many other skills.

Children must master basic timing before they can develop other basic motor skills, for example, performing a series of jumps, hops, or skips. Basic timing is also a prerequisite for learning most sport skills and for participating in music activities.

When and how is basic timing developed in young children? The skill of walking to the beat successfully is attainable by 2½ years of age. This capacity develops easily if parents, caregivers, and older siblings have mastered it themselves and know the importance of providing infants and toddlers with direct experiences in matching the steady beat. Those children who develop this capacity in the preschool years have had many opportunities to feel the movements of family members as they are matched with the steady beat in music rhymes, chants, and songs. These children have been rocked, sung to, patted, stroked, burped, and jiggled to the steady beat. They have been held or walked with their feet on the adult's feet as the adult walks or dances to music.

If this skill is developed so easily and automatically, why are so few young children able to walk to the steady beat? (In fact, in one kindergarten class observed by a High/Scope consultant, not a single child had attained this skill by the beginning of the school year!)

One major set of reasons this skill does not develop is the lack of "natural" play opportunities discussed in the opening of this piece. Another more specific reason why kindergarten children have problems in this area comes from experiences in which *rhythm* rather than *beat* is emphasized. When we say "rhythm," we are referring to the surface rhythm, the pattern of short and long notes and rests in a musical melody or the syllables and pauses in a chant or poem. Rhythm is uneven. Beat, on the other hand, is the underlying structure that the mel-

name will be used next. For example:

Susan, Susan, Susan, Susan
pat   pat   pat   pat

Timothy, Timothy, Timothy, Timothy
step   step   step   step

Be sure to work up to weightbearing stepping as you use this activity. ■

ody or chant is built on, a pattern of steady beats and regular accents. (For example, see the diagram, below, of the steady beats and rhythm in the common chant, Patty Cake.)

	Pat-ty	Cake	Pat-ty	Cake	Bak-er's		Man
Rhythm of words	x	x x	x	x x	x	x	x
Steady beat of rhyme	x		x		x		x

One common experience that actually hinders the development of basic timing is that many adults tend to stimulate children to the rhythm, rather than to the beat, of a musical selection or chant. For example, an adult who is clapping out "Patty Cake" with a child will clap nine times if clapping out the rhythm, but only four times if clapping with the steady beat. When attention is focused in this way on rhythm, rather than beat, the young child's hearing and feeling become attuned to the rhythm. We say in these cases that the child has been bonded to rhythm rather than beat.

The majority of today's young parents, caregivers, and early childhood teachers have been raised with this same emphasis on rhythm rather than beat. They remember their own childhood experiences, and it is natural that they would repeat them as they care for and work with young children. These adults need retraining to understand why it is important to provide frequent experiences that focus on steady beat and how to design such experiences.

Fortunately, the activities that can foster an awareness of steady beat in children are simple for teachers to design and conduct, once they understand the fundamentals. But since many adults themselves lack basic timing, High/Scope consultants often start their training experiences for early childhood educators and caregivers with a few activities that help the adults develop the ability to use the steady beat.

We've found that once adults become aware of the importance of basic movement capacities such as basic timing, they find many creative ways to foster them in their own work with children. A wide range of High/Scope curriculum materials and training options focusing specifically on music and movement are available to assist in this process (see materials list, page 297). ■

Music and Movement Throughout the Daily Routine

by
Ruth Strubank

Young children first communicate with the world by making sounds and moving their bodies. Since movement is one of the child's earliest modes of communication, adults need to continue to support this natural means of expression in the preschool years. In the High/Scope Demonstration Preschool, we provide music and movement opportunities for children throughout the daily routine. As always, our emphasis is on direct and active experiences.

In addition to developing physical skills, music and movement activities provide opportunities for developing a wide range of other skills. As children take part in physical activities, they are beginning to figure out how their world works and how they fit into it. As they move their bodies and show and tell others how to move, they may also pretend, make spatial observations, match, count, and use language skills.

Music and movement activities also provide children with opportunities for taking initiative, making choices and decisions, and solving problems. In music and movement experiences, as in all classroom activities, we try to strike a balance between teacher and child initiatives. We plan music and movement experiences by identifying children's interests and developing abilities, as well as by using our own interests and ideas. In addition, in the course of both teacher- and child-initiated activities, children make decisions about how they will move, and adults respond to and extend upon children's decisions. Throughout all these activities, we use the key experiences to help us identify the developing abilities children are using and to guide us in

Many movement experiences in High/Scope's programs are initiated by children and supported and extended by adults.

planning related experiences to support and extend children's interests and abilities.

In addition to providing many opportunities for children to develop a wide range of abilities, music and movement experiences are important because they give children and adults a focus. These planned and unplanned events help make transitions go more smoothly, and help children make good use of times when they must wait to do something else. Music and movement activities are not used as a means of controlling children but as a tool for managing them.

Following we describe some of the music and movement experiences, both planned and spontaneous, that have occurred during various parts of the daily routine at the High/Scope Preschool this year. Note that during each part of the day, either children or adults may initiate music and movement activities, or the activity may reflect a blend of child and adult initiatives.

Greeting Time (Morning Circle)

Child-initiated: As two children sit at the circle, one child moves her leg into a new position (e.g., leg tucked up) and asks another, "Can you make your leg look like mine?" Soon this becomes a turn-taking game as each child moves into a new position and the others imitate.

Adult-initiated: The adult reads books to children that are tied to songs, e.g., *The Wheels on the Bus* (Maryann Kovalski), *Abiyoyo* (Pete Seeger), *Down by the Bay* (Raffi), or that have repeating phrases or other predictable elements, e.g., *Chicka Chicka Boom Boom* (Bill Martin, Jr.), *Chicken Soup With Rice* (Maurice Sendak), *Over in the Meadow* (Paul Galdone). Adults encourage children to move their bodies to the beat of the song or repeated phrase.

Planning Time

Adult- and child-initiated: Adults and children make a "train" with their bodies and move through the work areas, dropping off "passengers" as they make plans to work in particular areas. The adults developed this planning strategy because one child had been engaging in lots of train play the day before.

Adult- and child-initiated: The teacher lays a "planning path" (made from long sheets of fabric) on the floor and asks children to choose a way to move their bodies along the path (e.g., crawl, hop, go backwards, jump, walk like a crab) to an area where they plan to work.

Adult-initiated: As children take turns stating their plans, the adult requests a child's plan by chanting: "Jerry, Jerry, Jerry, Jerry—It's your turn to plan if your name is Kerry," "Beara, Beara, Beara, Beara—It's your turn to plan if your name is Sara," and so forth.

Work Time

Child-initiated: A child who has brought in some taped music asks to listen to it during work time. Some of the other children extend on this by dressing up, building a stage, and singing and dancing to the music.

Child-initiated: A child moves from the computer area to the art area reciting "Humpty Dumpty" while doing a scissor step and opening and closing her arms overhead. As she arrives in the art area, another child joins in, reciting the rhyme and stamping the beat with her feet. This is an example of how children use music and movement themselves as a transition from one plan or area to the next.

Child-initiated: A child sings as she paints at the easel. She paints to the music she is creating, making large brushstrokes that rise and fall with the melody.

Adult-initiated: As a child jumps along the floor from the art area to the block area, the adult says *jump* each time the child's feet hit the floor. Later the child uses the language himself as he jumps to another space.

Adult initiated: While a child and an adult paint a box together, the adult spontaneously sings a song describing what they are doing: (to the tune of "Yankee Doodle") "We are painting red and yellow at the High/Scope Pre-school, I hope we can get it all done before it's time for clean-up."

Clean-up Time

Child-initiated: A child speaks rhythmically, "We are the clean-up kids!" Soon all the children join in the chant.

Adult-initiated: The adult sings, "We're putting away the toys, We're putting away the toys..." to the tune of "Farmer in the Dell." Soon

Transitions between different parts of the routine are a good opportunity for movement experiences—in this case, children go from the greeting circle to the planning table while moving like various animals.

children are singing the song to themselves as they are cleaning up.

Recall Time

Adult- and child-initiated: The adult asks a child to find something he or she worked with and to show the other children how it was used. Everyone then imitates the child's actions (using exaggerated motions) and sings about what the child did (to the tune of "This Is the Way We Wash Our Clothes"): "Steven worked with markers today, Stephen worked with markers today, Stephen worked with markers today, In the art area."

Adult- and child-initiated: The adult rolls a tennis ball to a child and sings (to the tune of "Yankee Doodle"), "David, David, catch the ball and tell us how you worked." The child who has just recalled then rolls the ball to another child and sings along with the adult.

Snack Time

Child-initiated: A child speaks rhythmically, "No more cookies and no more milk." The other children join in the chant.

Adult-initiated: The adult asks children who are helping pass things out to show or tell how they plan to move, e.g., a child says, "I'm going to hop over to the refrigerator and get the juice and walk back holding the pitcher like this."

Circle Time

Adult- and child-initiated: While playing recorded music, the adult asks children to choose different ways to move around the circle (e.g., walking, jumping, wiggling), describing their movements by showing and telling what they are doing.

Adult- and child-initiated: An adult sings a story song using the flannel board and felt pieces cut in the shapes of the objects and characters in the story. The story, sung to the tune of "Yankee Doodle," begins like this: "I wrote a letter to my love and on the way I dropped it, A little doggie picked it up and put it in the mailbox." Each time the song is sung, the adult changes the word at the end of the verse (e.g., *pumpkin*, *boot*, *heart*). The adult encourages children to choose other words and to make motions with the corresponding felt pieces.

Child-initiated: At a child's request, the group plays "Duck, Duck, Goose." The adult encourages the children to decide what text they will use as they pat their friends' heads. One child comes up with the words, "Slipper, slipper, slipper, shirt."

At circle time, this adult initiates an experience in moving with objects. Children take turns with the adult in leading the activity.

Small-Group Time

Adult- and child-initiated: The adult provides giant Tinkertoys for children to play with, planning to focus on encouraging children to be aware of and describe how they are moving. Christopher builds a barbell and uses it to imitate weightlifting. Another child builds a jackhammer; as he pretends to drill with it, he imitates the sound a jackhammer makes.

Adult- and child-initiated: An adult builds an obstacle course for children with tables, blankets, hula hoops, carpet squares, and large boxes. The adult moves a puppet through the course to demonstrate what an obstacle course is. Then she asks children to choose different ways to move through the course. The next day she provides similar materials and asks children to create their own obstacle course.

Outside Time

Child-initiated: A child sings to herself as she swings on the swingset. As a group of children ride the tire swing, they begin to chant, "Higher, higher, higher" as they push themselves.

Child-initiated: A child walks around a large tree in the crow's nest (round tree-house) reciting familiar nursery rhymes.

Child-initiated: A child invites an adult to walk on the railroad ties that border one of the play areas, using them like a balance beam. Soon a follow-the-leader game begins as other children join the pair.

Transition Times

Adult-initiated: To end morning circle, as the children put books away and find places at the circle, the adult sings (to the tune of "Here We Go Round the Mulberry Bush"), "Time to put the books away, the books away, the books away, Time to put the books away and find a yellow square."

Adult- and child-initiated: As children move from one activity to the next, adults ask one or more children to show or tell others how they will move their bodies to the next activity.

These examples illustrate the unlimited possibilities for music and movement activities during all parts of the daily routine in High/Scope programs. When adults support the movement experiences they see children engaging in spontaneously, as well as encourage children to add a movement dimension to ongoing activities, a rich variety of movement experiences will result. ■

The Daily Routine

· ·

Structuring a predictable daily routine that provides an orderly framework for children's learning experiences is a major concern of staff of High/Scope Curriculum programs. To be considered a true "High/Scope routine" the daily schedule must have certain elements—a *plan-do-review cycle* and times for *small- and large-group activities*—but the duration and arrangement of these components are not specified, and most programs also schedule other kinds of activities as well (e.g., outside play, naptimes, meals).

The plan-do-review cycle is the centerpiece of the High/Scope daily routine. The sequence goes like this: Children plan an activity at "planning time," carry out this and other activities at "work time," and later, at "recall time," review what they did. The first three selections in the chapter—by Michelle Graves, Mary Hohmann, and Mark Tompkins—discuss this sequence in depth: the first two authors explore the child planning process; the third, the recall process.

Other articles look at the specialized issues involved in designing particular kinds of daily routines: Bonnie Lash Freeman, Mary Hohmann, and Susan M. Terdan discuss general considerations for planning an appropriate routine for day care programs; Charles Hohmann and Jane Maehr discuss the daily schedule in High/Scope kindergartens. Underlining the message that the general elements of the High/Scope daily routine must be adapted by educators to meet needs specific to the group of children, the time of year, and the nature of the setting, the last article by Warren Buckleitner and Susan M. Terdan looks at the actual daily routine of a High/Scope preschool program on the first day of the school session.

Child Planning: Why It's Important, How to Get Started

by
Michelle Graves

The idea of preschool-age children "making plans" may seem like an impossible dream to those who see planning for children as solely the adult's role. Yet helping children learn to plan is a central goal of the High/Scope Curriculum because the planning process fosters so many important abilities in preschoolers.

In High/Scope programs, each child makes a daily plan at "planning time" that he or she then carries out in the subsequent "work time" period. At planning time, children and adults get together as a group, and each child gets the chance to choose an activity and discuss his or her plans with the rest of the group. For a preschooler, a plan can be as simple as just pointing to the art area or as complex as picking out a variety of costumes and props for fantasy play. The important thing is that the child gets the chance to initiate an activity that interests him or her, and, with the help of an adult, begins to think about how he or she will go about doing it.

Why is child planning so important?

• **Planning helps children see that they can make things happen for themselves.** This enables them to develop a sense of control over their own lives and to take responsibility for the consequences of their own choices and decisions. Findings from High/Scope's long-term Curriculum Comparison Study (see side column, next page) show that giving children opportunities like this to initiate their own activities promotes positive social behavior—including reduced juvenile delinquency—later on in a child's life.

• **Planning helps children develop a better understanding of time.** Planning requires them to anticipate the future and to think about what can be accomplished in a given time period. As an adult, you may find that there are often many tasks on your "to do" list that are left unfinished at the end of the work day. You know how difficult it is to organize your own time, so it's easy to understand why this is such a difficult, yet crucial, skill for preschoolers to learn. Planning time gives preschoolers the chance to begin to develop this ability.

• **Planning helps children develop language skills.** Children learn new words and phrases as they choose their activities and identify the materials and processes they plan to use. At first, a child making a plan may, for example, simply point to the dress-up clothes in the house area. Later in the year, the child will begin to attach labels to such choices: *fireman's hat, fire extinguisher, hose, slide down the pole.*

• **Planning gives children opportunities to acknowledge and use their own moods and feelings in constructive ways.** If a child comes to school excited about a visit from his grandparents, teachers can help him identify those feelings and make appropriate plans: "So you want to make an airport so you can watch Grandma and Grandpa's plane come in."

Because planning is important for so many reasons, it's worth some extra effort to get it off to a good start. Don't expect overnight results. The planning process does not usually go smoothly at first. Most children will need help and preparation. Expecting children to jump right in and plan on the first day of school is like expecting them to know that heavy rocks will sink to the bottom of a container of water before they've had the chance to experiment with them. Children begin the planning process by first ex-

Organizing the classroom into distinct areas, such as this music area, enhances child planning because it helps children see the choices available.

ploring the people, materials, and choices that make up their environment. Adults can help by using the following strategies:

• **Arrange your classroom in defined areas that are equipped with materials children can see and reach.** Choose a regular time and place for planning. Small-group gatherings on the floor or at low tables will encourage children to share ideas. Always follow planning time with work time, because children will be eager to act on their plans at once. It's not necessary to ask all of the children to stay at the table until each has finished a plan. Remember, you also want to encourage independence.

• **Help the children learn the names of the areas, the materials, and the other children in the room.** You can do this best by talking casually with children as they work: "Elliott, that's a very tall tower you made in the toy area with the large Legos. It comes up to your waist. I wonder how far up Ilana's body it will go?" In addition, plan group activities for other times of the day that help to orient children to the classroom, the materials, and the other children. For instance, plan a small-group time that introduces painting materials in the art area or sing songs at circle time that use the children's names.

· ·

Handy Aids to Child Planning

The planning strategies below were taken from a list developed by trainers and teachers in classroom settings throughout the country using the High/Scope Curriculum. Try them in your own classroom, or use them as a point of departure in developing your own ideas. Caution: most of these are "group planning strategies" whose purpose is mainly to engage the interest of the planning group as a whole. Adults should not get so caught up in the rituals of using strategies like these that they lose sight of the ultimate goal of planning: eliciting a thoughtful, in-depth plan from each child.

• **Paper cups**—You can use paper cups in many ways during planning. For example, give a cup to every child. Possible instructions: "Put the cup on something you want to play with." "Put something you want to use inside the cup." "Punch a hole in the bottom of the cup and use it as a telescope to look at the area of the room where you want to play."

• **Telephones**—Using two toy telephones, call children one at a time and ask them what they plan to do that day.

• **Tape recorder**—Using a microphone, let the children record their plans on tape. Let them listen to the tape and have them guess who is talking.

• **Roll the ball**—From a central point in the room, have each child roll a ball into an area he or she wishes to work in. You and the child can discuss what the area is called and what materials are near the ball that the child may choose to work with.

• **Signs**—Make a sign that represents each child. The sign usually has the child's name and should also have a symbol or shape to represent the child (and possibly his or her picture). Ask children to hang their signs in the area they choose to work in to indicate the choice they've made.

• **Planning sheets**—Children make pictures of what they plan to do. This can be done in any number of ways: the child draws one or more of the materials or tools to be used; the child traces the object; the child draws a portion of the object and the teacher fills in the rest (e.g., to represent scissors, child draws double circle, teacher adds crossed lines).

• **Planning sheets with area symbols**—Make planning sheets for children with little symbols or drawings to represent each area of the room. Then have children indicate where they plan to work by drawing the symbol in the appropriate space or circling the symbol.

• **Picture boxes**—Make a representation of each material or object in your classroom by cutting out pictures from catalogs, magazines, box tops, etc., by drawing small pictures, or taking photographs. Get a small box to represent each of the areas of the room and put each picture in the appropriate box. After children have told you the area they have chosen, ask them if they can find the pictures of what they want to play with in the box for that area. Ask them to arrange the pictures in the order in which they will use them.

• **Planning books**—Make "books" of planning sheets for each child to use in the week's planning. Each page has the name of the child, the day of the week, and instructions for you to read to children, such as "Trace around something you plan to work with"; or "I will work in the _____ area."

△ Name Monday	△ Name Tuesday	△ Name Wednesday	△ Name Thursday
Trace around something	I will work in the _____	Draw a picture of a person you will play with	I will use

• **Reinforce the concept of making choices whenever you can during the day.** Making choices and seeing alternatives is basic to all good planning: "Do you want to put away the wooden blocks or the cardboard blocks, Mia?" "It was a good idea, Joshua, to use your hands to pat your shoulders." "Rachel, where else could we pat our hands?"

• **Finally, and most important of all, remember that children have different abilities.** A planning strategy that works for one child may be too difficult for another's developmental level. Take your cues from the children. Observe their behavior carefully so that you present ideas and ask questions that they can process and understand. ■

The Many Faces of Child Planning

by

Mary Hohmann

Child planning has a central role in the High/Scope Curriculum. (At "planning time," a regular part of the High/Scope daily routine, each child discusses what he or she wants to do that day. At "work time," which follows planning, children carry out their stated plans.)

Through these daily experiences with planning, children learn to articulate their ideas and intentions. They develop a sense of control over their own actions and learn to trust their inner resources. Child planning also enhances the "learning potential" of the play that grows out of it. Motivational research suggests that children's intrinsic motivation to learn is greater in activities that they select themselves. In addition, specific research on the High/Scope Curriculum suggests that the play that follows planning is more complex and challenging than unplanned play.

Children's Plans: What to Expect

There are many good reasons, then, to encourage children to plan. As adults who wish to support child planning, we need to know **what to expect from young planners.** This article discusses some of the many possible forms that child planning can take and the implications for teachers and caregivers working to support child planning.

Over the years, we've become increasingly aware of the range and variety of children's plans as we've observed planning time in many different High/Scope settings: in preschools, Head Start programs, day care settings, and home visit programs. From observational re-

Research indicates that the play resulting from child planning is more complex and challenging than unplanned play.

search conducted in High/Scope Curriculum programs, we've also learned about the planning process. Many of the insights about planning reported in this article come from a study conducted by C. Berry and K. Sylva of the plan-do-review process in British classrooms .

One dimension of child planning that most of these observers have noted is that **plans can be both verbal and nonverbal.** When asked what they would like to do, some young children respond by pointing, looking at a friend or toy, or simply going to one of the areas and beginning to play. Other children respond in single words ("cars," "hammer"), phrases ("over there by David"), brief sentences ("I want to make something for my mom"), or whole paragraphs ("First me and Lena are gonna' play dentist again. I'm being the dentist and she's the little girl. I'm gonna' give her some special stuff so her mouth don't hurt"). Adults who value child planning are careful to acknowledge and support all

One-to-One Planning Strategies

• *Ask open-ended questions:*

Adult: Tell me what you're going to do today, Bill.

...

Adult: I see that you've brought something that you plan to work with, Angie. What do you plan to do with it?

• *Co-narrate (an alternative to direct questioning):*

Adult: I'm sitting right next to a little girl named Lou. She's watching her friend Betsy.

Lou: Betsy's bathing her baby.

Adult: That baby will be clean and happy when she's done.

Lou: My baby needs a bath, too. She's crying.

Adult: She's crying for her bath.

Lou: I better give her a bath.

• *Interpret and translate gestures into words:*

Adult: You're pointing to the book and writing area.

Terry: [nods yes].

Adult: Show me what you'll do there, Terry.

Terry: [picks up *Mr. Gumpy's Motor Car* from bookshelf].

Adult: Oh, you're going to read *Mr. Gumpy's Motor Car*.

• *Converse about space or materials:*

Adult: What will you use to make your monster house?

Dom: The cardboard blocks, the big wood blocks, and the others you can reach inside of.

Adult: You know, I see some other kids already using the big hollow blocks and some of the big wooden blocks.

Dom: I could use the pillows.

Adult: The pillows.

Dom: And maybe those boxes we had yesterday.

Adult: The boxes we used at small-group time.

Dom: Yes, they'll be the walls.

• *Talk about details:*

Adult: So your plan is to make an exercise machine, Jeff.

Jeff: I'm going to use the big, giant Tinkertoys and make some of those lifter things.

Adult: A lifter thing like a bar with weights on the ends?

Jeff: Yeah, I'll get a long Tinkertoy for the lifter and then put the round wheel things on for the weights. Then I'll make a part for your feet where you put them under and lift them like this.

• *Talk about sequences:*

Adult: What's your plan, Mira?

Mira: Play in all the areas.

Adult: All the areas. That's lots of places. What will you do first?

Mira: Go to the art area. Make a card for my mom. A "Happy Birthday" card 'cause it's her birthday. It's gonna' have flowers.

Adult: First you're making a birthday card with flowers for your mom.

Mira: Then put it in my cubby and read a book. ∎

plans that children make, whether or not they are expressed in words.

Children's plans also vary in focus and complexity. Based on their classroom observations, Berry and Sylva classified the plans children made into three different types: vague, routine, and elaborated plans.

Vague plans are minimal plans. In response to a question about what they are going to do, children just barely indicate a choice or beginning point, e.g., "Go over there," "House area," "Make something." Children who make such ambiguous plans seem to have an unclear picture in their minds of what they actually want to do. We have noticed that these children often end up doing one of three things: (1) going to a safe, unoccupied spot, picking up something like a doll or stuffed animal, and intently watching other busily engaged children; (2) wandering from place to place to explore the room and materials; or (3) seeking out an adult to join and follow them as they move about. Such children may be telling us: "I need to take in all the possibilities before I decide what to do" or "I want to do something really safe before I risk something new."

Routine plans are simple, specific plans in which children identify an activity, process, or material as their beginning intention, e.g., "Play with blocks," "Cutting—lots," "Computers." These children seem to have a clear picture in mind of themselves engaged in a particular experience or with a specific material. They know how they want to begin and generally get started right away, unless someone else is using the materials they had in mind.

Elaborated plans are more complex plans in which children mention an activity, process, or material as a beginning point, state a goal or outcome, and, in addition, mention one or more steps or materials needed to carry out their inten-

Writing and Planning

Adults demonstrate the value they place on children's plans when they write down (or record in some other way) a child's plan. This act says to the child: "Your plan is so important that I'm going to save it by writing it down." Some adults write down, word for word, what each child says, while others take briefer notes on clipboards, file cards, Post-it notes, planning notebooks, or on the computer. Whatever methods adults use, children see that the adults are writing and realize that adults value their ideas and intentions.

Children interested in writing will sometimes write their own versions of their plans. This works well when adults anticipate and appreciate a variety of drawing and writing styles and forms, including scribbles, tracings, outline shapes, designs, figures, common symbols, letters, and any combination of these forms of emergent writing. ■

tion. Here are some examples of elaborated plans:

> "Make a Robin Hood hat. With a feather, a real one like Michael's. "

> "Use the Construx. Make a telephone truck with a very tall ladder. And I think I'll put a cab for the driver. And balancers on the sides so it won't tip over."

These children have a more extensive mental picture of what they want to accomplish and how they will go about doing it. They are generally quite persistent in pursuing their original intentions in spite of problems that arise along the way.

Another dimension of child planning often noted by experienced early childhood staff is that **children's plans may be perfunctory or real.** Children are usually enthusiastic about planning. Adults can hear this enthusiasm in the tone of children's voices as they plan, and see it in their bodies as they lean forward eagerly to describe their ideas. There are times, however, when this enthusiasm is missing. Even though a child may clearly state an intention, he or she seems to be just "going through the motions" of planning.

A perfunctory plan is a signal that something is impeding or delaying planning. Perhaps the child cannot make a genuine plan until she shares an upsetting experience that happened on the way to school. Or a child may be waiting for someone: "Sometimes Noah just says something, anything, at planning, because I think what he really wants to do is play with John, who hasn't arrived yet." When adults are alert to the possible reasons behind a halfhearted plan, they can respond by discussing the child's concerns, suggesting to Noah, for example, that he wait until his friend comes and then make a plan.

When adults listen attentively as the child states an initial plan, they set the stage for an in-depth dialogue about the child's ideas and intentions.

Another variable that affects the kinds of plans children make is their experience with the planning process. Observant adults recognize that **children's plans change over time** as children become familiar with available materials and playmates and their own ability to make choices and follow through on them. Children's plans usually become increasingly verbal as time passes; they also become more focused and complex. In a 1984 study of the development of the planning process in young children, W. Fabricius reported, for example, that most 3-year-old children can keep a goal in mind, but generally work toward it one step at a time. They deal with problems as they encounter them, rather than anticipating and planning for them. Between the ages of 3½ and 5½, however, Fabricius reported that children gradually gain the ability to plan a multistep course of action, foreseeing problems and ways of dealing with them before they launch into action. For example, a 5-year-old might incorporate anticipated problems in her plan: "I'll make a bird house. I'll use the big cardboard blocks for the walls, but I'll need a big enough board or something else for the roof. If there isn't a piece of wood big enough, maybe a piece of cardboard will work."

Adult Support for Planning

Children's plans, then, come in a wide variety of forms. The range of strategies adults use to support child planning is just as wide. Here we discuss just a few of the most important support strategies you can use to enhance child planning. We don't focus on **group planning strategies**—ways of engaging the interest of the entire planning group as each child takes a turn to plan—but on **individual planning strategies**—ways of enhancing the conversation with each child about his or her intentions.

One of the primary ways you can make these individual conversations more meaningful is to **listen attentively as the child states an initial plan.** Rushing through planning can cause children to feel hurried and anxious. After you question a child about his or her plan, it is important to pause and give each child ample time to respond. Whatever the child says or does tells you something important and suggests ways you might respond. Listen and observe for both nonverbal and verbal planning. If the child's communication is nonverbal, you may want to restate it in words or engage the child in a dialogue to clarify his or her intentions. Listen also for vague, routine, and elaborated plans to gain some idea of how well the child is able to picture the desired action sequence. Then think of ways you might help him or her foresee it more completely. Listen for perfunctory plans and deal sensitively with the issues behind them, reassuring children who are not ready to plan that it's okay to wait for a while.

Once children have indicated a plan in some way, the next step for adults is to **encourage children to develop their plans further.** At this point it makes some sense to distinguish between two groups of planners, nonverbal/vague planners and routine/elaborate planners. Interestingly enough, Berry and Sylva's research suggests that adults tend to question the first group extensively, the second, hardly at all. In their analysis, adults tend to keep after the vague or nonverbal planners until they arrive at a more complete picture of what they might do, but pass up the opportunity to converse with and question children who have the potential for thinking through and articulating quite elaborate plans. It's important to remember that *all* children need the opportunity to expand on and clarify their plans—even those who've stated an initial intention fairly clearly. There are many ways adults can encourage children to develop their ideas further. For example, they can talk with children about where they will work, the materials they will use, the sequence of their actions, and other details, and they can discuss the child's prior related work.

Is there time for a thoughtful planning conversation with each child? Yes, there is. First, even though such conversations take longer than a routine question-and-answer exchange (e.g., "What are you going to do?" "Play with blocks"), they don't take that much longer. In fact, thoughtful planning conversations often go rapidly, because they are intense and full of the unexpected. In addition, when adults converse attentively with children about their plans, children are generally able to get started with less adult help—because many potential problems and choices have already been dealt with. This leaves the adult free to focus on conversations with other children about *their* plans. In this sense, in-depth planning with each

Two Steps to Success

Planning involves a series of highly personal, individual conversations that occur in a group setting. The following steps take into account both the "group" and "individual" aspects of planning.

Step one: Engage the attention and interest of the planning group through a game-like activity, a special task, or challenge. For example, children might explore a collection of new materials; take a guided tour of the center in a make-believe vehicle; use special props or materials while making a plan; use pantomime, drawing, or writing to plan; participate in games or role plays to decide whose turn it is to plan next (e.g., "Today we'll pass the planning pillow. When the music stops, whoever has the pillow will plan next").

Step two: Engage in one-on-one exchanges with each child. Talk about his or her plan. Talk to the child at his or her own level. Create an intimate, unhurried atmosphere by showing the child your genuine interest in his or her plan, and by listening and observing attentively as the child expresses an intention. Encourage the child to talk further about his or her plan by commenting or asking questions about materials, space, sequence, prior related work, and other details. Deal sensitively with any concerns that may be impeding planning. ■

child is a group management tool, since well-conceived plans generally lead the planner to a focused and appropriate set of actions. ∎

For more information on the research cited here, see Berry, C. F., and Sylva, K. (1987, unpublished), "The Plan-Do-Review Cycle in High/Scope: Its Effect on Children and Staff" (write Carla Berry, Chicago AEYC, 410 S. Michigan Ave., Chicago, IL 60605); and Fabricius, W. V. (1984, doctoral dissertation), "The Development of Planning in Young Children" (available from UMI, 300 N. Zeeb Rd., Ann Arbor, MI 48106).

A Look at Looking Back: Helping Children Recall

"Recall time used to be the most difficult part of the daily routine for me and the children. Somehow I was forgetting the principles of active learning. I would ask the children, one at a time, what they did during work time, and they would respond with three- or four-word answers. Then we decided to make recall time more active and cooperative by adding variety to the strategies we used. I can't believe the difference this has made. Now recall time is the highlight of the day!"

by

Mark Tompkins

This preschool caregiver, like many others who use the High/Scope Curriculum, has discovered that recall time can be one of the most rewarding parts of the daily routine for children and adults. The key to success is to approach recall time with the principles of active learning in mind.

In this article we explain the value of recall experiences and share strategies you can use to make recall time a more active learning experience for children. We also explore ways to encourage spontaneous recall experiences during other parts of the daily routine, and we share segments of a recall-time diary from the High/Scope Demonstration Preschool.

The Importance of Recall Experiences

Have you ever asked your own children what they did at school, only to meet with a blank stare or to be told, "I just played" or "I don't know"? Have you ever experienced similar responses when you asked children in your preschool or center to recall something they did?

A Look at Looking Back: Helping Children Recall · 129

In some cases like these, children may have difficulty recalling because their experiences haven't been personally meaningful. Children tend to recall what is vivid and exciting to them, and if adults make most or all of the decisions in a child care or classroom setting, children may "go through the motions" of the activities but not feel involved in them. At this age children are most likely to *encode*, or store, their experiences as memories when they work *actively* with materials or people—their encoding processes are tied to concrete, active experiences. If learning experiences are too abstract or do not reflect their personal interests (as with premature academic drills), children may simply not process them mentally and thus may be unable to recall them later.

But even when children enjoy what they are doing, they may respond with blank stares when asked later to recall their experiences. We must remember that children are *present-oriented*. No matter how involved they may have been in what they just did, their focus is on the *here-and-now*. **Nevertheless, when children recall their experiences as a regular part of their daily routine, as they do in the High/Scope Curriculum, the process of looking back becomes more natural to them.** When adults recognize the importance of and promote these regular recall experiences, children eventually begin to recall in greater depth and detail—assuming, of course, that the setting offers lots of experiences that they're excited about sharing.

Thus, the first steps for helping children to recall more readily are to **encourage children to take the lead in their own activities** and then to **provide regular times for children to review these experiences.** High/Scope's plan-do-review sequence, a key curriculum element, is designed to provide such opportunities. The process is based on the idea that children are

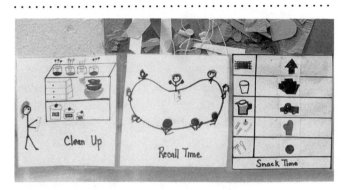

The capacity for reflection, fostered by providing children with opportunities to recall their experiences as a regular part of the daily routine, is an important foundation for later academic learning.

capable thinkers and doers, especially when they carry out activities of their own choosing.

Recall experiences, then, are part of a larger process of planning and doing that offers children **opportunities to initiate and reflect upon their actions.** By planning an activity, carrying it out, and then looking back at what they have done, children develop a sense of control over what happens to them. They can see the relationship between their plans and their activities, and they develop more awareness of their own ideas and the effects of their own actions. The process of talking about and representing their actions helps children evaluate and learn from their experiences; it also makes them more capable of drawing upon these experiences in the future.

The capacity for reflection, fostered in recall experiences, is an **important foundation for later academic learning.** At the primary school level, so many educational experiences emphasize rote learning and memorization of facts that children may not understand the context or function of the facts they are memorizing. Teachers of grade-school children frequently deplore their students' inability to "think" when completing assignments: "She can fill in all the blanks with

To spark your own creative thinking about how to make your recall times more active, we've included the following accounts of actual recall activities that took place at the High/Scope Demonstration Preschool in Ypsilanti, Michigan. Each of the "diary entries" presented here was reconstructed from notes teachers made during their daily planning and evaluation sessions. The dates are included to convey a sense of the development of the recall process over time.

Monday, September 18, first day of preschool. Curriculum focus: Familiarizing children with teachers, peers, the classroom, and the routine. Recall strategies: Bag of materials, singing. To help children become comfortable in their new environment, teachers encouraged relaxed exploration and play throughout the day. As the children were cleaning up their toys and materials, one teacher gathered several items that the children had used in their play and put them in a bag. Everyone then met as a large group. As children took turns pulling items out of the bag, teachers and children talked about where the item came from, who used it, and what he or she did with it. Teachers led the group in singing a song describing things children did (to the tune of "This a way, That a way.")

Wednesday, October 4. Curriculum focus: Spatial key experiences. Recall strategies: Musical carpet squares, motor encoding. Throughout the day the

the right answers, but she can't apply them—I just wish she would *think* more!" In contrast, High/Scope's plan-do-review sequence gives children experience with a recall process that is very different from simple short-term memorization or reactive thinking. We encourage children to remember and evaluate what they have seen, done, said, or thought. In so doing, they are learning a structure for their thinking that allows them to evaluate and apply what they have learned—valuable capacities for both academic learning and "real-life" success.

Recall experiences are also valuable for the wonderful **social opportunities** they provide. Children enjoy talking about, hearing about, and evaluating each other's experiences. In the process they improve their speaking and listening skills. They also discover new ways of doing things and interacting with others.

Now that we've discussed the importance of recall experiences in High/Scope programs, let's focus on how to make these experiences as beneficial as possible for children.

Enhancing Your Recall Times

As trainers in the High/Scope Curriculum, we sometimes hear teachers and caregivers complain that children are bored or uncooperative at recall time. We frequently find that these adults go through the same process every day at recall time: asking every child, one by one, the same set of questions ("What did you do today? What materials did you use? Who did you play with?"). As each child responds, the rest of the children are expected to sit and listen.

Like any teaching strategy that is overused, this way of conducting recall time can become an empty ritual. Another problem with this approach is that it demands a lot of maturity from children, since it depends heavily on language and since children must spend so much time listening quietly.

There are lots of other ways to help children recall. We suggest replacing such repetitive recall activities with recall experiences that are *active, social, cooperative,* and *conversational.* Here are some ideas for doing this:

First, make sure you have created an environment rich in materials that children can choose for their play. Earlier we said that children are most likely to recall their experiences when they are encouraged to make choices and direct their own activities. To support the process of making choices, children need a classroom setting that is well stocked with concrete, interesting materials: blocks, dress-up clothes, kitchen gear, art supplies, etc. **Collect materials that relate specifically to interests of the children that you know about,** such as musical instruments or props from fast food restaurants.

To promote recalling of particular experiences, you can **bring in materials that relate to things children have done:** For example, after a field trip to a farm, the teachers and children at one center collected farmers' caps, hoses, shovels, rakes, hoes, toy animals, and farm machinery. The teachers also brought in big boxes, and the children used them to make silos, farmhouses and barns—play experiences in which they recalled, or represented, their farm trip.

Another way to use concrete materials to facilitate recalling is to **develop recall-time strategies around materials children are using.** If you find, for example, that children are spending a great deal of time in play about airplanes, try this strategy at recall time: With your recall group in tow, take a toy airplane and "fly" around the classroom with it, stopping at each of the interest areas. At each stop, ask which "passengers" played there and talk with them about what they did.

teachers promoted spatial concepts such as "next-to," "beside," "on top of," and "behind." At recall time teachers arranged carpet squares (one red, the others, blue) in a large circle. As in a musical chairs game, the whole group marched around the circle to music, stopping when the music stopped. The child who ended up on the red square was asked to recall verbally. As that child talked, the teachers encouraged the other children to use exaggerated motions to imitate and re-enact what the child did (motor encoding). Throughout the activity, teachers made a point of using spatial language (such as "next to" or "on it"), repeating any spatial terms children used as they talked about their experiences.

Tuesday, December 12. Curriculum focus: Representation key experiences. Recall strategies: Maps and bears, drawing. The teacher asked one recall group to use a map of the classroom and small toy bears to represent their movements that day during work time: "Could you make your bear move to the different places you played in today?" In the other group, the teacher asked a few children, one at a time, to recall their activities. As each child talked, she sketched a partial picture of the activity the child described, then asked the other children to help complete the drawing.

In each of the above examples, teachers used two basic principles to plan for recall time: planning around a daily curriculum focus and using active recall strategies to implement this focus. ∎

Encourage Recalling Throughout the Daily Routine

Recalling doesn't just happen at recall time. Some ways to encourage recalling at other times:

Circle/Greeting time. Ask children questions about what happened to them before school: How did you get to school? Did you see anything unusual outside the car window? What did you eat for breakfast? (You can follow up this last question by helping the children make a chart of the foods mentioned.)

Planning time. If children are developmentally ready, encourage longer-term planning: ask them to recall what they did yesterday, and encourage them to make plans that build on what they did the day before.

Work time. Have children give directions (to you or another child) for something they have just done: "That's a tall building. Can you tell me how I can make one like that?" or "Can you tell Caroline how to make a mask on the computer?"

Small-group time. Have the group "write" a story about a common experience, e.g., "What We Saw at the Fire Station," on a long sheet of butcher paper. Ask each child to use part of the sheet to "draw and write" a part of the story. ∎

One way to make the recall process more meaningful is to concentrate on extended recall experiences with just a few children.

Another way to break away from a repetitive, question-and-answer format for recall time is to **concentrate on extended recall experiences with a few children.** This makes it easier for all the children to share in the experience and allows the discussion to take a more natural, conversational tone. It also gives the teacher time to use active recall strategies that involve more than just verbal experiences.

If Ehren is doing extended recall today, for example, the teacher might take the little blue shovel he played with at the sand table and hide it under a cloth. Then she could ask the children to feel the object under the cloth and guess what it was and who played with it. Next, Ehren could describe and demonstrate how he used the shovel, and the teacher could then lead everyone else at the table in imitating Ehren's shoveling: "Ehren said he poured the sand until it was a mountain. Let's pretend that we're all pouring sand and making mountains."

Recalling Throughout the Day

The above are just a few of the many possible ways adults can make recall times more enjoying and meaningful for children. It's important to remember, however, that recall time is not the only opportunity for recall experiences. Program staff also need to think about ways to **promote recalling during other parts of the daily routine.**

One such important strategy is to **support the naturally occurring opportunities for recalling that occur during children's play.** Play is the key activity in developmentally appropriate programs. As children play, they are often reenacting, restructuring, and recalling experiences they have had.

To support recalling during play, **become a partner in the child's play.** Imitate what they are doing by "playing" alongside them, using the same materials and some of the same language. This imitative interaction is a simple form of recalling in which the child sees his or her own actions reflected back. Later, you can extend on this reflective process by taking advantage of opportunities for conversation. You may ask, "What happened?" or "How did you do that?" or "Can you show me how I can build one like yours?"

Recalling during play is especially important for toddlers and younger preschoolers who are just beginning to recall or who may not be interested in recalling at recall time. As children mature, they are able to recall experiences that are increasingly distant in time.

Plan Recall-Time Strategies Around High/Scope's Key Experiences

Make recall time more active by tying your recall strategies into your key experience focus for the day. For example:

Key experiences in spatial relations: With your group, recall inside a block structure a child made at work time. This allows children to see both the block structure and classroom from a different spatial viewpoint.

Key experiences in representation: Use puppets or stuffed animals as props to stimulate conversation. For example, the adult pretends that her puppet says, "I saw Mary build a hamburger stand in the block area today. She made lots of hamburgers and vanilla shakes." Then the adult gives each child a puppet to continue the conversation with the first puppet.

Key experiences in movement: As a child talks about an experience, ask the child to show the group what he or she did by reenacting the motions. Then ask the child to tell you how he or she moved arms, hands, head, etc. ∎

It's clear that many opportunities for recall experiences occur throughout the High/Scope daily routine. Some of these opportunities are discussed in the side columns on pages 134 and 135. In these and other recall activities, the key to success is **planning with active learning in mind.** ∎

Planning a Daily Routine for Day Care Settings

The High/Scope Curriculum offers considerable flexibility in planning a daily routine. Though the curriculum has certain basic elements—the plan-do-recall sequence, circle time, and small-group time—staff of each program decide how much time to allot for each activity and how to order the various time segments. Despite this flexibility, developing a daily routine is still difficult for day care staff because so many caregiving tasks must be scheduled and because outside requirements (for example, licensing standards that may specify a fixed naptime) must also be met.

Yet many day care centers have found creative ways to meet all of these scheduling needs within the curriculum framework. The key is to think through each part of the routine from a developmental perspective. To do this requires setting aside staff time for daily planning—naptime is the usual time chosen. Such *team planning* is a "must" for centers using the High/Scope approach.

Below are additional suggestions that may be helpful in planning a daily routine for day care:

• **Consider all the tasks that must be accomplished in a given time frame and allow enough time so that routine tasks can be handled in a relaxed, unhurried way.** For example, early mornings can be especially difficult because there are so many things to do at the same time—greeting children, conducting health checks, getting special instructions from parents, supervising the group as each new child arrives, and setting up for breakfast. To start the day off right for both children and staff members, take

by
Bonnie Lash Freeman,
Mary Hohmann,
and
Susan M. Terdan

Sample Day Care Routine for Ages 3–4

7:00–8:15
Arrivals, health checks, limited plan-do-recall

8:15–9:00
Breakfast, clean-up, toileting

9:00–9:20
Morning circle: Stories, songs, announcements

9:20–9:30
Child planning

9:30–10:30
Work time

10:30–10:40
Clean-up

10:40–10:50
Recall time/Juice

10:50–11:05
Circle time: Music and movement

11:05–11:25
Small-group time

11:25–12:00
Outside time

12:00–12:45
Lunch and clean-up

12:45–1:00
Toileting, set up cots

1:00–2:30
Naptime (adult planning: 30-45 min.)

2:30–3:20
Toileting, snack, and story-time overlap as children wake up one by one

3:20–3:40
Circle time

3:40–4:30
Outside time

4:30–4:45
Transition to inside, planning time

4:45–6:00
Work time, clean up with parents, recall on way home. ■

Planning a limited plan-do-review at the end of the day is one way to involve busy parents in your routine. The child and parent pick up his or her play materials together and then discuss what the child did, continuing the discussion on the way home.

note of all these tasks and arrange your routine so you don't have to rush through them. One staff member can set up for breakfast and supervise children's play; another can greet parents and children and conduct health checks, making this a relaxed opportunity for a warm interaction with parent and child.

• **Plan overlapping activities to make transitions smoother.** Expecting all children to start and end a particular activity at the same time will result in some children having long waits and others being rushed. Instead, plan for gradual transitions. For example, don't expect all children to wake up at the same time from their naps. Instead, conduct a quiet activity as naptime winds down (for example, a small-group time, story time, or snack) so that children can wake up slowly, use the bathroom if necessary, and join the activity at their own pace.

• **Plan ways to encourage parents to be a part of your routine.** Because day care children are away from parents so long, it is especially important to plan ways to involve them in your daily schedule. One center we know of does this by conducting a limited plan-do-recall sequence at the end of the day. In late afternoon, teachers at this center offer children a few choices of activities; for example, they may leave just two interest areas "open." As parents arrive to pick up their children, they help children clean up the equipment they have been using and encourage them to recall what they have just done. Often this leads to a relaxed discussion of the whole day as parent and child ride home together.

This center's innovative way of ending the day is just one example of how a well-planned routine meets important needs for children, staff, and families. Thoughtful planning is the key to developing such a routine for your program. ∎

Planning the Kindergarten Day

by
Charles Hohmann

High/Scope kindergarten teachers who are planning a daily schedule often ask, "How can I fit it all in?" The schedule must not only accommodate basic structural elements of the High/Scope program—large-group activities, small-group "workshop" activities, the plan-do-review sequence—it must also assure that required content in science, social studies, math, and literacy is covered. At the same time, it must allow for such out-of-class extras as music, library, and physical education. No wonder teachers who want to plan a consistent schedule often feel overwhelmed!

However, the sample daily schedules for full-day and half-day kindergartens given in the side column, next page, show how readily these activities can be accommodated in a typical day. Of course, these are only two of many possible ways that staff of High/Scope kindergartens can schedule their activities—each High/Scope program designs its own unique schedule.

For those familiar with the daily routine of High/Scope preschool programs, the somewhat different nature of the High/Scope kindergarten schedule requires explanation. First, note that we use the term "schedule" rather than "routine." This shift in terminology better describes the organization of the kindergarten day, which is usually more flexible than a preschool program routine.

There are two main reasons for this greater degree of flexibility: first, the kindergarten has to accommodate more required activities than the typical preschool, and second, unlike most preschoolers, kindergarten children have the maturity to handle variations in the daily schedule. Since kindergartners can use time concepts such

Kindergarten children are sometimes able to use emerging writing skills to describe their plans.

Sample Kindergarten Schedules

Half-day kindergarten
8:30–8:50
Opening/circle

8:50–9:30
Plan-do-review

9:30–10:30
Language/math workshop

10:30–11:00
Outside play/snack/ physical education

11:00–11:30
Music/story

11:30
Dismissal

Full-day kindergarten
8:30–9:00
Opening

9:00–9:45
Plan-do-review

9:45–10:45
Language/math workshop

10:45–11:15
Music, movement

11:15–11:45
Lunch

11:45–12:00
Prep for outside

12:00–12:30
Outside play

12:30–1:00
Circle or theme activity (social studies or science experiences)

1:00–1:40
All read/all write

1:40–2:00
Physical education

2:00–2:20
Story

2:20
Dismissal ∎

as hours, days, and weeks more ably than preschoolers, they can handle a schedule that may change from day to day.

The increased maturity of the kindergarten child is also reflected in High/Scope's plan-do-review sequence, in which kindergartners plan activities using materials in one or more of the classroom activity areas (art, reading, writing, science, computers, etc.). Kindergartners typically develop more elaborate plans than preschoolers and, by the middle of the year, some may be writing their plans and recording their choice of center on a planning graph. Work time, during which children do what they have planned, accommodates the more involved projects and interests of 5- and 6-year-old children. When kindergarten children recall what they have done at review time, they not only describe what they did but also compare their work with the intentions expressed in their plans. They may reflect on the process of their work in some depth, often discussing problems encountered and solved.

Small-group activities in the kindergarten program are called "workshops" to reflect their more purposeful instructional focus. Like small-group times in preschools, workshops involve six to eight children and are planned by teachers around the High/Scope key experiences—in this case, the kindergarten key experiences. These activities often focus on concepts and skills in language, math, science, and other content areas. As in the small-group activities of the preschool, children participating in workshops are active— they *do* things, rather than listen passively. Unlike preschoolers, however, kindergarten children go to several workshop activities each day as the small groups rotate fromone workshop to another. In some of these workshops they may work intensively with the teacher; in others, they may work more independently.

The daily schedule of the High/Scope kindergarten thus emphasizes a continuity of appropriate child development practices in the transition from preschool to kindergarten. At the same time, it provides opportunities for the new levels of learning that advancing development and maturity invite. ∎

Day One: What We Did When the Children Arrived

by
Warren Buckleitner
and
Sue Terdan

There is no one "High/Scope daily routine" that works for all programs and settings. Instead, staff of each program are guided by curriculum guidelines and strategies as they develop a routine that meets the needs of their group of children. This article describes the daily routine of an actual High/Scope program. The program was a summer preschool for 3- and 4-year-olds we conducted in a public school building normally used for the Ypsilanti, Michigan, kindergarten program. It's important to note that the following account is not intended as a "recipe." Rather, it is an example of a specific routine, for a specific group of children, on a specific day, the opening of the school session. Depending on the nature of their setting, the time of year, and the needs and interests of their group of children, adults in other programs will structure their own unique routines.

A major consideration for us in planning this particular routine was the newness of the program to children and parents. Throughout the day we tried to keep in mind the mixture of fear, anxiety, and excitement that we knew most children—and their parents—would be feeling as they encountered a new place, new people, and a new routine. Here's how each part of the day went:

Greeting/circle time. Warren stood at the door of the school, greeting children and parents and passing out an information form. Because the classroom was down the hall and around the corner, we had run a strip of red tape at children's eye-level along the wall leading to the door of the classroom. We asked parents to follow the tape and walk their child to the classroom. When they arrived, Sue welcomed each child to the circle area where children's signs (each one cut in a familiar shape) were waiting. We asked each child to select a sign, wrote his or her name on it, and hung the signs on children with yarn. This made it easier to begin using children's names immediately. We also had our daily routine chart available to show to children and parents.

Planning time. We had decided to do both planning and recall as a large group for the first week, using very easy, concrete planning strategies. (Later, when children were used to the idea of planning, we divided them into two smaller planning and recall groups.)

Here's how we planned on the first day: From the circle, we made a "planning train" to help children explore the room and get an idea of what they wanted to do. Our "train" went through all the areas of the room, with the conductor (Warren) pointing out some of the things available:

> *"We're going by the water table. It's all full of water! . . . Now we're coming into the art area where we can paint a picture [chugs by the easel] . . . or use the modeling dough [holds up the modeling dough]. . . ."*

We found that we easily held the children's interest by keeping the train moving and by only using language directly associated with objects and areas. After the first trip around the room, the train made stops in each area, letting off children in the areas they selected. The caboose (Sue) noted each child's departure: "Scott is walking to the toy area."

Work time. In our first work time, we stressed helping children explore with the materials and learn and use relevant words: names for the children, teachers, areas of the classroom, and parts of the daily routine: "I see you planned

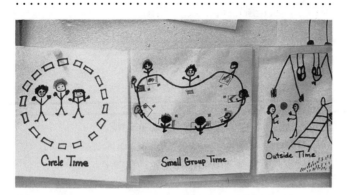

Pictures of each part of the daily routine can help children learn the routine at the beginning of a program session.

to work with *Lindsey* in the block area." "It's me, *Warren*. Can I come in to your house for a visit?" We made a point of giving a clear warning five minutes before clean-up time: "Soon it will be time to clean up." We also found these early work times to be excellent times for making our first general observations of children—we kept a pad handy to make brief notes to consider later.

Clean-up time. Because we had a hearing-impaired child, we signaled the start of clean-up by ringing a bell *and* flashing the lights. We modeled clean-up behavior, again emphasizing language: "I'm handing the blocks to Lindsey, who's in the block area." We were surprised at how smoothly clean-up went—could it have been our labels? During clean-up, we prepared for recall by collecting 10 or so objects that we had seen children use a lot (a pitcher from under the water table, a pair of scissors, a Bristle Block).

Recall time. With all the children gathered at the circle, each child took a turn pulling an object from the bag. We then sang a simple recall song that included the name of the child who had used the object during work time. For example, when a smock from the art area was picked, we asked, "Who played with this?" When Jimmie answered, we asked him "to show us what your hands did." Then we sang, "This is the way we paint with the brush . . . just like Jimmie," copying Jimmie's motions as we sang. At the end of recall, we divided the children into two predetermined groups for snack.

Snack time. Rather than talk at length about the "rules of snack," we modeled appropriate table behavior. For example, when Jimmie took a large handful of crackers, Warren pointed out how many of the children had no crackers and helped Jimmie decide how many each child could take. We also asked children to pour their own juice.

Small-group time. Sue's table worked with paper strips, glue, tape, and staples. The children at Warren's table each had two magnets and experimented with these and a variety of nuts, bolts, pen caps, inch cubes. In interacting with children, we focused on the ingredients of active learning and the language key experiences, both of which actively involved children and helped them learn about materials available to them in the classroom.

Circle time. To reinforce names, we sang, "Everybody do this, do this, do this. Everybody do this, just like [*child's name*]." Children provided the movement ideas. Before we went outside, we asked the children if there was a song they would like to sing. Several children mentioned "Eensy Weensy Spider" and several others suggested "Skinamarink." We explained that there was enough time to sing each song once and that then it would be outside time.

Outside time. The short walk down the hall from our classroom to the playground door was marked with yellow tape to encourage children to find their way independently. Once outside, we used this time to get to know each child better as we played with them until their parents came. The children were very excited about the playground, which has some unique play equipment (e.g., a large spinning dish that holds five children; a variety of different-sized balls).

For the first three weeks, to help children learn the daily routine, we had them move a large clip along our *daily routine chart* as they completed each segment of the day. We continued to work on familiarizing children with the routine, the areas, and the names for everything and everybody in the classroom. After a few weeks of experiencing a *consistent* daily routine and room arrangement, children began to show—through their plans and their general behavior—that they knew what to expect and where to find things. ■

C·H·A·P·T·E·R F·O·U·R

Environments for Active Learning

· ·

Settings for Active Learning — Ann Rogers

Home Day Care and High/Scope: A Natural Combination —
Bonnie Lash Freeman and Ruby Brunson

The Playground: An Outdoor Setting for Learning — Vincent Harris

Blocks, Sand, Paint . . . and Computers —
Warren Buckleitner and Charles Hohmann

Toward Multicultural Settings — Ann Rogers

Since adults in High/Scope programs do not rely on pre-structured activities to set the course for children's learning, one of the key ways they guide children is through careful planning of the environment. This involves dividing the space into defined *areas*, then stocking these areas with a rich array of inviting *materials*.

In the opening piece, Ann Rogers outlines some general considerations for arranging and equipping settings for active learning, using concrete examples from the High/Scope Demonstration Preschool. Rogers emphasizes the need for adults who are planning the physical setting to consider the general kinds of play that are typical of young children—including dramatic play, constructive play, exploratory play, and play with games. The fact that an environment for active learning does not have to be a classroom is underscored by the next two selections. Bonnie Lash Freeman and Ruby Brunson explore the issues that arise when early childhood programs in family day care homes are organized around High/Scope's *active learning* principles. Vincent Harris describes how playgrounds are transformed when educators view the outdoor play space as an active learning environment. Questions and concerns about the kinds of materials that are appropriate in early childhood settings crop up repeatedly at curriculum workshops; and the article by Charles Hohmann and Warren Buckleitner takes up some nontraditional materials—computer equipment and software—and looks at their role in developmentally based early childhood programs. The issue of how the environment contributes to learning about diverse cultures is addressed in the concluding piece by Ann Rogers, who discusses a common problem of early childhood programs: how children can learn about cultural diversity in a setting that serves a homogeneous group.

Settings for Active Learning

by
Ann Rogers

Children actively playing—together or alone, neatly or messily, quietly, or noisily—are busy learning about the world in ways that children are intended to learn—by exploring and working with people, materials, and ideas.

One of the most important responsibilities of adults who teach young children is to create and maintain a physical setting that encourages this type of *active* play. In this article, we offer principles and strategies for designing environments in which children can express their own plans, intentions, and interests by choosing materials and activities. The ideas we share can be implemented in all kinds of early childhood settings, including preschools, day care centers, and family day care homes.

Types of Play

In creating settings for active learning, it's helpful to think about the kinds of play typical of young children. Here are some general kinds of play, and some examples of them from the High/Scope Demonstration Preschool:

• **Dramatic or role play—pretending.** *Linda and Aimee act out a wedding all week long. They dress up in wedding finery, travel in hollow block cars, dance to taped music, and pretend to eat lots of wedding cake.*

• **Constructive play—using materials to make something, sometimes as a part of dramatic play and sometimes as an end in itself.** *Will uses paper tubes and tape to make swords for playing Teenage Mutant Ninja Turtles. Carole uses some of the plastic, interlocking straws and stars to make an umbrella.*

Providing materials for constructive play—making things—is a prime consideration for planning active learning environments.

• **Exploratory play—exploring the possibilities of materials and processes.** *Given large chalk sticks, water, and black paper, Deola explores them in many ways. She tries using the chalk (both with and without water) on the paper, on her hands, on her arms, and on the table. She notices the changing color of the water in her dish and spends a long time stirring different pieces of chalk in the water and observing the color changes.*

• **Play with games—board games, card games, action games like hopscotch, and other such games with rules.** (Young preschool children usually don't play these games conventionally—they are not naturally competitive, and following rules and taking turns may not be within their developmental range. However, they often enjoy playing with the pieces of a game set, making up the rules as they go along.) *Naaman loves to play "Memory," and he has an excellent visual memory so he is very good at it. However, when another player turns up a card, he excitedly indicates the correct match, not realizing that this diminishes his chance of winning.*

All these forms of play come naturally to young children and are important for their development. Here are some guidelines for arranging the space and selecting materials for early childhood settings that provide plentiful opportunities for these different types of play.

Defining the Space and Selecting Materials

The first step for adults in planning a setting for active learning is to **divide the classroom, center, or home into defined areas.** The boundaries of the areas should be clearly and visibly delineated—by furniture, walls, fences, shelves, masking tape on the floor, differences in floor covering, or by some other type of border. As much as possible, the names given to the areas should be understandable to children, e.g., "climbing area" not "gross-motor area."

The number of areas adults choose for their program should grow out of the particular needs and interests of their group. The curriculum does not demand a specific number of areas, nor does it designate specific names of areas. Here are the areas we presently have in the High/Scope Demonstration Preschool: block area, house area, art area, computer area, reading and writing area, toy area (for small toys), and bean table (also used for sand and water).

The basic consideration for program staff in defining the areas and stocking them with materials is to **look at the children—their interests,**

Locating the Areas

In making decisions about the size and placement of your areas, consider these factors:

Space. Allow enough space in each area for several children to play comfortably.

Noise level. Locate areas in which play tends to be more quiet—e.g., the space where children play with books or puzzles—at a distance from noisier areas, such as the block area.

"Cross-fertilization." If possible, place areas next to each other that have the potential for related play activities. For example, making house and block areas adjacent encourages interrelated role play.

Floor surfaces, running water. Locate art materials on easily cleaned surfaces, near running water if possible, to facilitate clean-up. Low-pile carpet cuts noise, but is still firm enough for building, so it is ideal for block areas.

Traffic patterns. Children need space to play and build without being obstructed by the flow of traffic from one part of the room to another.

Visibility. To help children see the choices available to them, make the dividers between the areas low enough for children to see over. Children also need to display and view their own creations, so provide space at children's eye level for such displays. ■

their developmental levels, their cultures.
Adults provide play areas and materials that support children's developing abilities and personal interests and that enable children to reflect upon and reenact their experiences in their homes and neighborhoods. In thinking about the physical setting, adults are guided by this maxim: "*Play with* equals *learn from.*" Here are some general strategies for selecting materials:

• **Adults choose as many "full-sized" materials as possible.** One view of children's play is that it is an attempt to make meaning out of their experience of the world. The adults a child is close to are very important in a child's world. That's why imitating adults—*by using the things they use and doing the things they do*—is such a persistent theme in the play of children the world over. It makes sense, then, for program staff to stock the areas with "real," adult-sized materials—real telephones, adult-sized cooking equipment and unbreakable tableware, empty boxes and cans of the kinds of food the children have in their homes, etc. These kinds of materials promote dramatic play that is based on children's real experiences and is therefore very engaging for them.

• **Adults keep children's cultures in mind as they select materials.** The materials should reflect the everyday lives of the children in the program, and therefore their cultures and heritages. If a program includes children whose parents make their living fishing, then fishing equipment would probably be popular play materials with that group. Asking parents to bring in materials and tools from their homes and jobs is one way to assure that the physical setting will reflect children's cultures. For example, if there are Asian children in a classroom, parents might bring in woks and chopsticks. A participant in a High/Scope workshop on multicultural educa-

*Children enjoy working with "real," adult-sized materials that they've
seen their parents using.*

tion recently stated, "You should be able to tell
something about the cultures of the children in
your program just by looking at the classroom
and the materials in it!" This goal is easier to
achieve if program staff enlist parents' help in
selecting and gathering materials.

• **Adults stock the areas with many "open-
ended" materials.** By "open-ended," we mean
materials that can be used in many different
ways. Some examples of open-ended materials
that we have in our demonstration classroom are
blocks, paper, cardboard, string, paper towel
tubes, twist ties, pipe cleaners, glue, tape (masking and transparent), boxes of all sizes, and
wood scraps. We also include Legos, Tinkertoys,
Bristle Blocks, and other small manipulatives,
which children can turn into anything they can
imagine. We emphasize these kinds of materials
because we believe they encourage problem solv-

Open-Ended Materials Encourage Creativity and Problem Solving

Open-ended materials —those that can be used in a variety of ways—encourage children to solve problems creatively:

Caleb, a 4-year-old from the High/Scope Preschool, decided to build a race car using the longest unit blocks and carpet squares. He needed a stick shift, but all the long unit blocks were gone, so he searched in the art area and found some paper towel tubes. To get the length he wanted, he needed two tubes, but didn't know how to stick them together. A teacher referred him to Chris, who is our resident tape expert. Chris helped Caleb fashion a stick shift two tubes long. To solve his problem, Caleb had to hold in his mind the characteristics of a stick shift that were important to him, and then find materials that matched his ideas—in this case the concepts of "long" and "narrow." He had the additional problem of figuring out how to fit together the tubes. None of this problem solving would have occurred if we had in the classroom one of the little plastic driving toys that simulate a car's dashboard and steering wheel. ∎

ing and creativity (as in the example of Caleb's activity described in the side column).

• **Adults sometimes choose materials with specific purposes in mind.** Sometimes children develop interests that are best supported by specific—rather than open-ended—materials. For example, when two children in the demonstration classroom were stung by yellow jackets nesting in a hollow log, we added several books about insects and some bug-collecting jars to our classroom.

• **Adults continually watch what children do and use these observations as they make changes in the areas or materials.** Sometimes children signal the need for new materials by their fascination with a particular activity—if several children are spending a lot of time "washing" their hands, then it's probably time to think of ways to provide waterplay in the classroom.

Some changes we're now considering in the High/Scope Demonstration Preschool illustrate how early childhood staff continuously try to adjust the physical setting to provide new challenges and accommodate children's changing needs. We've observed that many of our children are very interested in building with blocks—so many, in fact, that the blocks often run out before their ideas do! We've also noticed that many of the children are using the unit blocks as *accessories* (e.g., as motors or food) for their large, hollow-block constructions, and this is sometimes frustrating for children who want to build with the unit blocks. We also have many children who are creating things with wood scraps and tape from the art area. They seem ready to explore new ways of using wood. To meet these different needs for supporting children's constructive play, we're wrestling with several alternatives for changing our areas. We may decide to subdivide the block area into a large block area and a small block area and add additional unit blocks. Another possibility is to create a construction area—with a workbench and real carpentry tools—at one end of the block area. We don't have room to do both. Still another option, now that the weather is warmer, is to create a construction area on the playground.

To help us in making decisions about changing these areas, we'll continue to observe the kinds of play children engage in and to think about the best uses of our space and materials. Like other teachers and caregivers in High/Scope programs, we've discovered that the process of creating a physical setting to support children's active learning through play is truly never-ending! ∎

Home Day Care and High/Scope: A Natural Combination

by
Bonnie Lash Freeman
and
Ruby Brunson

Parents who want high-quality day care often choose family day care homes, especially for their youngest children, because these settings offer a homelike environment. These parents want care settings that are safe, nurturing, and stimulating—settings in which their children can grow and develop mentally, physically, socially, and emotionally.

Providers of home day care know that delivering the best possible care to children is a difficult task, especially when their programs must earn an income for staff while keeping fees low enough that families can afford them. Making the provider's task even more difficult is the need to maintain a comfortable home for family members while operating a bustling child care business in the same space.

In recent years, home child care providers have been tailoring the High/Scope Curriculum to meet their unique needs through their participation in High/Scope's Training of Trainers (ToT) projects. In fact, ToT participants in California, New York State, and New York City have successfully incorporated the curriculum within a range of home-based programs. The ToT projects are conducted by High/Scope consultants who train a cadre of home day care providers and early childhood supervisors to use the curriculum and train others to use it. Local trainees who successfully complete the ToT projects can then establish a network of trained home-based caregivers.

At the start of these training projects, providers identified and confronted a range of issues: *Why does a family day care home need a curriculum? How will the High/Scope Curriculum help me as a home provider? How does the High/Scope approach differ from the approach I am already using? Can this new approach help me improve my business?* As training participants generated and tried out curriculum strategies in actual day care homes, new issues emerged: *Will I have to spend more for equipment and materials? How do I use the curriculum with a mixed-age group? Is the High/Scope approach too structured/too lacking in structure for a home-based program?*

In the following pages, we'll explain how family day care providers have resolved these and related issues while using the High/Scope approach in their programs. Our discussion is organized around basic elements of the High/Scope Curriculum—it's **room arrangement principles, daily routine, assessment tools,** and **parent involvement strategies.** The examples are drawn from the actual experiences of High/Scope ToT participants and the providers they've trained.

Room Arrangement

Room arrangement principles are usually introduced early in the training process because they are concrete, easy to convey in a visual presentation, and easy to understand. As is typical of High/Scope training, ToT participants were shown videotaped examples of typical High/Scope room arrangements in one of their earliest training sessions. They reacted strongly, and their reactions were both positive and negative ("Labelling is a great idea. I can't wait to try it" "That will never work in my home—I don't have room for all those interest areas!")

As they worked through the process of planning actual room arrangements for day care homes, participants gradually realized the curriculum was flexible enough to adapt to their

Family Day Care Homes Evaluation Checklist

Note: This brief list is a condensed and adapted version of the High/Scope Room Arrangement Checklist. *It is written specifically for home day care settings.*

The areas
☐ Available space is divided into several distinct areas (house, block, art, toy, etc.).

☐ Location of the areas is compatible with their other uses (e.g., art area in the kitchen).

☐ The areas have adequate space for the expected activities.

☐ Traffic flow permits children to work without interruption.

☐ All areas allow for active play.

☐ An active learning philosophy underlies the planning of the setting.

Storage and labeling
☐ There are definite storage areas with appropriate labels, e.g., concrete objects, outlines, pictures, print, or a combination of these.

☐ Identical and similar items are stored together when possible.

☐ Space is provided for children's belongings.

☐ Children's "cubbies" are labeled and placed so children can use them independently.

Maintaining a comfortable home for family members while providing an active learning environment for enrolled children in the same space is a challenge many home providers have resolved through thoughtful planning of space and materials.

specific settings. But the process was time-consuming and complex. The providers had to consider the needs of family members as well as those of enrolled children in a wide age-range.

Some of the most common room arrangement issues that arose among the ToT providers are discussed next.

Use of space. In family day care homes, the space available for child care is usually limited and often has multiple uses. To make the best use of space, ToT providers often decided to use more than one room to house the interest areas: for example, a living room could contain the block area and house area; the kitchen or laundry room could be used for messy activities like sand-and-water play or art activities. Bedrooms could be used for quiet play or naps. When work areas were arranged in more than one room, caregivers often found they had to limit the choices offered to make it possible to watch all the children: "This morning the cooking area, art area, and bookmaking area [all in the kitchen] will be open. After lunch we'll work in the basement and you can use the toys and water table there."

Materials and equipment for a wide age range. The broad range of ages of the children served in day care homes created special problems for the ToT providers in selecting and arranging materials. For example, one room arrangement issue that arose in many of the day care homes was that of infant care. The infants often required extra equipment—cribs, playpens, highchairs, baby seats, walkers, and so forth—and these required extra space. The providers usually found it worked well to integrate the infant equipment with that of the older children, cribs and cots in the same space, for example. Many providers eventually discovered that they made less use of restrictive equipment like play pens, because, with the High/Scope approach, they had more time to spend interacting with the children. Children who had more choices and who did more things for themselves required less help with routine tasks; thus, adults could spend less time restricting, directing, and "doing for" children and more time down on the floor, playing with them.

The arrangement of materials was another problem that took on a new dimension because of the wide age range served in family day care homes. In home day care settings, just as in High/Scope classrooms, an important principle is that materials are arranged so that children can get them out and put them away themselves. To accommodate the different age groups they served, many providers planned to place materials for infants and toddlers on bottom shelves

Materials and equipment
☐ As much as possible, materials are easily accessible to children.

☐ Only useable, safe materials are within children's reach.

☐ There are a variety of materials available for children to use in achieving their goals.

☐ Unstructured materials are available in all areas.

☐ Materials that can be manipulated and explored are available.

☐ Materials are available for pretending and representing.

☐ "Found" materials are available (pots, dress-up clothes, plastic containers).

Parent involvement
☐ There is a clearly stated method for informing parents of the children's daily routine and activities (bulletin boards, notes home, informal contacts). ■

and materials for older children on higher shelves. This way, even crawling babies could get out their own materials. In addition, providers often learned that having materials for younger and older children in close proximity encouraged the older children to help out the younger ones as needed.

Costs for materials. Budgeting for equipment and materials was another important issue for ToT home caregivers. Most of the providers were on limited budgets and couldn't afford expensive, school-type equipment. Because the High/Scope Curriculum recommends offering children a wide variety of materials, many providers at first assumed wrongly that they must buy expensive toys and equipment. As they learned more about the curriculum, however, they began to understand that we actually endorse a "natural" environment in which children play with many "real" things: pots and pans, house plants, clothes for dress-up, etc. Materials like this can be collected at little or no cost, especially if parents are enlisted to help. The providers eventually realized that they were not expected to make the home into a school, but rather to choose a stimulating range of materials that fit within a home setting.

Family needs for space. Day care activities are bound to impinge on the possessions, privacy, and personal space of other family members. Balancing family needs for space with those of the enrolled children was one of the most important room arrangement issues faced by providers. To maintain the integrity of the family's home, many providers decided to store day care materials on movable shelves so that they could be pushed out of the way in the evening. Other providers stored materials in hanging devices on the backs of doors or on low shelves in a closet that was left open during the day. Limiting the space that could be used for day care was another strategy used by some providers to preserve the family's privacy. Some providers, for example, reported reserving one or two special rooms for family members only.

The Daily Routine

The ToT providers also dealt with many issues in incorporating the High/Scope daily routine within their home-based programs. A consistent daily routine is recognized as a priority for all early childhood programs. A routine is especially important for family day care providers, who often work alone and must rely on the organization of the day to provide order.

In home day care, the plan-do-review sequence is the central element of the daily routine, just as it is in center-based programs. But ToT providers found they often needed special strategies to adapt the plan-do-review sequence to a home setting serving a wide age range. For example, a planning board illustrated with photographs helped to structure planning in situations where children couldn't see all the work areas because the areas were located in different rooms. Such planning boards were particularly successful with toddlers, who could point to pictures of the toys and play areas they desired. For babies, planning often meant simply crawling to where they wanted to play. Once the baby arrived at a play space, the provider used language to label the baby's choices.

One aspect of the High/Scope daily routine that home caregivers found especially useful was its emphasis on encouraging children to recall the order of the day and to predict what would happen next. When providers made an effort to help children learn to predict the next activity in the day, they found that many management problems disappeared. For example, if Tommy knew that toothbrushing would be

The Daily Routine: An Organizing Tool

Home day care providers using the High/Scope approach report that the predictability of the daily schedule makes it easier for them to organize and accomplish such routine chores as cooking, cleaning, and diapering. Many of these activities can be integrated into small-group time. For example, a small-group activity could be structured around making sandwiches for lunch (see "Key Experiences," side column, next page).

Caregivers also report that a predictable routine encourages older children to make transitions independently, freeing the provider to give younger children extra attention. For example, while older children independently clean up their toys and begin to prepare their cots for a nap, a sequence that happens at the same time every day, the provider can diaper and sing to an infant. ■

The Key Experiences in Family Day Care

Just as in center-based programs, providers of home day care use the High/Scope key experiences as a framework for planning activities and interacting with children. For example, one home caregiver chose the spatial key experiences as her focus for the day. The following small-group time plan shows how she developed this focus in a pre-lunch activity.

Key experiences:

• Rearranging and reshaping objects and observing the changes

• Experiencing and describing relative positions, directions, distances

• Distinguishing and describing shapes

Materials: Bologna and cheese slices, crackers in several shapes, blunt knives

Procedure: Encourage the children to make "cracker sandwiches" for lunch. As they work, model and encourage language describing spatial positions and shapes: "Athi is putting a round cracker on top of a triangle of cheese. What do you have in between your crackers, Sara?" Watch closely as children rearrange and reshape the materials and encourage them to notice and describe the changes that occur as they twist, roll, stack, stretch, fold, and cut the lunchmeat and cheese. ∎

For a baby, expressing a "plan" might simply mean creeping to a toy she wants to play with. Adults may then use language to label the baby's choice.

followed by an opportunity to play outside, he was more likely to cooperate with the process.

Assessment

Unlike teachers in preschool or Head Start programs, who routinely must use reporting forms, many of the ToT home day care providers were not initially comfortable with the High/Scope assessment system, in which early childhood staff use anecdotal notes and the COR (Child Observation Record) to record children's developmental progress. Many had never before considered using a formal assessment system. To these providers, a paper-and-pencil record seemed too academic and "school-like"—they saw it as having no place in a family day care home. However, once caregivers had used the High/Scope assessment system for a while, they began to see it not as a premature inventory of academic skills but simply as a useful way of gathering concrete examples of children's maturation. The caregivers also found that having these written anecdotes about children made it easier to provide useful information with parents. This led to stronger parent/provider relationships.

Parent Involvement

Family day care providers have to create viable reasons for busy working parents to become involved in the daily working of the home or most parents will say they "just don't have time." Using a bulletin board as a parent involvement tool (see side column) is just one example of the efforts ToT providers have made to communicate effectively with parents. In general, the providers found that parents became more supportive of the new curriculum approach as they learned more about it. For example, the New York City providers often used curriculum materials to explain to parents how activities are designed to enhance children's learning. The caregivers found that if they shared with parents the overall curriculum goals, the active learning checklist, some small-group time plans, the key experiences, and samples of children's work, for example, parents came to understand and support what providers were attempting to do. Parents began to realize that the home was not a babysitting service, but a setting for active learning. At the same time, providers worked hard to reassure parents that a homelike environment would be maintained and that the implementation of the curriculum did not mean the program would be overly structured and "school-like."

Providers also found that the support the curriculum generated in parents became a marketing tool, strengthening the business side of their programs. Parents quickly recognized the value of a program that had a visible structure

The Bulletin Board: Focus for Parent Involvement

The bulletin board that is available in most day care homes is an important parent involvement tool—parent/caregiver conversations about children often start here. The bulletin board contains examples of children's work; reminders to parents; special instructions to the caregiver; private notes to parents, often with anecdotes about individual children; the menu for the week; the daily schedule; special notices; a lesson plan for the day or week; and extra paper so that parents can write messages to the caregiver. ∎

and a clearly defined approach to children. The national reputation of the High/Scope Curriculum also attracted many parents.

...

The experiences of caregivers described in this article show that the High/Scope Curriculum and family day care can be a natural combination. **Organization**—of the setting, of the daily schedule, and of the provider's approach to children—is the key to a successful family day care operation, and the High/Scope Curriculum provides a useful framework around which a program can be organized. The curriculum not only improves services, but also serves as a marketing tool that helps the program to succeed financially. ■

The Playground: An Outdoor Setting for Learning

by

Vincent Harris

The young child encounters two significant learning environments at preschool—the classroom and the outdoors. While
educators typically devote ample time and energy to organizing and equipping their classrooms, they often overlook the importance of the
second environment, the playground. They may
view the time spent outside as a break from the
serious educational business of the classroom, a
time for children to "let off steam" and for adults
to socialize or sit and relax. When educators
begin to recognize the learning that can and
should take place outdoors, however, they find it
easier to make a commitment to improve their
outdoor play space and to find ways to work
with children outdoors so that curricular objectives are met.

In a High/Scope setting, young children are
active learners both indoors and outdoors. During outside time children not only exercise their
large muscles; they also observe, interact, explore, and experiment. This is a time for running
and riding, for balancing and building, for discovering nature, for adventurous role play, and
for quiet play with small objects. The playground should be designed and equipped to support this wide range of experiences. Next we
present some general guidelines for setting up
an "outdoor classroom" and for working with
children outdoors.

Playground Design

The overall site for your playground is usually the first consideration in designing a new
playground or revamping an existing one. All el-

ements of the natural environment should be considered. Ideally, the early childhood outdoor play area allows children to explore and appreciate a rich variety of **landscape elements** (hills, valleys, sunlit areas, shaded areas, grass, rocks, gravel, water) and **plant life** (trees, shrubs, bushes, vines, flowers). Contrasts in shape, color, and texture create an environment that young children are eager to explore and talk about. A weedy area that is left unmowed will stimulate children's exploration. A small tilled bed can be used for children's gardening. Try to make the entire playground site pleasing to the eye. Chain link fences can be improved, for example, by placing shrubs or trees in front of the fences or growing vines through them.

Play materials and equipment are another prime consideration in playground design. For a really exciting playground, you'll need more than the traditional swings, slide, and climber. Children do enjoy these **stationary structures,** but a playground should also offer **loose manipulative materials** that invite children to build, pretend, explore, and experiment. See page 172 for a list of both large-motor play equipment and structures and loose materials that may be included in your playground plans. It's also important to evaluate materials and equipment for **safety** (for detailed information on evaluating the safety features of play equipment see other High/Scope resources listed on page 297).

Layout of the playground requires careful planning. We recommend arranging the playground in well-defined **areas** similar to those we have inside a High/Scope Curriculum classroom. For example, swings, a climber, a sandbox with a nearby water supply, a paved area, and a garden could each be thought of as separate areas.

If possible, arrange the areas around the perimeter of the playground, leaving an open area

On the playground, "loose" materials that children can manipulate are just as important as stationary structures.

in the center. This open space allows children to move freely between the areas without colliding with stationary equipment. This central area is also an ideal vantage point for children, who can see all the choices available, and for adults, who can observe children in several areas at once. Within each area, space and equipment should be arranged so that adults can see children and get to them quickly. Although children need to have quiet retreat spaces outdoors, there should be no enclosed spaces so small that adults cannot see into them and get into them if necessary.

In deciding which areas will be adjacent, take care to separate incompatible play areas, for example, swings and riding vehicles, and the spaces for quiet sand play and noisier physical play. Compatible areas should be located next to each other to promote interactive play; for example, you can locate a sand area next to a play house, and a platform structure next to a symbolic boat. Consider the traffic patterns; allow ample space, for example, in high traffic areas, like the spaces around swings and slide. Don't forget to consider noise levels as well. The playground is a place for running feet and outside voices, but it should also provide spaces for quiet thought.

You can define **area boundaries** by changes in surface materials (wood chips under high equipment, hard surfaces for wheeled toys) or actual physical boundaries (low shrubs around swings, railroad ties around the sandbox). The fence or barrier that defines the entire play area should not only provide for children's safety but also should block unpleasant sights, such as streets or parking lots.

Storage always becomes an issue when loose materials are included in the playground. Try to store materials so that children (including handicapped children) can get them out and put them away themselves. Place materials on low labeled shelves in a shed or in a labeled outdoor container. If outdoor storage is not possible, try storing outdoor materials near the classroom door in a closet or on shelves.

The Adult's Role Outdoors

Adults should **work with children outdoors in the same ways they do indoors,** keeping in mind the greater freedom possible in outdoor play. Adults in High/Scope preschools use language to expand upon children's outdoor experiences. Though there may be no formal time to plan outdoor activities, adults can talk with children about what they are going to do on the playground while they are getting dressed to go outdoors. Once outdoors, they allow children to set their own course. Adults first observe and listen to the context and language of children's play and then support and extend children's experiences by asking open-ended questions, restating ideas in different ways, and helping children expand their observations and experi-

Stationary play structures should be carefully evaluated, for both safety and the number of play options they offer children.

ments. Adults do not interrupt children at play or try to change the direction of their activities without good cause. Adults are **active participants** in play—not play leaders, but play followers and enhancers. Adults also guide children to use equipment safely.

Discipline problems, such as fighting, chasing, and difficulty taking turns, are often symptoms of poor playground design: the playground may not offer enough materials or play options. If the only things available are single-function, one-child-at-a-time play structures, and if the only other things children can manipulate on the playground are their own bodies, play will naturally be rough.

Discipline problems may also mean that adults need to be more involved in children's play. Outside time should not be thought of as the adults' break or social time. Adults may prevent or reduce conflict by using the following strategies: *encouraging communication between children* ("Mary, tell Jamie what you want to do. Screaming and grabbing the handlebars won't work"), *encouraging children to see other points of*

Materials: The "Right Stuff" for Outdoor Play

A well-equipped playground should include some materials, equipment, and structures from each of the following categories:

Large-motor equipment and structures:

• **Climbing equipment**—jungle gym, net climber, ladder, fireman's pole, low trees.

• **Elevated structures**—places to get on top of and look out from, such as platform structures, low tree houses, hills, sturdy crates, tree stumps, boulders, snow piles.

• **Swings**—commercial swing set, multi-person tire swing, rope swing, tree swing, toddler swing for younger or handicapped children.

• **Sliding equipment**—commercial slide, fireman's pole, low cable ride, watered plastic sliding track for summer, sleds for winter.

• **Materials to jump on or over**—inner-tube trampolines, old mattresses, piles of leaves, ropes.

• **Structures for balancing**—rows of railroad ties, bricks, or rocks arranged in a variety of ways: single rows, parallel rows, straight rows, curving rows, zigzags.

• **Wheeled vehicles**—a wide range, to provide varied coordination experiences and minimize conflicts over toys, for example, tricycles, scooters, wagons, strollers, pullcarts, wheelbarrows, cars with steering wheels, vehicles with pedal steering.

• **Bouncing and rocking equipment**—spring-based toys that allow both side-to-side and front-back movements; spring-based or curve-based teeter-totters. (Traditional-style teeter-totters can cause spinal injuries.)

• **Equipment for children with disabilities**—play structures and toys that handicapped children can operate without assistance, for example, climbers accessible by wheelchair, play houses and tables that accommodate wheelchairs, and special wheeled vehicles designed for use by handicapped children. (Also, be sure that your playground has some paved areas to make it accessible by wheelchair.)

Loose manipulative materials:

• **Unstructured materials** to manipulate, transform, and build with—sand and sand tools, pebbles, water, shells, small boards, cardboard, plastic foam, boxes, boards or packing pieces, string/rope, old sheets or blankets, large interlocking toys.

• **Role play props**—including both "real" things (pots and pans, flowerpots) and toy objects, with an emphasis on those that are generally used outdoors—goggles, helmets, backpacks, make-believe telescopes.

• **Sports and games equipment**—balls of all sizes, bean bags, low-hung basketball hoop, pails, buckets, boxes, bullseye painted large and low on a fence or wall.

• **Art materials**—an outdoor painting canvas made from an old bed sheet and washable paints to use with it, large-scale weaving frame with large pieces of fabric or rope, colored chalk, clay for texture imprints, food coloring for snow dyeing.

• **Music and rhythm materials**—pipe chimes, bells, trash can drums, margarine tub maracas. ■

view ("Sean, Matthew says he isn't really through with the swing—he just got off to tie his shoe"), and *helping children find other ways to accomplish their goals* ("Christian is using that truck now, Erin. Can you think of another way to haul those rocks?"). It's also very important to *set clear limits*. Decide in advance what shall be permitted (Can children climb up the track of the slide? Will you allow superhero play? Where is running permitted?) Let children know the reasons for each rule, and be firm about enforcing them.

With careful attention both to playground planning and the ways adults work with children outdoors, you'll enhance both the learning and fun that take place on your playground. ■

Blocks, Sand, Paint . . . and Computers

by
Warren Buckleitner
and
Charles Hohmann

Today I went to the computer area. I made a crown. Then I went to the art area, cut it out, and colored it. I put the crown on and I was the king. Then I made a castle with Jeremy.

— Chris, age 4

The use of computers in programs for young children offers exciting possibilities, some of which are illustrated by the experience of Chris, above. Note that Chris uses the computer as a vehicle for creative expression; his computer play leads naturally to his work with art materials and his role play with another child.

We view the computer as just one of many tools and materials that can provide valuable experiences in a developmentally oriented program. Computers fit comfortably within the High/Scope Curriculum framework because computer activities can be planned and conducted in the context of the High/Scope key experiences.

Attitudes Toward Computers: How We've Changed

Our belief that computers can provide exciting and worthwhile activities for young children grows from experience. The fall of 1988 marked the fifth year we'd worked with computers in the High/Scope Demonstration Preschool, and the third year we'd provided training for early childhood educators who wanted to use computers in their own programs. As we look back on these experiences, we can see how our views on the possible role of computers in early childhood classrooms have developed and changed.

We find that the educators that we work with fall into three groups in their attitudes toward computers in the classroom: the **skeptical,** the **curious,** and the **enthusiastic.** Over the years, we've belonged to all three of these groups ourselves. Here's a short history of how our own attitudes have changed.

Getting started: our skeptical stage. While we, as adults, were fascinated with the potential of computers, we initially had real doubts about whether they were workable or appropriate for 3- and 4-year-olds. We thought that computers might be too complicated for young children to use successfully, and we feared the children would damage expensive machines and software. We wondered whether the two-dimensional, TV-like computer screen was a developmentally appropriate medium for children in the preschool years who build knowledge primarily through direct, "hands-on" experiences with materials. In addition, most of the commercial software (computer programs) we had seen were just too expensive and too low in quality to appeal to us.

In spite of our doubts, we went ahead with plans to add computers to the High/Scope Preschool on an experimental basis, and as always, we found that children are the best teachers. We started our experiment by adding a "computer area," to the classroom with three computers arranged in a semi-circle. The computers were available as a choice during work time, and we also used them in occasional small-group activities in which we introduced new software.

Curiosity: our next stage. Watching 3- to 5-year-olds working at computers quickly turned our skepticism to curiosity. Early on, we observed that all the children liked to go to the computer area. Some used the computers more than others, but even the youngest children (who were not yet 3) sometimes made plans to go to the computers. Children had few problems using the regular keyboard, mouse, or joystick, and despite fears to the contrary, we found that computers did not turn some children into isolated "hackers." Instead, we found that computers actually stimulated social play. Children enjoyed working with partners at the computer, and "expert" children often helped out other children with their computer problems. Finally, we found that the machines rarely broke down, despite daily classroom use.

Enthusiasm: our third stage. Over the years, these positive experiences with computers have continued. As a result, we're now enthusiastic about using computers in early childhood programs. We find that after a year in our preschool, most of our preschoolers have mastered a long list of computer skills: they can use menus, use important keys on the keyboard, operate the mouse and the printer successfully, and use all of these skills well enough to operate a half dozen or so programs on their own. Through these programs, they've had many valuable learning experiences. Most of these children have used the computer to create attractive art projects; to learn to recognize all the upper- and lower-case letters; to practice counting, matching, comparing, and memory strategies; and to explore the sound/symbol relationships of written English.

We've found that young children engage in these kinds of learning activities at the computer by choice, without pushing from us. We've also noticed that the presence of computers doesn't diminish the use of traditional materials. We've concluded that working at computers is compatible with the active, "hands-on" learning style that comes naturally to this age group. No longer do we think of the world of computers as an abstract version of the "real world" far removed from young children's thinking. Instead, we see it as a *different* world, with its own special opportunities for learning.

Quality Software: The Key to Success

The selection of high-quality software is essential to offering these kinds of learning opportunities to preschoolers and kindergartners. Since we began our experiment with computers, the availability of good early childhood software has increased tremendously to the point that we now have at least five good programs for each major key experience area. To select programs of high quality, we suggest looking for the following characteristics:

• **Easy to use**—Select programs whose activities start as soon as the computer is turned on, or that begin with a simple picture menu. Instructions should be brief and keyed to the children's level. Programs should require children to use only one key at a time.

• **Interactive**—The best programs require frequent reactions, decisions, or creative input from the child.

• **Childproof**—The designers of good software know that children will experiment with all the keys. Good programs can handle busy fingers and an occasional elbow without "locking up."

• **Designed with features for teachers and parents**—Look for codes adults can use to control the sound, add new challenges, or review what a child has done while using the program. Well- designed programs give adults such options.

• **Strong in content**—If you can't put your finger on the learning content, it's probably

Noteworthy Early Childhood Software

For the Apple II and compatibles
• Animal Alphabet and Other Things (McGraw-Hill Media)

• Color Me (Mindscape Educational Software)

• Counting Critters (MECC)

• Easy Street (MindPlay)

• Explore-a-Story Series (D.C. Heath & Co.)

• Mask Parade (Queue, Inc.)

• Muppetville (Sunburst Communications, Inc.)

• Observation and Classification (Hartley Courseware, Inc.)

• Picture Chompers (MECC)

For IBM and compatibles
• Color Me (Mindscape Educational Software)

• Kid's Stuff (Stone & Assoc.)

• Mask Parade (Queue, Inc.)

• Math and Me (Davidson and Assoc., Inc.)

• Mixed-Up Mother Goose (Sierra On-Line)

• Muppets On Stage (Sunburst Communications, Inc.)

• Number Farm (DLM)

• The Playroom (Broderbund Software)

For Macintosh
• KidsTime (Great Wave Software)

• The Playroom (Broderbund Software) ■

This child's drawing,
and the description he
dictated to accompany
it, depict his experience
with the computer in the
High/Scope Demonstra-
tion Classroom.

The best software programs are interactive—that is, they require frequent reactions, decisions, or creative input from the children using them.

*This is a mask and I
made it in the computer
area.*

*Then I took it to the
block area and I wore it
and this is a block to
show you I had the mask
in the house. James and I
made it [the house] with
blocks.* ∎

weak. Worthwhile programs give the feeling
that they're about something: shapes, words,
patterns, classification, numbers, for example.

• **Child-controlled**—A program should
never leave the child feeling trapped into continuing to the end of an activity. It should be easy
for the child to pause, finish up quickly, go on to
another level of activity, or stop altogether (for
example, the ESCAPE key often provides a quick
and easy way out of an activity).

• **Designed to aid learning**—Clear pictures
and interesting sounds related to the learning activity, not just fanfares of color and sound, are
signs of a good program. Programs that offer
novelty each time they are used and provide
feedback on success and failure are superior.
Some programs even adjust themselves automatically to a child's performance, moving down a
level to help the child who repeatedly makes mistakes and moving up a level for a child ready for
a greater challenge.

• **Worth the price**—The price of the program must be weighed against what you get for
your money. Check whether the price is above or
below the average price of software, how many

activities you get for your money, and what the program "package" includes. Consider also the longevity of a program—how long it might hold a child's interest or how much classroom use it will get.

Adult Support of Computer Learning

Once you've selected quality software, the other essential for effective computer activities is **gentle, non-intrusive adult support.** We stress non-intrusiveness because we've noticed that many teaching adults tend to hover protectively over children working at computers. These adults often fear that without constant supervision, children are likely to damage the machines or become frustrated with the exacting tasks the computer presents. Yet our own experiences have convinced us that, *given appropriate software,* young children will become adept at using the machines without extensive adult help.

Children working independently at computers quickly become familiar with the little tricks of operating the equipment. Children find out through experience that there are moments when the computer is unresponsive. They learn to wait a moment and try again.

To prepare for children's independent work at the computer, we recommend that adults introduce basic computer skills and new programs in a series of teacher-led small-group times. Once children are introduced to a program, they should then need only occasional adult help in operating it on their own—again, providing the program is developmentally appropriate.

When children do hit a snag at the computer, we suggest that adults, whenever possible, encourage the child to get help from another child. This way, the child with a problem gains a non-threatening helper, the helper builds his or

Overheard in the Computer Center: Typical Adult Statements

Inappropriate:
"You can use the computer yourself, but I or Mrs. G. must help you." (*Hovering*)

"Your four minutes at the computer is up. It's Alex's turn now." (*Over-scheduling*)

"Don't touch anything but the number keys and the spacebar." (*Discouraging experimentation*)

"When you get stuck this way, you should hit the spacebar like this. Then hit the arrow key like this. Then hit the other arrow key like this. There, it's all fixed." (*Doing it for them*)

Appropriate:
"Why don't you see what happens when you press this key?" (*Letting the child do it*)

"I see. You're pressing the spacebar to move the cursor." (*Labelling a child's actions*)

"Erin, can you tell Josh how you got your picture out of the printer?" (*Referring one child's problem to another*)

"The program we used to draw with at small-group time today will be on the computer tomorrow for anyone who wants to play with it." (*Encouraging choices and exploration*) ∎

her sense of competence and self-esteem, and both children gain a friend.

This potential for stimulating cooperative play is just one of many ways computers can enhance a developmentally based curriculum that stresses child-initiated learning. If you think computers could be an asset to your program, the next step is selecting appropriate equipment and software.

Computers: What You Need to Get Started

What kind of equipment do you need to introduce computer learning in your early childhood program? Our recommendations for equipment and software are based on an approach in which computer activities are available in the regular classroom as one of many possible choices children can make. This contrasts with the "computer lab" approach, in which computer equipment is set up in a separate room, and each class in the school or center visits the lab at a scheduled time.

To conduct computer activities successfully within the regular classroom, we recommend that the program have about **one computer for every 6 to 8 children.** We do know of programs that have used computers profitably with only one machine shared by 12–24 children. Having more machines available, however, makes it easier to offer the computer as a free-choice item during work time. When we first started our program, we had only one computer for a group of 18, and teachers had to use a scheduling system.

Each computer should have **at least 1 megabyte of internal memory** (128K is adequate for the Apple II and its compatibles) and a **floppy disk drive** (choose 3.5-in. for IBMs and compatibles, Amigas, and Apple Macintoshes and 5.25-in. for Apple IIs and compatibles). Internal hard drives, with the storage capacity of hundreds of floppy disks, are not strictly necessary for these machines, but will greatly simplify the start-up and operation of programs. A **color monitor**, however, is essential, since much of the impact of good preschool software comes from colorful graphics. A **mouse** for each computer is also recommended.

It is also desirable to have at least **one printer per classroom.** A printer enables adults and children to use the computer (with certain programs) to produce typed words or sentences and to print out their drawings on paper. Having these printed creations to show for their computer efforts gives children special satisfaction; the capacity to print also makes the computer a resource that can enrich children's play

. . . .

Computers in a Home Day Care Program

Andrea Scheib, a home day care provider and High/Scope endorsed trainer in Livermore, California, reports that computers have enriched the High/Scope Curriculum day care program she provides for children ages 10 months through 12 years. Scheib has three computers, a Commodore 64, an Atari and a Coleco, but uses the Commodore most because of the lack of educational software available for the other two machines. Typically, Scheib will introduce a new program to her 4- and 5-year-olds at small-group time. The next day she makes the program available as a choice during work time. Scheib relies heavily on the children themselves to help out their peers at the computers. She notes that 4- and 5-year-olds help children as young as 14 months to use the computer.

Scheib's day is organized around two plan-do-review sessions, one in the morning and one in the afternoon. The computers are available to toddlers, preschoolers, and kindergartners during the morning session. In the afternoon, older children who come to the program after school get "first dibs" at the computers. Scheib's three children, ages 7, 14, and 18, are often available to help children at the computers during the afternoon program. The only reservation Scheib expresses about computer learning concerns the problem of finding good software, especially for her toddlers and younger preschoolers. "I find it difficult to find really good programs that don't give me the feeling that I'm working with a ditto," she says, adding that she feels the selection of programs for older children is better. ∎

. . . .

elsewhere in the classroom (examples: using the computer to make masks for role play, or cards for birthdays or special occasions).

Which system should you buy? **The prime consideration in choosing a system should be the software available for it,** and there are preschool programs available for all popular personal computers. As there is more good early childhood software available for the somewhat dated Apple II computers than for any other system, these and the compatible Laser 128 make good choices and can be attractive low-cost options.

Newer and more up-to-date equipment— like the Macintosh LC, (which, with an Apple II option board and additional 5.25-in. disk drive can run Apple II software) and IBM PS/2 Model 25 and compatible machines—also make good choices. These newer and more capable computer systems, are likely to be the ones for which innovative software for young children will be developed, and there is already a considerable body of good early childhood software that can be used with these machines.

How much software will you need? It is essential to have **at least ten programs** that meet the criteria we have described for quality software. Programs cost about $30 each. Try to choose a range of programs that cover a variety of curriculum areas; try also to select programs in a variety of formats (these range from workbook-style matching and counting games to open-ended drawing and storymaking programs). For recommendations on specific programs, see the sidebar or consult the High/Scope materials on computer learning listed on page 297.

The recommendations we've given here for choosing equipment and working with children at computers reflect our belief that computer activities are a feasible and potentially exciting

To allow computer activities to be one choice available to children at work time, a ratio of one computer for every six to eight children is recommended. The computers and a printer should be arranged in a clearly defined area.

option for many early childhood programs. Computers will not make a weak early childhood program an effective one, but they can enhance an already strong program. ∎

Toward Culturally Diverse Settings

by
Ann Rogers

A participant at a High/Scope workshop recently asked us, "I know it's important for all children to grow up valuing our multicultural society. But my preschool serves only white, middle-class children. How can our staff help the children gain an appreciation of other groups and cultures?"

The issue this teacher raised is a common one for preschool and day care programs. An environment that includes a broad range of children may be the ideal setting for learning about various cultures, but attracting a diverse mix of children is not a possibility for all programs. Staff of centers that serve relatively homogeneous groups may wonder if there are experiences they can plan or materials they can introduce to broaden children's cultural outlooks.

In cases like this, we believe there are many things staff can do to help children learn about cultural diversity. But before considering the program's activities or materials, we suggest that staff first look at their own attitudes about human differences. Probably the most important thing we want children to learn is that all people are the same in some ways and different in many others, and that these differences are *normal* and *okay*. Sometimes adults are uncomfortable when children notice or mention such differences as someone's skin color, disability, size, etc. Their discomfort is communicated to the children, who then feel that there is something wrong about the difference. A first and ongoing step for all of us, then, is to **examine and openly discuss with other adults our own feelings about**

Even if their group is fairly homogeneous, staff can discover and build on the cultural variations within their group. For example, if music is an important part of a child's family life, staff can provide materials so the child can share her interest with the group.

human differences so that we can avoid passing on such negative feelings to children.

The next step for staff is to **capitalize on the differences that do exist among the families of their group of children.** For example, they can invite parents and children to share their special interests, particular holiday traditions, or favorite foods. Another idea is to help each child make a book about his or her family that contains pictures of family members, the home, the parents, and workplaces; box sides from their favorite breakfast cereals; pictures of what they do on weekends, etc. Staff can share the books with all the children and make them available in the center.

Should staff go beyond this step and make efforts to introduce children to a more diverse range of people? This is not easy to do, when one considers that preschoolers have difficulty form-

Open-Ended Materials Promote Multicultural Awareness

Open-ended (nonspecific) materials enable children to reenact experiences they've had with their families and share them with adults and children in the center. In turn, this enables the staff and children to learn about the everyday lives and cultures of diverse families:

Scott came in to the High/Scope Demonstration Preschool one recent Monday very excited over the "Monster Truck" Show he had attended over the weekend with his parents. Since then, he and his friends have planned to make and drive "monster trucks" nearly every day. Since we do not have any toy monster trucks in our classroom (in fact, the teachers had never before heard of them), Scott and his friends have had to think hard about the features of these trucks that were important to them and the materials they could use to make the trucks. They've made gear shifts from long unit blocks and paper towel tubes and short wave radios from Bristle Blocks. The availability of these nonspecific materials enabled Scott to share a very specific experience with other children and adults. ∎

ing concepts about things they cannot directly experience. One thing adults *can* do is to **make sure that the books, pictures, and dolls they use and make available in their setting depict as wide a variety of people as possible** in all occupations, roles, and races, represented without stereotypes. In choosing materials, staff should also remember to avoid the "tourist" approach to culture, in which special-occasion costumes and celebrations are presented out of the context of people's everyday lives, leading to misunderstandings and stereotyping.

The strategies given here are valid both for diverse and homogeneous groups of children. They are intended as a starting point—through a continuing process of team planning, staff will develop many other strategies for promoting multicultural awareness. ■

The Team Process: Child Observation, Team Planning, Assessment

· ·

Effective Team Teaching: Working Together Works Better —
Warren Buckleitner, Bonnie Lash Freeman, and Ed Greene

Sharing Your Workload: Creating a Sensible Division of Labor —
Warren Buckleitner, Bonnie Lash Freeman, and Ed Greene

Observation and Feedback: Why They're So Important for You, for
Children — Mary Hohmann

Assessment: A System That Works for You, Not Against You —
Mark Tompkins

Child-Oriented Lesson Plans: A Change of "Theme" — Mark Tompkins

Getting Started: The First Day of the Rest of the Year —
Warren Buckleitner and Susan M. Terdan

T his chapter takes up the professional concerns that early childhood staff deal with on a day-to-day basis: how to work together as a team, how to provide feedback to team members or trainees on their effectiveness in working with children, how to assess children's progress, how to improve the program. In the opening article, Warren Buckleitner, Bonnie Lash Freeman, and Ed Greene offer an overview of the process of working and planning together in High/Scope programs and make some suggestions for strengthening the team process. In the second article, the same authors offer practical suggestions to teams on how to allocate duties fairly and effectively.

Child observation is emphasized throughout this chapter as the key activity that unifies and guides the team process. Discussing the basic principles of observation and feedback, Mary Hohmann points out that child observation is the starting point for both training/staff development activities and the team planning/child assessment process. The theme of child observation is developed further in two selections by Mark Tompkins. The first article discusses the High/Scope assessment system, which is based on collecting anecdotal observations of children, and the second describes how early childhood staff can develop lesson plans around children's interests, building on themes they observe in children's play.

The last article by Warren Buckleitner and Susan M. Terdan offers a specific illustration of many of the principles presented in other articles in the chapter. The authors provide a "case history" of effective team planning as they describe the steps they took to prepare for the opening of a preschool session.

Effective Team Teaching: Working Together Works Better

by

Warren Buckleitner,

Bonnie Freeman,

and

Ed Greene

The Lone Ranger and Tonto, Sears and Roebuck, Rogers and Hammerstein, the Boston Celtics—these are all examples of successful teams. Whatever their profession, people can often achieve more by working together than by working alone. In the High/Scope Curriculum, we advocate a team approach to working with young children because it enables adults to pool their talents and build upon one another's strengths.

A team may include teachers, paraprofessionals, curriculum assistants, specialists, parents, student teachers, older children, senior citizens, in fact, anyone who is involved regularly or occasionally in the ongoing classroom program. Each member brings unique skills and credentials to the team, and these should be acknowledged and used by the other team members. For example, one team member may be recognized as a skilled pianist who can lead movement and music activities, another team member may have a rich knowledge of the local community that can be useful in efforts to increase parent participation. Through the process of planning as a team and recognizing one another's strengths, each member becomes an equally important contributor to the classroom program. When teaching adults work in a team, children experience not only a varied program but also a unified one.

Building a Strong Team

Building an effective team isn't easy. The merging of separate personalities to strengthen a classroom program can be challenging. That's why we're offering some suggestions for building a strong teaching team that have worked well for us.

At High/Scope, **we work to strengthen the team by focusing on a shared commitment to the curriculum approach** and the task of applying it in the classroom program. Although all members of a team will have personal likes and dislikes and different working styles, focusing on the *curriculum* provides a common ground for building team cohesiveness. For example, child observation is a key element in the High/Scope Curriculum. We find that child observation helps improve team relationships because it keeps the focus on *children* and shifts it away from the individual needs, hang-ups, and "axes to grind" of team members. Trust will grow as team members go through the process of observing children, sharing these observations, and planning activities based on curriculum goals. Team members will learn to communicate openly and support one another. But this is a long- term process, and perfection won't be achieved overnight. Next, we discuss some steps you can take to get your team moving in the right direction.

Plan together at a consistent, mutually acceptable time. Daily planning is best, but some teams can meet only every other day or once a week. If necessary, plan during naptime or ask parent volunteers to help watch children as you plan. Your time together is precious, so use it wisely. Make sure your team does the following:

• Evaluate what worked and what didn't in the previous day's plans.

• Plan for group activities.

• Pool observations; supplement one another's knowledge of individual children.

• Evaluate whether classroom expectations are consistent from team member to team member.

A shared commitment to the curriculum approach and the task of applying it to the program for children is the basis of team cohesiveness in the High/Scope approach.

• Establish the responsibilities of each team member.

• Set daily and weekly goals for individual children.

In sum, daily planning sessions are the time when team members turn the successes and problems of one day into plans and strategies for the next.

As you go through this planning process, organize yourselves by selecting a focus for your discussion at any given time. Your overall focus can be to relate the curriculum framework to the experiences children are having in the program. You can break this big task down by concentrating on specific topics for part of all of a meeting (for example: a particular grouping of key experiences; elements of the room arrangement and daily routine; your observations and plans for two or three children).

Develop your observation skills. Accurate observation of children is essential to the team planning process. Learn to look at what children are doing, how children are learning, and which materials they are using. Knowing this information will be shared later in the planning meeting will motivate you to remember the little things that happen during a day. For example, you may decide to carry a small notepad to write down your observations as they occur throughout the day.

Make decisions systematically. Define the problem; discuss the alternatives; allow all team members to contribute their ideas. After discussion, try to reach consensus on a possible solution. Once a decision is made, communicate it clearly to all affected. If you can't reach an agreement on some issue, make plans to try out alternative solutions and review them later.

Set clear and consistent expectations and limits for children's behavior in each segment of the daily routine. When is running permitted? What are the ground rules for taking turns at the swings? What if a child won't clean up? Decide in advance how *all* adults will deal with such issues, set consistent policies, and communicate them to children.

Capitalize on your human resources. Find out about and use each others' strengths. People who are especially skilled in certain areas should use their skills regularly—for example, a teacher whose hobby is carpentry should be encouraged to lead an effort to set up a construction area.

Decide together on the forms and tools you will use to document the planning/observation process. What will you use to record your daily plan and your observations of children's problems and progress? You may wish to develop forms yourselves or you can use the planning forms and observation/assessment records developed by High/Scope: The High/Scope Child Observation Record (COR) and the COR Anecdotal Notecards. You'll also need to decide how often you will make notations on these forms and who will be responsible for filling them out. We recommend that you use part of your daily planning session to record plans and observations as you discuss them. This discourages procrastination and encourages all team members to share the recordkeeping tasks.

Carefully assess your division of labor and rotate tasks among team members. Team members should view one another as *colleagues*, without a rigid hierarchy, regardless of their official titles. Take a close look at *who does what* and *what needs to be done*. List duties and divide them up sensibly, making sure each team member's special talents are used and that nobody gets too many housekeeping duties. Rotate roles when possible.

Get to know one another well. Persons who like one another make better teams. Team members don't have to be fast friends to work together successfully, but personal issues can have a negative affect on teamwork. If you are having problems working with one of your team members, try spending some informal time alone together; you could suggest that you go out together for a cup of coffee or that you drive together to a local early childhood association meeting. Try to iron out your differences by learning more about what makes each of you "tick."

Periodic Evaluation

Evaluate your teamwork occasionally. Like a sailboat moving through the sea, your team may need to shift course or "adjust sails" periodically as you move through the school year. So plan for periodic reviews of how well your team is working and make whatever adjustments seem appropriate.

Following these guidelines for team teaching and team planning will help you create an environment in which each team member's experience is valued, in which all individuals'

Setting Clear and Consistent Expectations for Children

One planning task for early childhood teams is to decide on expectations for children. For example, a team might want to discuss and develop consistent expectations in the following areas:

Can a child go to a new area without indicating a plan?

Should children clean up before moving to a new area?

Where is running permitted?

How loud is too loud for indoor play?

Can materials be taken out of the interest area?

Can children go to the bathroom themselves?

What if a child won't clean up?

Must all children participate in small-group time? In circle time?

Do children have to clean up only the materials they used themselves, or should they work until the whole room is cleaned?

How do we deal with hitting, biting, or grabbing?

What do we do if a child disrupts a group activity? ∎

ideas are considered and used, and in which individual problems are taken seriously. The team process also will help you achieve the following goals:

• Reduce the dependence of teacher aides and teachers on head teachers, trainers, curriculum specialists, or other outside "experts."

• Encourage identification with the curriculum model.

• Break down status differentials among staff if they act as barriers to honest communication.

• Make better decisions based on the input of the total group.

• Provide opportunities for team members' professional development. ■

Sharing Your Workload: Creating a Sensible Division of Labor

O ne of the most important planning tasks for early childhood teams is to find out **what needs to be done** and decide **which team member will do it.** Creating a well-thought-out division of labor that makes the best use of individual strengths and talents and encourages team members to develop as professionals will have a long-range positive impact on your program. Here are some suggestions for creating a fair and effective division of labor.

First, look at what each of you is doing in your present situation. You may be surprised by what you discover. In centers staffed by both teachers and aides, a "top-down" pattern of leadership often emerges. The teachers plan, lead, and evaluate activities, doing most of the direct work with the children and parents, while the aides take care of the housekeeping duties.

This division of responsibility is incompatible with the High/Scope teaching philosophy, in which all adults in the classroom are expected to work with children, offer ideas, and participate in group problem solving. When you make a team member a "go-fer," you lose out on the valuable experiences and skills he or she has to offer. For example, while a teacher may have more years on the job, the aide may have some new ideas from a training workshop she recently attended. Then, too, an aide may be more effective than others in working with certain children, parents, or other staff members, so it makes sense to spread the "people work" around.

To evaluate who is doing what, we suggest you think carefully about each part of the daily routine and list in detail each small job to be

by

Warren Buckleitner,

Bonnie Lash Freeman,

and

Ed Greene

Which Team Member Does What?

It's a good idea for early childhood teams to list all the tasks to be done in their programs and then to decide systematically who does what. Some tasks may be handled by particular individuals, others by the group as a whole, and other rotated on a regular basis among team members. Here are some items from a typical list:

Who talks with the program supervisor?

Who fills the paint jars?

Who waters the plants?

Who stocks the paper?

Who makes the snack?

Who records daily observations of children?

Who arranges program publicity? Who talks with parents when they pick children up?

Who greets children?

Who reads to children?

Who leads small-group time?

Who selects new materials?

Who decides how to arrange the classroom?

Who visits children's homes?

Who cleans the floor?

Who gets out toys for children?

Who handles child management problems?

Who writes the parent newsletter?

Who arranges field trips?

Who greets children in the morning?

Listing in detail all the tasks that must be done in the daily routine and which team member is going to do them is a good starting point for evaluating the team's division of labor.

done. Then construct a list of questions like those offered in the side column, and answer them honestly, specifying, in writing, which team member is now doing each of the duties listed. Then look over the results, and reassign duties if necessary. It's often most beneficial to rotate many of the responsibilities among team members.

Dividing and sharing roles and responsibilities can also enhance the team planning process itself. For example, a different team member each day can act as discussion leader for each team planning session, taking responsibility for keeping the group on task and making sure all ideas are considered. Another way to divide up the job of planning is for each team member to take responsibility for a particular area of the classroom or segment of the daily routine. For example, assign each team member to assess and refurbish the materials in the house area, or to observe there the next work time. After a designated time period (perhaps two days or a week) reorganize again. You can also rotate the roles of conceptualizing and handling practical details: One team member can plan the content of a small-group time, while another gathers the materials; the next day, they can switch roles. The responsibilities for record-keeping can also be rotated—for example, each day a different team member can write down children's accomplishments on the proper forms as you talk about your observations.

Sharing roles in this way doesn't mean that team members' special qualifications, such as in-depth training in the curriculum model, are discounted; rather, it means that all team members' special credentials are valued by the group, whether the credential is a different home language or a master's degree. Sharing responsibilities gives all team members the opportunity to grow professionally. ■

Who changes diapers?

Who answers the phone?

Who checks to see if doors and windows are locked?

Who sets IEP goals for special-needs children?

Who cleans up spilled juice? ■

Observation and Feedback: Why They're So Important for You, for Children

by
Mary Hohmann

In the High/Scope Curriculum, adults use the dynamic processes of observation and feedback dialogue on a daily basis—both in working with children and in training others to do so effectively. In both cases, these processes are used in remarkably similar ways.

Observation in the High/Scope Curriculum is a way of capturing, in words or on film, what a child does and says during a specific period of time, in as much objective detail as possible. *Feedback* is the process of two or more adults talking about and analyzing an observed situation to discover which opportunities for a child's growth and development are present and to find ways to support and/or expand them.

Ideally, all adults involved with children—parents, day care providers, home visitors, aides, administrators, trainers— take part in observation and feedback discussions. These processes start with the adults who work with children on a daily basis, and may extend to adults who are not as directly involved. In this respect, our curriculum differs from other approaches in which observation and feedback are conducted primarily by "outsiders."

Are such careful observations and feedback dialogues really necessary? Are these processes really so important in our approach to educating children and working effectively with adults? Yes they are! Here's why.

Observation and feedback discussions provide ongoing support for children and adults. Adults support children by looking closely at what they are doing, by sharing insights and understandings with them, and by generating ways

Child observation is the starting point for the observation/feedback process—regardless of whether the goal is to work with children effectively or to train or supervise others who are working with children.

to help children build on their strengths, interests, and successes. Adults support each other by sharing their detailed observations of individual children and by designing strategies that will enable them to act on their observations.

Observation and feedback discussions encourage teamwork. By teamwork we mean the close working relationship of all the adults involved with any particular group of children. Adults who consistently observe, share, and plan together will strengthen their ability to appreciate and support both children and peers. Because everyone on the team observes and leads feedback discussions, everyone on the team builds both leadership and teamwork skills.

Observation and feedback discussions encourage adults to focus on the curriculum. As they discuss their observations, adults draw upon the curriculum to confirm and clarify their impressions and ideas. The curriculum describes key learning experiences to look for in children's activities and principles to follow to support them. It provides a framework for observing children and designing subsequent support strategies.

Using the curriculum as the major reference point enables team members to make objective, detailed observations and to engage in feedback dialogue that is rich in insight, ideas, creativity, and usefulness.

Principles of Observation and Feedback

Observation and feedback discussions in the High/Scope Curriculum are guided by the same principles, regardless of who is doing the observing or participating in the feedback session. For parents, teachers, trainers, supervisors, volunteers, assistants, and coordinators, the same principles apply—because all are observing and giving feedback to each other in support of children's development. Here are the hallmarks of our approach to observation and feedback.

Children are the subjects of observation. For adults who work closely with children each day in their day care homes, home-based programs, classrooms, or wherever, this principle probably seems obvious. However, adults who are somewhat removed from daily work with children may feel that observing adults rather than children provides a stronger basis for improving staff teaching skills.

The curriculum breaks the whole into manageable parts that the team can focus on and discuss. For example, a team member might choose to observe how Noah uses materials at small-group time.

In our experience, the best way to support the growth and development of both adults and children is to focus observations on children. Child observation not only tells us what we need to know about children but also provides a basis for discussing the observed effects we have on them. Adults from outside the classroom also find that child observation allows them to see child development "in action" and contributes to a strong sense of teamwork among classroom adults.

Curriculum guides observation. The critical elements of the High/Scope Curriculum—the ingredients of active learning, room arrangement principles, daily routine sequences and roles, the key experiences—focus the observations. Thus, the observer is not overwhelmed by everything that is going on with every child at any given moment.

The curriculum breaks the whole temporarily into manageable parts. An observer might choose, for example, to focus on "active learning at small-group time" or "how Jimmy and Joey use materials during work time." Yet the parts can be reassembled later to represent the whole picture of the opportunities for growth and development that occur within a particular child-care setting.

Observations record factual details. Writing down or videotaping observations preserves situations so that the adult team can put them to good use. Writing frees adults from relying totally on memory to recall in detail situations they

· ·

Effective Feedback Discussion Techniques: "Real-Life" Stories From the Field

Across the country, High/Scope trainers are using the constructive feedback process. Here are some scenes that illustrate feedback in action.

Scene I: Brooklyn, NY. *Four women (two classroom staff, trainer, center director) are reviewing room arrangement and materials as children used them that morning during plan-do-review. Enthusiasm is high. The dialogue flies back and forth. Discrete, clearly defined, child-centered problems are presented and solved. A sense of "We can do it!" fills the air.*

Fleeta: It seemed to me that Julio and Carlotta left the house area play because there weren't enough materials there. What materials can we add to the house area to support the Christmas role play?

Mrs. H: Gift boxes, wrapping paper, a large platter for the turkey.

Mrs. B: Toys around the tree. We could have the children wrap up the

toys. This would be a good spatial problem for them to solve.

Mrs. H: Candles. We could ask children and parents to bring things in. This way, everyone's culture would be reflected in our house area.

...

Fleeta: When the children were working with modeling dough, I noticed they were having problems sharing materials.

Mrs. B: We should have had enough spoons for everyone. And a separate bowl for each child—more individual containers.

Fleeta: On their own, the children did add pots and pans from the house area. They know where things are and that it's okay to take materials from one area to another.

...

Fleeta: How can we highlight the numbers on the clock so that children can see them more easily? I couldn't see the numbers when you pointed

to the clock at clean-up time. I knew
Maria and Paula couldn't see them,
even though they had asked you to
show them how you knew what time
it was.

Mrs. B: Magic-marker the numbers. Lower the clock.

Director: Take my clock and give
me yours. Mine has nice big numbers
that the children will be able to identify much more easily.

Scene II: Uniontown, PA. *As
Cindy and Becky share their observations
of a small-group time that Becky did earlier in the morning, the unexpected turns
in their dialogue are particularly strik-
ing. For example, throughout the small-
group time Cindy had noticed a number
of disruptions—children leaving the
group, children joining the group, children needing to be taken to the bathroom.
To raise this issue, Cindy asks an open-
ended question:*

Cindy: Was there anything that
distracted you during your small-
group time?

Becky: Yes. I was really preoccupied with the questions I wanted to
ask children. Also, Jackie (volunteer)
was wandering in and out of the
room. I wanted her to join one of the
small groups.

*Cindy is surprised by Becky's an-
swer, because she had assumed that
Becky had been distracted by the same
things that had distracted her. Recognizing that she had made a false assumption, Cindy follows Becky's train of
thought. For the next few minutes,
Cindy and Becky talk about the issues
Becky has raised—how to promote child
language and how to train volunteers.
Cindy decides to save the distractions she
had noticed for the next training session
she is planning on small-group time.*

Scene III: Your town. You can
write your own real-life feedback
scripts. All you need are your team
members, a curriculum focus, dialogue, enthusiasm, and a dose of the
unexpected! ∎

. . . .

want to share and discuss. Although videotaping
can be somewhat awkward, it has the advantage
of being detailed and factual. It presents what
happened, period! Written observations, like videotaped ones, should be as detailed and factual
as possible.

Feedback is reciprocal. Effective feedback
involves dialogue—talking, listening, giving,
and taking. Although the observer has the most
complete set of factual, detailed notes, other
team members often make important contributions because they can recall the same incident
from different points of view. Since such team dialogue involves a spontaneous exchange of
ideas, one can never be sure what will happen

during a feedback session. The outcomes will depend on the contributions of each participant.

Feedback results in mutually agreed upon action. People participating in effective feedback sessions do three things: (1) report and agree on children's actions, (2) determine the extent to which children are engaged in active learning and key experiences, and (3) guided by the curriculum framework, decide which actions to take next. This last step is often the most difficult. Sometimes the observer has a predetermined idea of what needs to be done and tries to "dictate" the idea to the rest of the group. Sometimes the only action necessary is "more of the same." Often, team members will refer to situations suggested in High/Scope curriculum materials in generating solutions.

In the best of situations, the feedback team agrees to try a number of new actions or strategies, some of which will work and some of which will, after trial, be discarded. The point is to proceed through all three steps because each step—reporting, analyzing, planning for action—is integral to effective feedback. ■

Assessment: A System That Works for You, Not Against You

"If I could change one thing about teaching here, it would be to limit the busywork of evaluating children. I feel like I spend the whole first month out in the hall testing one child at a time, when I should be in the classroom with all the children. To top it off, once I've finished the testing, the information that I'm left with is not that useful in my teaching. What I need is something meaningful that doesn't take so much time."

by
Mark Tompkins

The issue this teacher is struggling with is not whether assessment should take place but, rather, *what form it should take*. Most early childhood educators recognize the need to evaluate children's progress. Assessment gives us objective information on individual children and helps us to judge the effectiveness of the overall program. The assessment process should be easy, fast, and, above all, useful.

This article discusses some of the problems many preschool educators have experienced with conventional testing and assessment methods and introduces an alternative—the systematic observation method used in the High/Scope Curriculum. High/Scope's assessment instrument is called the COR (Child Observation Record). The COR is used by teachers trained in our curriculum to assess curriculum outcomes through observations of children's performance. It is filled out at periodic intervals.

In completing the COR, teachers use observations they have recorded daily on a special observation form. They can design these forms themselves or purchase them from High/Scope. Because teachers must integrate the process of re-

As the last child leaves for the day, Pam gets the observation notebook and sits down with her assistant teacher, Jose. They spend the next 15 minutes talking about what the children did that day. Pam begins the discussion: "I remember seeing you with Carol in the house area today—what happened?" As Jose begins to answer, Pam turns to Carol's page in the observation notebook. On the page with Carol's name is a form with nine key experience categories. Brief notes are jotted down in most of the categories.

"I was playing restaurant with Carol," says Jose. "The most interesting thing that happened was that she decided to make a menu. She got the pencil and paper, drew some pictures on it, and asked me to write the words spaghetti, pop, *and* corn flakes.*"*

"Let's see," says Pam, "where should I write that observation?"

"We could put it under LANGUAGE or REPRESENTATION," says Jose.

"OK, let's write it under REPRESENTATION." Pam makes the entry: "12/19— Used paper and pencil to make a menu for a restaurant. Dictated spaghetti, pop, corn flakes.*"*

Pam and Jose write their observations on a Carol's page in the notebook. In the notebook is a similar form for each child in the class. The notebook is kept within easy reach. Classifying and recording

cording anecdotal notes into their daily teaching *before* they can begin to use the COR, most of this article focuses on this note-taking process.

What Preschool Educators Say About Assessment and Testing

In two recent workshops on the High/Scope Curriculum attended by teachers, assistant teachers, administrators, and trainers, we asked the audience to describe the concerns they have about their current testing and assessment methods. Their responses were remarkably consistent with what we have heard and experienced ourselves over the years. Here are the problems cited most often:

• **Standardized testing often concentrates upon goals and skills that can be readily tested, ignoring the developmental appropriateness of the testing procedures.** Since the teacher's performance is often evaluated on the basis of children's test scores, teachers naturally are driven to "teach to the test."

• **Information generated from the tests and assessment procedures may not be useful if the curriculum approach is not reflected in the content of the test.** If teachers can't use the results in planning activities for children, the time and energy spent on assessment seems wasted.

• **Frequently, a child can't do something in a testing situation that a teacher has seen him or her do spontaneously in the classroom setting.** Teachers trust their own observations of what children are doing in the classroom more than they trust the results of a 20-minute test.

• **Test scores are often misused, resulting in labels and comparisons that can have a long-term negative impact on children.** A test score may be taken to mean that a tangible, unchang-

Discussing observations of children and recording them by key experience category is a crucial process for child assessment.

ing characteristic of the child has been identified, even though the test only reflects performance on a specific set of tasks on a particular day. Such misinterpretations of testing create labels that can follow the child for years, creating low expectations in teachers and parents that become self-fulfilling prophecies. Rather than focus attention on children's abilities and strengths, most assessment tools highlight what children can't do. In turn, this tends to focus the teacher's energies at remediating deficits rather than enhancing strengths.

 • **Some evaluation procedures are very difficult to administer, especially to young children.** If the person administering the test has not had the special training needed to do it properly, the results are highly questionable.

 • **Teachers and caregivers are often told which evaluation tools to use, when and how to use them.** If they are not asked for input when decisions about assessment are made, they don't develop a sense of "ownership" in the process.

their observations in this way helps them plan follow-up activities.

Pam and Jose, for example, decide to build upon Carol's menu idea by making "menus" for planning and recall time the next day. Each menu shows symbols representing the various areas of the classroom, with the words for each area written underneath. Each menu also provides some blank space. The next day, the children use the menus in various ways: some children circle the appropriate symbol to plan where they want to play (or to recall it later); some "order" out loud from the menu as a way of planning which objects they want to play with and where; others trace objects they want to play with on their menus.

The use of recording forms to document observations of each child is central to the observation process Pam and Jose use to evaluate and give focus to their day-to-day teaching. The next stage in this evaluation process involves longer range assessment of child progress using High/Scope's observation instrument, the COR (Child Observation Record). Pam and Jose use the information recorded in their observation notebook to fill out a COR on each child twice a year. ∎

This can result in apathy and lack of interest that can sabotage the assessment effort.

- **Tests and assessment procedures can be biased against minorities.** Most tests reflect white, middle-class values and attitudes, and may not be meaningful for minority children with different linguistic and cognitive styles, values, and experiences.

What Anecdotal Note Taking Offers to Teachers

The cornerstone of the High/Scope assessment system is a system of taking anecdotal notes on children's daily activities. We recommend that adults make dated notes each day on specific things children have done. They then classify each notation into one of nine categories reflecting the major key experience areas in the curriculum—*language, representation, classification, seriation, number, space, time, movement,* and *social development.* To make this process of recording and classifying observations easier, we recommend that staff develop a recording form for each child with nine columns, one for each key experience category, leaving space in each column for recording anecdotes about the child.

A form available from High/Scope—the Child Observation Record (COR) Anecdotal Notecard—can also be used for this purpose. This card is divided into six columns, for notes in six broad areas of child development: Initiative, social relations, creative representation, music and movement, language and literacy, logic and mathematics. This notecard was developed as a generic form that all developmentally oriented early childhood programs could use, regardless of the curriculum approach, so it is not organized around High/Scope's key experience categories. It may be easier for staff of High/Scope programs, who use the key experiences as their frame of reference for understanding child development, to develop their own observation forms around the key experience categories.

Regardless of what form you choose to use to record your observations, the important thing is to get started in the process of taking notes, discussing them in child development terms, and recording them in some systematic way. This task may seem intimidating, but keep in mind that you don't need to record notes on every child, in every category, every day. Instead, we recommend that teachers record just a few observations a day on a few children. We go into the process of taking the anecdotal notes in more detail in the side column; but first let's consider some of the advantages of using such notes in teaching and planning:

• **As written and dated records, anecdotal notes allow teachers and caregivers to see children's progress and development over time.** These notes can help you remember the steps of children's growth accurately, and to think of children in terms of their present abilities.

• **The daily process of completing these notes develops teachers' "objective" observation skills.** Subjective statements like "She was very happy today" have no place in such notes; they are replaced with factual observations, such as "Carrie smiled as she passed out the cups during snack time, and later said it made her feel good when she helped." As teachers learn to observe more accurately, they become more responsive to the varied needs of individual children.

• **An anecdotal record form can be quick and easy to use since it relates directly to the classroom curriculum.** If you are conducting a program based on the High/Scope key experiences, using a form divided into key experience categories to record your notes is a natural out-

Tips for Anecdotal Note Taking

Teachers from the High/Scope classroom and others we have worked with during training have contributed the following tips to simplify anecdotal note taking.

• **Always date your entries** and write them objectively and in a way that helps you remember what happened—but keep them brief.

• If you are afraid of forgetting incidents, **carry around a small note pad to jot down observations** during the day.

• **Make recording your anecdotal notes a part of your team's daily plan.** Budget 15 minutes for talking about and writing entries.

• **Don't try to talk about every child every day;** instead, just talk about what you saw and did. On some days you may make 4 entries and on other days, 12.

• When you first begin classifying your observations by the key experiences, **don't spend too much time choosing "just the right category"** for each observation. For most entries, there are several key experiences occurring, so there are many possible "correct" choices. To jog your memory, tape a list of key experiences on the inside cover of your observation notebook.

• If you don't meet as a team daily, **make entries at any time or in any place that is convenient for you.** Collect and record these notes later in one place. ■

growth of the observing, discussing, and planning that you are already engaged in. This kind of assessment system does not require teachers to set up artificial testing situations or to fill out lengthy checklists; it takes only a few minutes a day.

• **Anecdotal notes provide essential information for planning.** When teachers have an accurate record of what children have been doing, they are better able to plan and provide *developmentally appropriate* experiences for children. Planning then becomes a process of finding out what the children have been doing and are interested in and using that information to plan for the day or week. Rather than make an arbitrary decision to focus on a theme like "community helpers," adults using this approach are building upon and extending the interests of children.

• **A record of anecdotal observations is an excellent tool for sharing information with parents** because it forces teachers to describe children in specific terms, without vague generalities, jargon, abstract numerical scores, or rating scales. Parents can readily understand how the specific incidents recorded in the notes relate to development and learning.

• **Anecdotal note taking helps teachers and caregivers discover children who are not getting enough attention.** As you review your notes during daily planning, you may notice that one child's record form has very few entries. This gap can be a signal to get to know this "hidden child" better.

• **Anecdotal note taking helps teaching adults learn the key experiences and understand child development.** As you categorize your observations by the key experiences, you will learn about them. This kind of day-to-day practice with the key experiences is more involving and meaningful than just reading about them. The process of applying the key experi-

Assessment in the High/Scope Curriculum does not take place in restrictive and limiting testing situations but grows out of observations of children engaged in spontaneous play.

ences to your daily observations can make child development theory come to life.

• **Anecdotal note taking helps identify needs for teaching and further training.** In reviewing a set of anecdotal note forms, teaching team members and/or their supervisor may notice that certain key experience areas are filled out more often or with a greater variety of entries than others. This pattern may indicate that the team is overlooking some areas in classroom planning or that further training in a particular area is needed.

• **Filling out records of anecdotal notes provides a systematic way of collecting data that can be used later to complete the High/ Scope Curriculum assessment instrument, the COR (Child Observation Record).** The COR is a checklist of tasks in six broad developmental areas, such as creative representation and social development, that enables teachers to see the patterns of children's development over a number of months. The COR provides a basis for systematic assessment of each child's progress and evaluation of the program as a whole. Note that *the COR is a complex instrument—to use it properly, High/Scope COR training is recommended.*

Taking anecdotal notes is a simple process that can be a powerful agent of curriculum change. These notes help staff recognize and discuss *what* is happening in their classroom, *why* it is important in terms of the key experiences, and *how* to use this information in planning. ■

Child-Oriented Lesson Plans: A Change of "Theme"

It's "Yellow Week" at Everytown Day Care. The lesson plan posted by the door lists many activities, materials, and experiences that the adults have planned to help the children learn about yellow. Some of the planned activities include making yellow modeling dough, putting yellow paper on the easel, telling the parents to dress their children in yellow clothes during the week, and reading stories and singing songs about things that are yellow like the sun, corn, and flowers. In creating the plans for this year's "Yellow Week," the adults used curriculum resource books, materials they had stored in a curriculum file cabinet, and last year's lesson plans.

by
Mark Tompkins

Every teacher of young children faces the challenge of planning what to do the next day or week in the classroom. One of the most common ways to create lesson plans is the theme-based approach, in which adults choose a theme (like "community helpers," "dinosaurs," or "yellow") then plan their activities and materials around this focus.

This theme-based approach to planning is used in the majority of preschool programs today. Early childhood educators often cite many advantages of using themes: They are a convenient vehicle for organizing and planning activities; they insure that the program has tangible educational content; and they enable adults to expand children's horizons by introducing new topics and materials.

But despite the widespread popularity of theme-based planning, the themes adults choose are not always developmentally appropriate or

Child-Oriented Themes: One Preschool's Experience

Below we discuss some recent planning themes that teachers at the High/Scope Demonstration Preschool drew from observations of children.

Transportation. Colin, a preschooler, had seen a blimp at the local airport, and when his parents expressed interest, the crew had invited the family to come inside for a tour. Visiting the blimp was a very exciting experience for Colin, one that he represented at preschool by building his own "blimps"—large, enclosed block structures—in the block area. Usually, he would invite four other classmates to join him in his blimp (the blimp he had seen had had five crew members). Colin and the crew members would then pretend to fly the blimps over football games, over states they had visited with their families, and to other familiar destinations.

The teachers built on Colin's interest by gathering picture books about blimps from the library and reading them to the whole class. Many of the books they read also pictured cars, trains, planes, hot air balloons, helicopters, and so forth. This intrigued the children, who began to represent blimps and other forms of transportation in their play and artwork.

Teachers continued to build on children's expanding interest in transportation. For example, the teachers noticed one day that children had become especially inter-

meaningful for young children. For children to make sense of a theme, it must be relevant to their interests and experiences. There is no guarantee that a theme invented by a teacher, chosen from a book, or taken from last year's lesson plan will match children's interests, experiences, or developmental levels. Sometimes, too, adults may be so preoccupied with the chosen theme that they fail to recognize the children's own interests and preferred play activities. "Blinded" by the theme, adults may miss opportunities to support and extend what children are doing and thinking about.

Let's return to the Everytown Day Care for an example of the pitfalls of overemphasizing a theme. A group of children were using cardboard tubes, shoeboxes, and small counting bears of many colors, pretending that the bears were "cave exploring." Because it was "Yellow Week," the teacher working with the children was more interested in having children identify which bears were yellow and what the yellow bears were doing than in participating in children's cave-exploring play. The children's interest in cave exploring presented many possibilities that the teacher could have extended later in the week: for example, by bringing in big boxes to "go exploring" in, by finding books on caves or songs about bats, and by using flashlights as planning or recall props. Instead, the adult focused on *her* agenda—yellow—and missed these opportunities for building on the children's play.

An Alternative — Child-Oriented Planning

In an alternative approach to lesson planning that we have developed at High/Scope, adults identify children's interests and developing abilities, then build their lesson plans on these observations. Throughout this process, adults use the High/Scope key experiences to help clarify the developmental significance of children's actions and to suggest related experiences that may be appropriate for children.

Making the transition to a child-oriented planning system may be difficult for teachers and caregivers accustomed to planning in the more traditional way. To help adults make this shift, we often suggest they start with what is most familiar—which, in most cases, is a theme-based approach. We help adults see that we don't reject themes; rather, we encourage them, as much as possible, to get their theme ideas from the children's experiences.

This requires that the adults in the classroom become daily observers of children to discover what is meaningful and important to them: What kinds of objects and materials do children like to play with? What books, songs, and fingerplays are they familiar with? How complex is their play? What kinds of roles are they enacting? What ideas, experiences, or events do they talk about the most?

Once such observations are made, adults need a systematic way to record and discuss them. To do this, teachers in the High/Scope Demonstration Preschool meet daily after the children have gone home to discuss their observations of children and record them in a notebook containing a one-page observation form for each child. Each form provides space for adults to classify children's actions according to the High/Scope key experiences. Adults do not make notations on each child's form every day, but instead review the major happenings of the day and record them on a few children's forms. In programs that do not use observation forms like ours, adults sometimes keep daily logs or portfolios on children. This process is similar to our recording process in that these adults are, likewise, developing objective observation skills,

ested in making different kinds of vehicles out of blocks, small Legos, and materials from the art area. They decided to build on this theme throughout the next day's activities. They planned a small-group time in which children made "maps" and drove small cars on them, and they used vehicle-related strategies ("Let's drive our planning truck to where you will play today") for planning and recall times. They also made available a computer program that allowed children to make simple maps and "drive" small cars on them.

Insects. Three children, unfortunately, were stung by bees one day in the preschool playground. This experience led to lots of interest in bees, beehives, and being stung, as well as in other insects like ladybugs, wasps, ants, and flies. The day after children were stung teachers brought in several books about insects. Children were fascinated. Parents also contributed by bringing in old hives, and the staff gathered some jars for the children to collect bugs in. "It's too bad that children were stung—but it led to a wonderful learning experience," said one teacher. ■

relating what they observe to the classroom curriculum, and using the information they have recorded as a starting point for discussions with each other. Whatever the system adults use for discussing and documenting their observations of children, the next step in establishing child-oriented planning is developing plans for the next day that build on these observations.

A Typical Play Theme

An illustration of how teachers incorporate their observations into plans occurred recently at the High/Scope Demonstration Preschool. A telephone repair crew arrived one day to fix some telephone wires connected to the classroom building. The children were fascinated as they watched the crew climb up the telephone poles and use the lifts on the truck. They were also interested in the crew's special equipment and clothing: their spiked boots, hard hats, and tool bags. For the rest of that day, the children represented the experience of the telephone repair crew in a variety of ways—pretending to be repairmen themselves by wearing hats, making and wearing "tool belts," and climbing on chairs to fix the "wire." During that day's planning session, the teachers noted the children's obvious interest in this experience and made plans to use the theme of the telephone repair crew all during the rest of the week.

The adults' role during lesson planning was similar to their role during work time—they explored ways to support and extend children's interests and abilities, using the High/Scope key experiences as a reference for understanding the children's actions. All during the telephone repair crew play, the teachers had observed what the children did and how they did it. They recognized that the children had been engaging in representation key experiences (*imitating actions and*

If several children in the classroom have new brothers or sisters, adults may want to encourage children to expand on the theme of new babies by bringing in baby-related play materials and asking one of the parents to demonstrate bathing a baby for the class.

sounds, role playing, pretending) so they recorded what they had seen the children do in the representation category in their observation notebook. The teachers had also observed that when some children watched the repair crew at work and climbed up on chairs to imitate them, they were involved in spatial key experiences (*experiencing and describing relative positions, directions, and distances; observing from a different spatial viewpoint*).

In planning ways to extend on this play, the adults decided to create additional opportunities for children to continue their representational

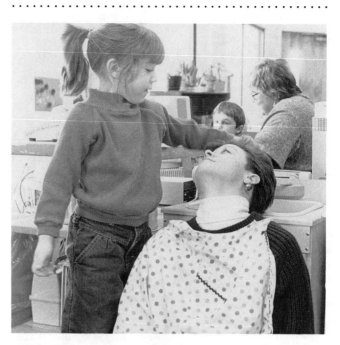

The beauty parlor play that this child is engaged in could provide a starting point for team planning to extend on the same play theme.

and spatial learning in the context of the telephone theme. For planning time, for example, they decided to ask children to plan by talking to one another on toy phones and by stretching "wires" (pieces of string) to the places they wanted to play in. They planned to observe whether children's interest in representing the telephone experience would continue and whether they would describe positions, directions, and locations as they discussed their plans. They also decided to give children additional opportunities to represent the telephone experience by planning two small-group times: one in which children made "construction belts" (the adults brought in old belts and children fastened objects from the classroom on them) and another in which children used modeling dough (the teachers planned to observe whether children would make models of telephones and phone wires with the modeling dough).

In concluding, it is important to note that the telephone theme was not the only focus for adults and children that week. In fact, children engaged in many different kinds of play, both individual and cooperative, that the staff also supported. Some children were interested in making spiders from pipe cleaners; others were attracted to a new computer program that was available; and several spent time wrapping "presents" for family members. Staff recognized and supported all these interests as they interacted with children. The telephone theme stands out because it was the basis for so many classroom activities, but adults didn't focus exclusively on this theme in working with children.

Whether or not a child's activities reflected a prevailing "theme," **the guiding principle for these adults was to be responsive to children.** Adults used children's ideas and interests as the source of inspiration, both in interacting with children individually and in creating lesson plans. By using the framework of the key experiences to understand the developmental significance of what they had observed about children's interests, ideas, and abilities, they insured that the resulting activities were developmentally appropriate and in tune with children's needs and interests. ■

Getting Started: The First Day of the Rest of the Year

by
Warren Buckleitner
and
Susan M. Terdan

It's 8:25 a.m., and your program is about to begin for another year. Off in the distance you hear the children's voices . . . some excited, some crying. The voices become louder and more distinct. As you take one last look around the room, in walks the "grand marshall" of the parade of new faces . . .

Whether you are a new teacher/caregiver or a seasoned veteran, the beginning of a new year is often filled with a mix of excitement and anxiety. You've planned and prepared, and yet you still have that "I-wonder-what-I-haven't-done-yet" feeling at the opening of a new program session.

What constitutes ready? How can you make sure that you and the children start the year off successfully? How do you set up the classroom? What is a typical daily routine for the first day? These are only a few of the questions that early childhood staff face at the opening of a new program or session. In this article we describe how we dealt with some common issues faced by early childhood teams as they plan for opening day. The case in point was a High/Scope summer demonstration preschool program. Because High/Scope's regular demonstration classroom was being renovated, the program had to be held in a local public school building, the Perry Child Development Center. Thus, we had to "start from scratch" to get the classroom ready for the summer session. We hope that reading about our experiences in preparing for and opening the session will help offer some insight on how early childhood teams can start a new session on the right foot.

Building a New Team

Building a new team was an important part of our preparation process because this was the first time we had taught together. Because we had only a short time to set up the classroom, we decided to tackle all of the start-up issues together as a team; this hastened the process of team building. By the time our first day of teaching arrived, we were already comfortable with each other's styles and had worked through numerous problems together. Following, we describe the "countdown" plan we followed as we got ready for "day one."

Getting Ready: The Countdown

TWO weeks to day one—We identified and approached others. Since the school we were teaching in was new to both of us, our first step was to contact the principal. We wanted to make sure we were firmly connected to existing channels of communication and administrative support. Especially because ours was the only classroom in the school doing the High/Scope Curriculum, we very much wanted to have the principal and staff feel a part of our efforts. Here are some other things we did—either before the session began or throughout the first month—to build the support and involvement of important "outsiders":

• **We showed administrators and school custodians in advance how we planned to set up the room and a typical daily routine.** We tried to be responsive to their needs; for example, we agreed to put chairs up on tables at the end of the day to make it easier for cleaning staff to vacuum.

• **We personally called all parents** before the program opened to double-check addresses, go over program hours, and find out about any

*Identifying and approaching all those who have contact with a program —
including administrators, parents, custodial staff, and teachers in other
parts of the building—and inviting them to visit the classroom helps to
build channels of communication and support for the program.*

special concerns they had. We made a home visit
to a family that had no phone. As well as initiating a good relationship with families, these contacts yielded some useful information: one child,
we found out, had been dismissed from a day
care program for biting; another child had a significant hearing loss.

• **We made consistent, continuing efforts
to offer tidbits of information to other staff:**
what children were doing; what room arrangement ideas and materials were working/not
working; how parent contacts were going, etc.

• **We offered frequent invitations to visit
the classroom** to teaching staff, administrators,
parents, not just to observe special events but to
participate or observe on regular days as well.
Our goal was simple: **No surprises** for anyone.
We made everyone involved aware of what we
wanted to do and how we planned to do it.

**FIVE days to day one—We took a hard
look at the classroom.** To remind us of basic
room arrangement issues, we first consulted the
High/Scope preschool manual *Young Children in*

Action and the High/Scope "Room Arrangement Checklist." (The "Room Arrangement Checklist" is available in the *Study Guide to Young Children in Action*, listed on page 297.) Working first on paper, then in the real room, we evaluated the overall space in our new classroom and divided it into basic areas—house, toy (quiet), block, and art. We followed the principles from the checklist in setting up the areas. For example, we placed the block and house areas next to each other to encourage interrelated play, and we visualized the traffic flow in the room to see how best to prevent collisions and avoid noise problems.

FOUR days left—We assessed materials. Fortunately, we had a supply of materials from the former demonstration classroom available to us. But this was a new, slightly older group of children, and we decided to add some materials that would challenge the older children in the group: rulers and lined paper in the art area, magnets and a scale in the toy area. While we wanted to offer a rich variety of materials, we were careful not to overdo it—we didn't want the first day to be overwhelming. After all, new materials and interest areas can and should be added later in the year. Here are some things we kept in mind about materials:

• **Variety**—We made sure we had several different sizes and textures of paper in the art area, for example, and we assessed each area to make sure there was a range of materials.

• **Quantity**—Enough materials were made available so that children could work together, if necessary; for example, since we had 19 children enrolled, we put nine place settings in the house area.

• **Easy access**—We made sure that all the materials in each area were accessible from a child's perspective. Could a child see what was in the container at the top of the shelf? We also

Getting Ready for "Opening Day": Tips for Teaching Teams

• Hasten the process of team-building by tackling all start-up issues together—make all decisions as a team. Make a list of classroom tasks—including everyday tasks, weekly jobs, and one-time jobs—and divide them equally.

• Identify and approach other building staff to inform them of your plans for the program. Continue to keep them informed.

• Contact all parents to get acquainted, introduce them to the program, and find out about special concerns.

• Offer frequent invitations to visit the classroom to teaching staff, administrators, parents, etc.

• Take a hard look at your classroom and materials, and arrange and equip your physical setting to meet the specific needs of entering children.

• Get help with labeling materials, if necessary.

• Make specific plans for the first day that will accommodate children's needs to learn about the setting, the materials, and the people in it. ■

carefully checked to make sure that things we *didn't want* the children to use, such as our non-erasable markers, were in the room next door or hidden in a high cupboard.

THREE days to go, but who's counting? — We made labels. Clear, well-placed labels that tell children which materials go where are important for many reasons: they give children a sense of control over their surroundings, help them work and clean up independently, and encourage the development of symbolic reasoning skills. Just as important, labels make classroom management much easier for adults!

Nevertheless, labeling all the materials in the classroom can be an incredibly big job for two people. We made it easier and more fun by hosting a pizza lunch for parents, other teachers, and available High/Scope staff. This strategy worked like a charm. In one afternoon, we were able to label almost all of the shelves, racks, containers, etc., in the classroom.

We stressed the importance of simple, clear labels to our helpers, showing them examples of the various types of labels we use: traced outlines of objects, pictures from toy catalogs, a few word labels to go along with the pictures. We asked our labelers to put clear contact paper on both sides of the labels to make it easy to move them in the future. We also traced and cut out sets of simple symbols, such as triangles or stars, to be used as children's identifying "mark." We made four of each symbol—one for a child's nametag, one for his or her cubby, one to take home on the first day, and one spare. We also made some extra symbols so each child would have a wide selection from which to choose.

TWO days left!—We planned for the first day. Our classroom looked great. Now it was time to plan our routine. Using *Young Children in Action*, we roughed out a 2½-hour daily routine,

*Contacting each child's parents by home visit or phone call **before** the program begins gives staff an opportunity to double-check addresses, go over program requirements and routines, and find out about any special concerns of the family.*

discussed it, and finalized it. We made a list of classroom tasks and divided them equally. These included one-time jobs, such as making a snack chart and designing a planning board; everyday jobs, such as greeting parents and cleaning up paint; and weekly jobs, such as doing the parent newsletter. After a last-minute shopping trip for snack and art supplies, we were as ready as we could be! ■

C·H·A·P·T·E·R S·I·X

Reaching Out to Other Settings and Caregivers

· ·

Continuity: Building Bridges Between Settings —
Ed Greene

Parent Involvement: It's Worth the Effort —
Patricia P. Olmsted and Marilyn Adams Jacobson

Involving Busy Parents —
Marilyn Adams Jacobson and Patricia P. Olmsted

Kindergarten: Thorns in the "Child's Garden"? —
Jane Maehr

E arly childhood programs do not exist in a vacuum, and program staff cannot serve children well if they are out of touch with the other settings and caregivers in children's lives. The need for early childhood program staff to develop close ties with parents, other caregivers, and staff of other programs in a community is especially critical today, when so many children are served in multiple care settings.

In the opening article, Ed Greene takes a general look at the ways early childhood staff can build these linkages. The next two articles, both by Marilyn Adams Jacobson and Patricia P. Olmsted, suggest ways to strengthen ties between programs and parents. Extending High/Scope's developmentally based approach from preschool into the kindergarten is the subject of the concluding article. Jane Maehr outlines some of the problems and pressures educators face in preparing for today's kindergartners. She describes the difficulties of meeting the public's demand for educational accountability while serving entering kindergartners whose previous education and care experiences have been in broadly different settings. Maehr argues that High/Scope's developmental approach can address these difficulties, and she echoes the other articles in this section in stressing the importance of forging close relationships among all programs serving young children.

Continuity: Building Bridges Between Settings

by

Ed Greene

It is early spring and the parents of a 2-year-old have just enrolled their child in next year's preschool class. How can the teacher help the child and family prepare for a smooth transition to preschool?

...

Because both of his parents work outside the home, a child who attends morning preschool is picked up regularly by a day care provider. The parents have complained to the teacher that they feel out of touch with what is happening at school. How can the teacher improve communication with the parent?

...

The mother of a graduating preschooler tells the child's preschool teacher that the local elementary school, after testing her child, has recommended that he take another year of preschool instead of starting kindergarten. She wonders whether holding children back a year is ever appropriate. How can the teacher advise her?

All of the above situations involve important transitions in young children's lives. Whether the transition is from the home to preschool, from one preschool setting to another, or from preschool to primary school, the child will experience a major change. Such changes can be disruptive, but they can also bring exciting new challenges. Much depends on how carefully parents and early childhood staff prepare for a transition.

The need for staff working with young children to plan carefully for transitions between settings is especially urgent today, because children are involved with so many programs and services. Early education in a variety of forms is reaching many more children than ever before in this country, and it is reaching them earlier in their lives. However, there are few systematic linkages among the programs that serve children who are younger than school age. And there are even fewer formal linkages between these early childhood settings and the next level of educational programming, the primary school.

Much of the literature on child development and early education supports the view that continuity between settings is an important component of high-quality early childhood services. Behind this view are two assumptions: (1) Growth and learning are gradual and continuous processes, and (2) Development is enhanced

Preparing Children for a New School

To help children make a smooth transition to kindergarten or another care setting, the key words are *information* and *experiences*. Children adapt more easily to change if they know what to expect and if they've had concrete experiences that help them to anticipate what the new setting will be like. As you plan for such experiences, keep in mind the key experience *recalling events, anticipating events, and representing the order of events*. Remember that young children tend to focus mainly on the present. With adult encouragement, however, they'll begin to think about and prepare for future events. This is a valuable process because it helps children gain a sense of control over what happens to them.

When you introduce children to the theme of getting ready for a new school, remember that even older preschoolers think in concrete terms. They are just beginning to use adult time units like days and weeks. Concrete examples of what might happen in the new setting will be more meaningful to a child than statements like "In September, right after Labor Day, you'll start kindergarten. You'll be learning a lot there."

One way to get children thinking about an upcoming transition is to **read books to them that discuss the experience of going to a new school** (for example, *The Kindergarten Book* by Stephanie Caimen). After reading, ask open-ended questions that encourage discussion: "Can anybody remember what it was like to come to preschool for the first time? Does anybody have a sister or brother who is in kindergarten? What does your brother/sister like about kindergarten?"

It's also helpful to **plan a field trip to the local kindergarten** or **encourage parents to visit the new school or care setting with the child.**

Ideally, children should have the opportunity to play in a kindergarten classroom, to meet the kindergarten teacher, and to see other areas of the building—the playground, gym, or cafeteria. Take photos while you are at the school, and after the field trip, **add play materials to the classroom that might encourage pretend play about the new school** (examples: a cafeteria tray, a toy school bus).

After the visit, **encourage children to recall and discuss what they saw at the school.** You might ask them to compare the new school with the preschool: "Did you notice anything at the kindergarten that is the same as/different from something we have here?"

Another useful activity is to **encourage children to dictate or "write" experience stories about the trip to the kindergarten or new care setting.** Ask children to describe some of the things they've seen at the school or center and some of the things they imagine they'll be doing there. Write down what the child says or encourage the child to write about the experience in his or her own way using scribbles, drawings, words, or other forms of emergent writing. Collect children's experience stories in a binder and illustrate them with photos taken at the school and children's drawings of the field trip. Just before this year's graduates leave, you can add their photos to the book, making them copies to take with them. The creation of such a book can be a "rite of passage" in which every child has a role.

These are just a few of the ways teachers can help children prepare for attending a new school. Teachers should encourage parents to follow up on these readiness activities at home. ∎

when each new learning experience is planned to build upon a child's previous experiences and achievements.

What can educators and caregivers do to insure continuity in children's educational experiences? In the late 1980s, the federal Administration for Children, Youth, and Families convened a national commission to study the transition from preschool to elementary school. This group identified four common-sense strategies for fostering continuity:

• Provide program continuity through developmentally appropriate curricula for preschool and kindergarten children.

• Maintain ongoing communication and cooperation between preschool and kindergarten staff.

**Important Transitions
in Young Children's
Lives**

Home → Preschool

Preschool → After-
school Program or
Caregiver

After-school Program
or Caregiver → Home

Preschool → Kinder-
garten ■

• Prepare children for the transition.
• Involve parents in the transition.*

Though these strategies were developed for the preschool-kindergarten transition, they are equally valid for transitions between other settings (for example, when a child moves from a morning Head Start program to an afternoon day care setting). In the rest of this article, we discuss these strategies in terms of our experiences with children in programs using the High/Scope Curriculum.

Fostering Continuity Through Developmentally Appropriate Curricula

Developmentally appropriate programs, by their very nature, foster continuity in children's learning experiences. In the High/Scope Curriculum, for example, learning activities are geared to individual children's developmental levels and thus build upon previous developmental advances. In addition, the fact that children choose many of their own activities in High/Scope programs insures that learning experiences will be related to and continuous with other experiences in children's lives. Children do change as they develop, of course, and it is often appropriate to introduce new activities and materials. But since teachers introduce new experiences only when children are ready for them, and in ways that are personally meaningful for each child, children experience such new activities as exciting rather than disruptive.

---

*From "Easing the Transition from Preschool to Kindergarten: A Guide for Early Childhood Teachers and Administrators" (Washington, DC: Administration for Children Youth and Families, Head Start Bureau, 1986), p. 4.

Getting to know staff of kindergartens and other preschool programs in the community at professional meetings and open houses builds ties that are useful later when exchanging specific information about children and programs.

But even if we strive to foster continuity by making our own programs developmentally appropriate, we can't guarantee that other care and education settings will do the same. However, there are a few things we can do *to increase the likelihood that a child will receive developmentally appropriate care* in other care settings he or she is involved with now or will experience in the future. Consider the following strategies:

• **Share information with other providers on a child's developmental progress, as well as on appropriate activities that the child has been particularly involved with in your program.** This will help the other caregiver recognize and strengthen the child's emerging skills, strengths, and interests. For example, tell a child's new kindergarten teacher about the developmental information you have recorded on the child's COR (High/Scope Child Observation Record).

When early childhood educators take a leadership role in bringing together kindergarten teachers and staff of preschool and day care programs in the community, they are helping pave the way for a smoother transition for children.

• **Help parents understand the components of developmentally appropriate care and education** so that they can make better decisions about settings and caregivers. For example, organize a parents' meeting around this theme, using a videotape, such as High/Scope's *Lessons That Last*, (see resource list, page 297) to focus your discussion.

• **Educate yourself about the developmental changes that occur in the years immediately before and after the preschool years.** Learn about appropriate expectations and activities for each age group. For example, the teaching team might decide to devote several team meetings to studying the similarities and differences between preschool and kindergarten children. This could lead to a discussion of age-appropriate activities and ways to assist the child and family who are making a transition.

Communicating and Cooperating With Staff of Other Early Childhood Programs

Building professional bonds with your colleagues in the community is the starting point for developing linkages between programs. Here are some steps you can take toward this goal:

• **Get to know staff of kindergartens and other preschool programs in your community** at local educational meetings (AEYC meetings, directors' associations, PTO meetings). Invite local early childhood staff to an open house at your school. Continue to build your relationships with them through letters, phone calls, and other contacts.

• **Use your contacts with colleagues in the community to find out as much as you can about local kindergartens and about other early childhood programs** in the community. Share this information with parents.

• **Develop a short fact sheet describing important elements of your program.** Both you and program parents can use the fact sheet in contacts with other educators, caregivers, and parents.

• **When a child leaves your program, get permission from the parents to write to the teacher or director at the new setting.** In the letter, you could share information about your program and about the child's abilities and interests. You might conclude by inviting the teacher to visit or call you for more information.

• **At a professional meeting in your community, suggest the formation of a "transition committee"** that will explore ways to ease the transition between local preschool and kindergarten programs. Examples of things the committee might do include planning kindergarten visitation days for preschoolers, developing a parent guide to local preschool programs and kindergartens, and planning ways kindergartens and preschools can share facilities and resources.

Involving Parents in Transitions

As the negotiators of all the transitions children make between settings, parents are the key link in the chain of educational continuity. Many of the strategies already discussed involve parents. Here are a few more ideas:

• **Share your observations about other settings and caregivers with parents.** For example, you might recommend a particular kindergarten teacher that you know at the next school a child will attend.

• **Encourage parents' continued involvement in the child's education/care experiences.** For example, you might set up a parent meeting on the transition to kindergarten in which the following topics would be covered: how to be an advocate for your child's educational needs; how to arrange an observation at your child's kindergarten; what to look for when you observe a program.

• **Help parents network with one another to share information about other settings.** For example, if a parent wants information on a particular kindergarten teacher, put her in touch with another parent from a previous preschool session whose child has that teacher.

By building links with parents and with staff of public schools and other early childhood settings, you've laid the groundwork for your preschoolers to make a smooth transition to other settings. You'll also need to prepare children directly for the changes they'll be experiencing through classroom activities, reading and discussions, and if possible, visits to the future care setting or kindergarten. ■

Parent Involvement:
It's Worth the Effort

When you hear the term *"parent involve-ment,"* what are the first words that come to mind? *"Important." "Difficult." "Good for the children." "Time-consuming."*

These responses reflect the conflicting feelings most early childhood professionals have about parent involvement. We've often heard staff at many early childhood centers say they know parent participation is important, but that there never seems to be enough time to plan and carry out activities with parents. Staff at other programs express a wish for better relationships with parents, along with the fear that too much family involvement can interfere with the program's educational activities. Other teachers or day care staff are unsure of how to develop and maintain a parent involvement program when parents are busy and have multiple time commitments.

Though all these concerns are realistic, we believe it is possible for staff of any early childhood setting to develop a parent involvement program whose benefits will outweigh the difficulties entailed. We'll discuss some of these benefits in the section that follows, and after that, we'll outline a realistic approach early childhood staff can take to strengthen parent involvement in their education or care program.

Note that everything we say here applies not just to parents but to all adults who are children's primary caregivers, whether they be grandparents or other relatives, foster parents, or guardians. It's important for early childhood staff to be sensitive to the fact that many children today do not live with their natural parents. Education and care programs should encourage the

by

Patricia P. Olmsted

and

Marilyn Adams Jacobson

participation of the important adults in the child's household, whether or not they are the child's actual parents.

Parent Involvement: Even More Important Now

Why is parent involvement so important? Parents are the child's first caregivers and teachers, the first adults to play a significant role in the child's development and learning. The home is the first learning environment the child experiences. Today, when young children are also involved with so many other caregivers—relatives, babysitters, home day care providers, preschool teachers, day care staff—often in settings outside the home, it is critical for the adults in a child's home to communicate well with these other significant adults. Strong linkages between parents and the child's other caregivers are helpful in many ways. For example, such linkages can

• Help the child make smooth transitions from setting to setting.

• Help parents understand the types of activities that occur in the school or day care setting.

• Help parents see how they might contribute their time and effort to the setting.

• Help parents, teachers, and caregivers understand behavioral changes they may see in the child.

• Help parents, teachers, and caregivers ensure that behavioral expectations, teaching and caregiving styles, discipline practices, and daily routines are as consistent as possible across the different care settings.

Parents and the High/Scope Approach

Parent involvement is especially important for programs using the High/Scope Curriculum because parents' own experiences with traditional schooling often don't prepare them for the daily routine and approach to teaching that they encounter in High/Scope programs. Parents may not understand why teachers are not drilling children on letters, numbers, and colors, or how a program built around children's choices prepares children for academic learning.

But when parents begin to understand the High/Scope educational approach, they often make changes in their own styles of interacting with children. While parents may not use curriculum components in the structured way we do at school, our general educational approach does transfer easily to the home. For example, parents will probably not want to have a formal planning time at home, but they can encourage children to make simple plans as the need arises: choosing what TV programs they want to watch that week or helping make a shopping list for groceries.

Research on Parent Involvement

As educators, most of us feel intuitively that the effort it takes to really involve family members in an early childhood program pays off for all concerned. This belief is strongly supported by research findings.

Studies have been conducted on parent involvement programs in a variety of educational and care settings during the past 20 years. The majority of studies have focused on publicly funded early childhood programs (e.g., Head Start) or child care centers serving ethnic minority families or children from low-income neigh-

Ways Parents Contributed to a Recent High/Scope Summer Demonstration Preschool Program

• A mother bathed and fed her baby during work time, sparking lots of baby-related role play.

• A father and his son built a sturdy stand for the sand timer teachers and children had made with plastic pop bottles.

• Parents served as drivers for a field trip to the pet store and joined the class on a walk to the farmers' market.

• A parent brought in a pasta machine and made noodles with the children.

• A father videotaped segments of the day—we showed the tapes at the parent meeting. ∎

Research suggests that the efforts early childhood programs make to involve parents in their activities have many benefits—parent involvement is associated with positive effects on children's academic performance, self-esteem, and motivation to learn.

borhoods. The findings of these studies have included the following as effects of parent involvement:

For children—

- Positive effects on academic performance
- Positive effects on self-esteem and motivation to learn

For parents—

• Improved understanding of child development, parenting, and education
• Larger support network

For teachers—

• Greater understanding and more positive support from parents for policies, procedures, and activities in the program or center
• More parents volunteering to work with children in the setting

While most of the children in these studies lived with their natural parents, the findings are equally applicable to children living with relatives, foster parents, guardians, or other adults.

High/Scope's own studies are among those that confirm the benefits of family involvement. In High/Scope's well-known Perry Preschool Study, for example, we have been following the lives of young adults from poor families who had a high-quality preschool program at ages 3 and 4. The long-term benefits to the young adults who had preschool—including improved school performance, reduced delinquency, and increased lifetime earnings—have been widely publicized. What many people don't know, however, is that the Perry Preschool Program included a strong parent involvement component consisting of weekly home visits by teachers. We can't say whether the positive effects the researchers found were directly related to these parent activities, but these results do suggest that involving parents is an important part of any effective program.

Steps Toward Effective Parent Involvement

Step one: setting goals. If you are planning to implement a parent involvement program in your preschool or center, your first step should

Parent Involvement in Action

One teacher sends home a one-page flyer—"Friday Notes"—at the end of each week. The flyer includes brief descriptions of things individual children have been doing in the classroom that week. The teacher is careful to mention each child at least once. She includes each child's sign next to his or her name, so the children can participate with their parents in reading the flyer.

...

The director of a K–3 program in a Northern Wisconsin school was looking for ways to involve fathers in the program. He made a point of finding out about parents' special skills, interests, and cultural backgrounds. This led to a unique winter activity: several fathers, who were Native Americans, volunteered to build an igloo on the school playground out of iceblocks. (The school was located next to a large lake that was frozen all winter—parents cut the ice blocks from the lake.)

Children used the igloo all through the winter. Igloo-building became an annual activity that was central to the school's parent involvement program. For the parents, it was a unique opportunity to preserve a valued part of their cultural heritage while making a significant contribution to their children's school. ■

be establishing the goals of the program in light of your needs and those of the families.

If possible, ask a few families to meet with you and jointly set these goals. For example, both parents and teachers may feel a need for better two-way communication about the development of each child. Or, teachers may wish to have parents become better informed about the policies and activities of the preschool or center. Perhaps your preschool or center serves ethnic minority families from a culture with which you are only minimally acquainted (e.g., Vietnamese), and you would like to have more activities that reflect this culture.

In each of these cases, there is a stated objective for the parent involvement program for which specific parent involvement activities can be developed. You may decide on two or three different objectives for your parent involvement program, but we suggest that you begin with a small number and add more only after the program is under way and running smoothly.

Step two: developing activities. Now you're ready to develop two or three parent involvement activities for each of the objectives you have set. For example, if you have selected *better communication between teachers and parents* as an objective, you might decide to take a more systematic approach to talking with parents when they drop off or pick up their children. One way to do this would be to keep a weekly "family contact checklist" on which you would check off the names of each parent you talk with during that week. Another possible strategy for meeting the same goal might be to schedule more frequent teacher-parent conferences.

For any strategy you adopt, you'll need to select activities that fit the situations of your families and children. For example, if some children are dropped off and picked up by babysitters,

Improving two-way communication between parents and teachers is one goal you might select for a parent involvement program. Staff can document how well they are achieving this goal by noting down when they have substantive talks with parents.

you may have to resort to written notes or phone calls to keep in touch with the parents.

Step three: taking stock. After a few months, take a careful look at the parent involvement activities you have developed and assess how well they are working. Do you feel there is more parent involvement using the activities you have developed? For example, Are parents spending more time talking with teachers when they drop off or pick up their children? Do parents seem to understand the program better? Are parents and teachers sharing information about children's strengths or problems more often? Do you need to try different activities? Do you feel that the initial portion of your parent involvement program is running well enough that you can now add an additional objective and develop activities to meet it?

This process of evaluating your program will go more smoothly if you keep systematic notes on parent participation in the activities you've developed. For example, you can note down how many parents you have a substantive conversation with each week or how many parents attend meetings or fundraisers.

Step four: fine-tuning. As time goes by, the activities in your parent involvement program will have to be reevaluated, adjusted, and possibly expanded. Like classroom activities for children, parent involvement activities must be tailored to the needs of a changing group of families. Evaluation and fine-tuning of your parent involvement program is a never-ending process. ■

Involving Busy Parents

E ven teachers and caregivers who have a strong commitment to working with family members and many creative ideas for involving them in their programs are finding it more difficult these days to encourage parent participation. Whether because of job or school schedules, career training, or other responsibilities, many parents say they "just don't have time" to volunteer in the classroom.

by
Marilyn Adams Jacobson
and
Patricia P. Olmsted

Even busy parents usually *want* to share in their child's preschool/day care experience, but they may need extra help and encouragement to make this wish a reality. Here we discuss some ways to make it easier for busy parents to become involved.

Give plenty of advance notice about special activities such as parties, performances, or field trips. Some parents may be able to make special arrangements or rearrange their days off to participate.

Schedule regular face-to-face meetings with individual parents. These might include a *home visit* before the school year begins and *parent conferences* two or three times a year. Use these meetings to make plans to stay in touch with parents and to solicit their involvement with the program. These face-to-face meetings typically focus on the child; but you should also use them as an opportunity to find out about the parents' needs, concerns, and interests relating to their participation in the school or center. Find out who will be picking the child up at school and, if that person isn't one of the parents, make plans to contact the parents through phone calls or notes home.

Send out a newsletter to program families to keep parents informed of the classroom activi-

Ways Parents Can Contribute Outside Classroom Hours

- Serve as the classroom repair person.

- Make story tapes to accompany the books in the classroom library.

- Assist in the construction of playground equipment.

- Participate in a local school board meeting on the importance of early childhood education.

- Regularly check books out of the public library to add to the classroom library.

- Prepare special materials: the snack on a given day, labels for classroom shelves, a batch of modeling dough (teacher provides recipe and ingredients).

- Send in everyday items to be recycled as art materials or props for role play: boxes, plastic bottles, fabric scraps, typewriter ribbon spools, computer printouts, old clothes, old telephones or cameras, hair rollers, etc.

- Make doll clothes, spare mittens, and hats.

- Take classroom pets home during weekends and vacations. ∎

ties: e.g., key experiences you are focusing on, content themes, special events, and suggestions for home follow-up. Also, you might occasionally send parents copies of articles and handouts on themes of particular interest to families (e.g., how to overcome struggles at bedtime, how the school deals with superhero play, the recipes for favorite school snacks).

Videotape what children are doing in the classroom and make tapes available to be checked out for home viewing. You can also make audiotapes of songs children are learning in the classroom and loan them to parents.

When you send home the child's work, include a brief note explaining the context of the project or its developmental significance.

Maintain a classroom photo album with snapshots of the daily routine, field trips, and special events. Encourage children to bring photos from home to add to the album. Suggest that parents borrow it overnight so their child can tell them about the pictures.

Distribute a class list with family phone numbers and addresses to all families (be sure to ask each family for permission to give out their name and address). This helps parents arrange child care, carpools, play days, etc.

Provide a handout on tips for conversing with your child about school: names and signs of classmates, who is in the same small group, the names of each part of the daily routine, names of the areas of the classroom, and suggestions for possible discussion starters.

Suggest ways parents can contribute to the program outside regular classroom hours. When it is impossible for parents to spend time in the classroom during regular school hours, let them know that their help at other times is just as welcome. There are many ways parents can help out during evenings and weekends—a few possibilities are listed in the side column.

A working parent may not have time to volunteer in the classroom, but she might be able to contribute outside classroom hours—for example, by sending in special materials for an activity.

When soliciting parents' help, keep in mind that many children today do not live with their birth parents—the responsible adult may be a grandparent, sibling, stepparent, foster parent, or guardian, and the extra child care responsibility these adults have shouldered may make them exceptionally busy. Be sensitive to these special family situations when you solicit the help of these key adults.

Finally, whatever way a parent or other important adult chooses to take part in your program, let the parent know you appreciate their participation. It's important to acknowledge the contributions of **all** parents, even the donation of an occasional cereal box. There are many ways to say thanks: a phone call, note, or card; a photo that shows the effect of the parent's efforts; special recognition at a parent meeting; a mention in the center newsletter; a special certificate or plaque. Acknowledging the efforts of parents is one way to demonstrate that you are sensitive to their scheduling problems. When you let parents know you are aware of the extra efforts they are making to be a part of the program, you encourage their involvement. ■

Kindergarten: Thorns in the "Child's Garden"?

The word *kindergarten* and the concept it names suggest a setting in which children are nourished and helped to grow through group activities, materials, and play. But in many schools today, the "child's garden" no longer provides the same kind of experience that was envisioned by Froebel and other shapers of the kindergarten. In fact, there are many thorny issues facing the kindergarten today.

The kindergarten, more than any other division of the elementary school, seems "caught in the middle," with well-meaning parents, administrators, and other interest groups pressing for change, often in opposing directions. Recent calls for educational reform and accountability, voiced at national, state, and local levels, have encouraged a trend toward skill-based kindergartens. These newer kindergarten programs, which usually emphasize the direct teaching of discrete skills in reading and math, are in many cases replacing programs emphasizing play and social adjustment.

As this trend continues, the debate over its appropriateness is intensifying. The frequent, nonexplicit use of such terms as *academic* and *child-centered* to describe the different approaches has tended to exaggerate the differences between them. This polarity has contributed to a climate that scarcely suggests a child's—or anyone's—garden.

The Children

Part of the controversy stems from the diversity of today's kindergarten population. First of all, too many children of the 1990s enter kin-

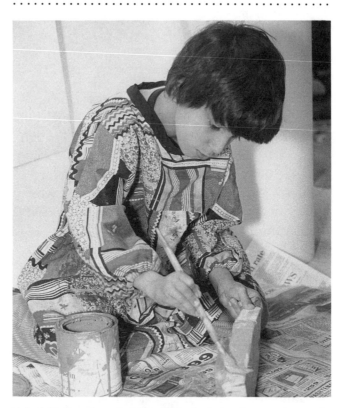

Today's kindergartners come from diverse backgrounds: some are unused to organized programs, others have had a surfeit of structured educational experiences. Regardless of their backgrounds, they share a need for active learning experiences that they can direct themselves.

dergarten poorly prepared for learning. Frightening statistics describe children who have already become victims of abuse, inattention, and ignorance. The problems of fragmented families, homelessness, and substance abuse result in many children arriving at school without language skills, without resources for learning, even without breakfast.

At the same time, many other children are entering kindergarten after two to five years of out-of-home child care—experiences that, for many, began in infancy. These children have had a wealth of early social experiences, and, in some cases, these experiences have come at the expense of quality time with families. In some cases, too, these early day care experiences have been excessively structured, preparing children to adapt easily in groups but giving them few opportunities to gain self-control or self-direction.

Many of these children have also attended preschools that have mistakenly equated social adjustment, adaptation, physical size, and a wealth of early group experiences with cognitive and social maturity. In a misguided effort to deliver a prepared student to the kindergarten, such preschool programs have too often replaced valuable early opportunities for children to play, explore, and plan with passive activities based on packaged craft projects or standardized worksheets.

In addition, many children of busy parents have participated in a variety of enriching but structured activities—gymnastics, music lessons, arts and craft camp, and so forth—leaving them with little that is novel to experience; indeed, they have become jaded, "gourmet" 5-year-olds.

The Schools

The schools face several dilemmas as they prepare for this diverse range of entering kindergartners. First, the disparities of the school population are widening. The children with little preparation for learning are scheduled for the same kindergartens as those with extensive group experiences—children who've attended day care, preschool, and art classes and have already encountered worksheets. Yet neither group has been permitted to take initiative, to solve problems independently, or to choose and carry out activities that grow from their personal interests.

The schools also face enormous pressures for accountability that contribute to a "spiraling down" of academic expectations to the kinder-

Useful Resources for Kindergarten Teachers and Administrators

Bredekamp, S., & Shephard, L. (1989, March). How best to protect children from inappropriate school expectations, practices, and policies. *Young Children.*

Charlesworth, (1989, March). "Behind" before they start? Deciding how to deal with the risk of kindergarten "failure." *Young Children.*

Egertson, H. A. (1987). The shifting kindergarten curriculum. *ERIC Digest.*

Gullo, D. F. (1990, May). The changing family context: Implications for the development of all-day kindergartens. *Young Children.*

Hatch, J. A. & Freeman, E. B. (1988, October). Who's pushing whom? Stress and kindergarten. *Phi Delta Kappan.*

Pellegrini, A. D., & Glickman, C. D. (1990, May). Measuring kindergartners' social competence. *Young Children.*

Shephard, L. A., & Smith, M. L. (1989, November). Escalating academic demand in kindergarten: Counterproductive policies. *The Elementary School Journal, 89* (2).

Smith, M., & Shephard, L. A. (1988, Fall). Kindergarten readiness and retention: A qualitative study of teachers' beliefs and practices. *American Educational Research Journal, 25* (3).

garten. Skills that are scheduled for assessment after second or third grade are now being taught in the first grade, to assure that nothing will be missed. In turn, much of the traditional content of first grade has been shifted to the kindergarten. Demands that kindergartners write conventionally on lined paper, fill in math workbooks, and participate in phonics and letter recognition drills are among the premature skill requirements that have "trickled down" to the kindergarten. But the thorny issues do not stop here. Many well-meaning educators are aware that not all 5-year-olds will be mature enough to sit at desks and complete traditional first-grade work; so they have begun screening out the less mature students. They realize that in kindergartens that are really *not* kindergartens, the rigorous conditions put many children at risk for failure—both those who have had little preparation for learning and those who've had copious learning experiences but few opportunities for self-direction. As a result, "pre-kindergartens," programs for "young fives," and other extra-year arrangements abound.

To provide an added age advantage, parents also frequently choose to "hold out" age-ready children. And many teachers, also for humane reasons, argue to retain young students for a second year of kindergarten or to provide additional transition programs—all to protect young or "unready" children from the observed stress of participating in early childhood programs that were originally designed for them.

The High/Scope Approach to Kindergarten

How does the High/Scope Curriculum address the dilemmas facing today's kindergartens? High/Scope has developed a curriculum model for K–3 education that offers broad educational experiences tailored to the diverse needs of today's entering kindergartners and that is responsive to the content and assessment needs of the 1990s. The High/Scope approach urges a **partnership** developed between the kindergarten program, the children, the staff, and the parents. In this way, the "garden" is reclaimed for all children who enter.

The program. The High/Scope kindergarten program seeks to strengthen and broaden the child's emerging intellectual and social skills by promoting the spontaneous and constructive process of learning. The curriculum does not emphasize skills at the expense of socialization; rather, the curriculum considers socialization to be a valuable part of the process of active, generative, problem-focused learning. At the same time, in focusing on the broad intellectual skills that are emerging in a particular point in a child's development, the curriculum does not ignore traditional goals in reading, writing, and math. Instead, the curriculum assumes that children will move toward and attain standard academic skills as they engage in the process of active, constructive learning.

The program uses developmentally sequenced **key experiences** to guide learning activities that are organized around content areas such as language and literacy, math, and science. These key experiences provide frequent opportunities for children to use sensory and manipulative materials, in an environment that is arranged to be functional. The classroom is rich in print materials and in hands-on math, science, and writing materials, which children are encouraged to explore. This active learning approach provides for children who are at varying learning levels. High/Scope's key experiences are also used by teachers as a guiding framework for observing children within the active learning environment, providing a basis

Spodek, B. (1988, November). Conceptualizing today's kindergarten curriculum. *The Elementary School Journal, 89* (2).

High/Scope K–3 Curriculum Series (available from the High/Scope Press, 600 N. River St, Ypsilanti, MI 48198):

Blackwell, F., & Hohmann, C. *K–3 Science.*

Hohmann, C. *K–3 Mathematics*

Maehr, J. *K–3 Language & Literacy.*

NOTE: High/Scope has also produced a series of K–3 videotapes: *Classroom Environment, Language & Literacy, Mathematics,* and *Active Learning.* And two more curriculum guides—*K–3 Classroom Environment* and *K–3 Program Overview*—will be released in January 1992. ∎

for the systematic assessment schools are seeking.

The program, then, makes it possible for a wide range of children to participate at whatever level is appropriate for each of them. Children of diverse backgrounds and preparation for learning are able to pursue their interests, and teachers plan workshop sessions to support them. At the same time, the progress children make is documented and further appropriate instruction is planned.

Child participation. Another element of the High/Scope Curriculum that addresses the critical issues facing today's kindergartens is the emphasis on **child participation** in the learning process. The curriculum offers the opportunities for child-initiated learning that all kindergartners need, but not in a "laissez faire" climate of total freedom. Instead, **teacher-student collaboration** is fostered in all learning experiences. In the daily **plan-do-review** period, children are encouraged to articulate a plan, carry it out, and evaluate what they have done. Throughout this process, the teacher looks for opportunities to help children clarify their understanding and extend their thinking, for example by offering additional art or science materials that might help children broaden their goals.

Through the plan-do-review cycle, children are encouraged to reflect on what they have done. In the process, they recognize relationships between ongoing experiences and previously held knowledge and they test new conclusions. This reflective process is especially valuable because heterogeneous kindergartners find a wide range of things to learn and many ways to learn them. These opportunities for participation enable children to see themselves not as pawns in a powerful, highly structured institution—school—but as participants in a partnership with adults, sharing control of the learning experience.

The staff. In our approach to the kindergarten dilemma, **teachers** and **administrators** are also part of this partnership. The staff play a key role. They are committed to working together within the curriculum framework. They share a common perspective about what should be taught and how; they promote an active learning climate in the school; and they respect the ideas and opinions of both children and parents.

To build support and acceptance for the model and to insure smooth transitions between the kindergarten and other programs for children, teachers in High/Scope kindergartens seek to assume a leadership role in the educational community. Administrators are ready and willing to assist and support teachers in their efforts to educate colleagues about the program.

High/Scope K–3 programs actively reach out to establish collaboration with existing preschool programs. Kindergarten staff schedule visits to local preschools to find out about their philosophies and to discuss with preschool staff the maturational and readiness expectations that the High/Scope program holds for entering kindergarten students (see side column). When possible, kindergarten teachers or administrators make joint plans with preschool teachers for activities that will smooth the transition between their programs. High/Scope teachers and administrators are also prepared to articulate an informed view of kindergarten to first-grade teachers or school officials who might hold unrealistic expectations, or who mistakenly argue for extensive retention of kindergarten students.

Teachers are best able to educate colleagues and parents about the curriculum when they are secure in their understanding of child development, of the curriculum perspective, and of the implications of current research. This assumes that teachers use opportunities for inservice training, summer institutes, and workshops, so

Ready for School?

Getting together to discuss appropriate developmental expectations for children's kindergarten readiness is one way kindergarten and preschool teachers can assure a better transition for children. The attached checklist of expectations prepared by Lawrence Schweinhart of High/Scope Foundation can be a starting point for such discussions.

Children are ready for kindergarten:

1. If they can communicate and get along with other children.

2. If they can communicate with adults.

3. If they are able to share and wait until it's their turn.

4. If they know their full name and possibly their address and telephone number.

5. If they have self-management skills—such as the ability to button, snap, and zip clothing.

6. If they can understand concepts of space (near, far, up, down).

7. If they have a general understanding of the concept of time (e.g., understanding the difference between a short time, and a long time—clocks and calendars can come when they are older).

8. If they can follow simple directions.

9. If they can complete a task they began.

10. If they can identify similar objects or distinguish between different objects. ■

The plan-do-review process is central to High/Scope kindergarten programs. When the classroom writing center is equipped with a typewriter, children who are ready to try writing have another option open for producing written plans.

that they remain knowledgeable about the curriculum. Likewise, administrators support teachers by insuring that they have opportunities to attend further training. Administrators, too, make an effort to keep abreast of curriculum innovations and new research findings.

The parents. For successful implementation of the High/Scope Curriculum, High/Scope kindergarten staff actively reach out to **parents,** both to educate them about the curriculum and to show the value they place on working with them. Teachers welcome parents in the classrooms and are committed to strengthening communication between school and home. Meetings are scheduled at times when parents are available, in locations that are accessible to parents, and where child care for younger siblings can be provided. Teachers also help parents develop the skills they may need to actively participate as partners in the child's learning experiences. For example, teachers may plan workshops focusing on how to support children's emerging literacy skills in the home.

...

In sum, the High/Scope Curriculum can provide some answers to today's dilemmas of diverse kindergarten populations, inappropriate curricula, unrealistic expectations, and inappropriate assessment. Educators involved with High/Scope kindergartens maintain that the kindergarten must be prepared to accept the children who are "age-ready." They argue for developmentally appropriate, yet well-defined, content-oriented programs. They insist on well-designed materials and methodology. They inform themselves about current research knowledge. They support and encourage parents to extend the work of the school in the classroom and at home. High/Scope's approach is based on a program partnership of children, teachers, administrators, and parents. The result can be a "child's garden" that is both stimulating and geared to each child's level of development. ∎

On Skill-Based Kindergartens —

"The forces which have led to the development of skill-based programs are reactive and largely ignore the early childhood research base. Redefinition of the kindergarten-primary curriculum from a developmental perspective is more beneficial for children than the use of retention and extra-year placement. Advocates of developmental kindergarten programs should emphasize the effectiveness of an active learning setting for advancing children's growth and development."

—Harriet A. Egertson in "The Shifting Kindergarten Curriculum," ERIC Digest, 1987. ∎

C·H·A·P·T·E·R S·E·V·E·N

Questions From the Field

. . . .

O ver the years, High/Scope consultants have worked with thousands of early childhood practitioners both at training workshops and conferences and during on-site consultation visits. This section presents answers to many of the questions posed by early childhood staff during these sessions. Most of these questions originally appeared in the "Ask Us" feature in *Extensions*, although a few appeared elsewhere in the newsletter.

The subject of child management always inspires many questions, so we have chosen to open with this controversial area. Other selections contain questions relating to the High/Scope key experiences, the daily routine, planning and equipping the learning environment, day care, and child observation/team planning/staff development.

Child Management

S everal children in our program engage in a lot of superhero play, which involves make-believe weapons and aggressive language and behavior. I want to be responsive to children's interests, but my co-workers and I are uncomfortable with this kind of play. Any ideas?

—A day care provider

Young children often engage in behavior that is incompatible with adult values and standards. Adults' responses to such behaviors may be influenced by many factors, including safety concerns, noise level, and the adults' own degree of comfort with or tolerance for what they consider aggressive or boisterous behavior. Because of these concerns, some adults in High/Scope programs choose to ban or limit superhero play. Other adults may feel quite comfortable allowing children to engage in superhero play—they may even participate in it themselves as a way of learning more about children's thinking and helping children expand on their ideas.

However adults choose to handle behavior of this kind, it's important for them to recognize that children's play reflects their current interests, feelings, and experiences, as well as their developmental levels. Children need to know that their interests and feelings are acceptable, even if the ways that they express them are not.

In superhero play, young children act out and experiment with feelings of power, control, anger, or fear. Adults can convey their acceptance of and sensitivity to these feelings by reading stories with children that focus on these feelings. They may also encourage children to explore these same feelings in alternative ways: e.g., acting out their feelings with dolls or puppets, creating their own superhero play props with many kinds of open-ended materials, or making up stories about superheroes that incorporate everyday experiences.

—*Amy Powell*

Children often "lose it" when they get frustrated with something. How can we support children when they are being difficult?
—*A day care teacher*

Frustrations, disappointments, and conflicting desires are natural occurrences in the course of children's play. When his block tower won't balance, Mickey kicks the block shelf; Minna beats on the stapler because no staples will come out; Lydel and Hank come to blows because they both want to be the dad in their make-believe game.

Adults who approach such negative acts patiently, firmly, and kindly, encourage children to make cause-and-effect connections—for example, between a very small base and a tower that topples, between what is inside a stapler and what comes out of it, between what happens when two children want the same role in a game and what might happen if they added a new role.

It's incredibly important for children to learn to make such connections. But these are not easy lessons to learn. It takes many real-life experiences and ongoing adult support for children to develop the capacities to anticipate and deal effectively with the rough spots they encounter on their own. So don't expect instant results. If you continue to model a patient, matter-of-fact attitude and encourage children to use problems as opportunities for learning, they will begin to develop the habit of confronting and managing problems for themselves. By the time they reach adulthood and face adult problems, they will have the skills and tools they need, the habit of using them, and the confidence gained from their years of experience and support.

—*Mary Hohmann*

When I visited the High/Scope Demonstration Classroom, I was surprised because I didn't see a "time-out" chair. Why? I use this with my children and it really helps them to behave.

—*A preschool teacher*

Although we don't doubt that it helps children "to behave," you did not see a time-out chair in our classroom because we don't have one. We feel that putting a child in a time-out chair is inconsistent with our belief that children need experiences that enable them to make choices about controlling their own behaviors. Most such time-outs are not connected to the actual "misbehavior," isolate a child at precisely the time he or she most needs help, and do not create an opportunity for a child to learn new ways of dealing with similar situations. In addition, there is always the risk that a child will refuse to stay in the chair, thus setting up a power struggle in which there may be no winners.

However, there are times when behavior can be so upsetting to all involved that a momentary break from the action is necessary. While it is true that we don't have a designated time-out chair, we will sometimes separate a child from the group. For example, after trying other management strategies (for example, explaining why a behavior is inappropriate), we might say to a disruptive child: "Jenny, if you kick the table one more time, it will let us know that you are not able to be close to the others, and we will then ask you to move away." Then we would ask Jenny to choose a nearby place to sit, where we can keep an eye on her and where she can see the activities she is missing. In such cases, it is important to keep the time away from the group *short* and, when the child is ready, to help him or her re-enter the group with the least amount of embarrassment.

—Michelle Graves and Ruth Strubank

Key Experiences in Child Development

I prefer a developmental approach to writing, but I'm under a lot of pressure to prepare children for paper-and-pencil work in first grade. If I don't provide a lot of practice in writing on lined paper, I'm afraid my children will not measure up next year. How can I handle this?

—A kindergarten teacher

Take the professional initiative and meet with parents, administrators, and first grade teachers to describe what you are doing and why. Explain that to concentrate on letter writing on lined paper is to select one isolated skill for development to the exclusion of many others that play an important role in literacy. Assure parents, teachers, and administrators that the research indicates children's free exploration of writing on unlined paper will eventually result in correctly spaced writing.

—Jane Maehr

Parents are usually very concerned when their child reverses single letters or words and often tell me that they've asked the child to practice writing the letters correctly. How should I respond?

—A kindergarten teacher

Try to help parents concentrate on viewing errors as indicators of what children already know rather than what they have not completely mastered. Parents will often associate reversals with dyslexia (a reading impairment), when it is more likely their children are still gaining control over a newly developed skill. Suggest to parents that children's attempts to form letters are a positive sign that they are moving along the literacy continuum and are beginning to attempt conventional writing. Also suggest that it would be more valuable to read alphabet books and stories to children and to encourage awareness of the print found in their surroundings than for children to spend time practicing—unless practicing is what a child chooses to do.

—*Jane Maehr*

I have two children who are not very verbal. I spend at least 15 minutes every other day with them—labeling and describing language stimulation pictures and playing picture lotto. Progress has been extremely slow. Do you have any ideas for me?

—*A preschool teacher*

Children are more likely to stretch, expand, elaborate, and develop their language skills when they are actively involved in what they are doing. Your activity is passive—the children are on the receiving end. They should be the DOERS. Encourage them to choose activities and materials, make statements and suggestions, and ask questions that are related to their activities. Label and describe their actions and encourage other children to do the same.

Some children are naturally shy and need to be cajoled into verbal interactions. Plan specific times during each part of the routine when you will look for opportunities to engage them in conversation. Remember that language flows from children's interactions with people and things, as they are challenged to find new words to define and describe new experiences.

—*Bettye McDonald*

A child whose home language is Japanese is joining our program. No one on our teaching

team knows Japanese. How can we help him feel comfortable and encourage him to learn English?

—A preschool teacher

Think of this child as a resource, as well as a special challenge. Some suggestions:

• **It's a good idea for members of the team to learn a few phrases in Japanese** (e.g., the words for *hello, goodbye,* and *show me,* and labels for the interest areas). This shows respect for the child's language and makes it easier to communicate with him. You can also ask the child to teach classmates a few Japanese words.

• **Introduce English in a natural manner, focusing on communication.** Don't drill the child on vocabulary. If the child is planning with an English-speaking adult, for example, he might point to the area and toys he is interested in. The adult provides the words: "I see, you want to play with the trucks in the block area."

• **Speak to the child slowly, in a meaningful context, and allow him plenty of time to listen before expecting him to respond in English.** Getting a physical response should be your first goal: "It's your turn to pass out the cups." "Show me what you want." "Bring your painting to the table for recall time."

• **Set up opportunities for the child to work cooperatively with other children on tasks that don't require language:** putting the cover on the sand table, tracing bodies on the floor, cleaning the guinea pig cage, helping each other with coats. Watch for opportunities to help the child enter play situations with peers.

• **Don't correct the child when he makes a language error**—just model correct speech in your reply to him and reward effective communication by showing you understand what he said.

• **Invite the child's parents to the classroom** to share a game, song, or skill with children; to lead a cooking experience; read a story; bring in their infant to bathe or diaper.

—Marilyn Adams Jacobson and
Bonnie Lash Freeman

How do I convince teachers and parents that the High/Scope Curriculum does teach children the traditional math skills that they need to know?

—A High/Scope trainer

First of all, stress that one of the goals of the High/Scope Curriculum *is* to help children learn traditional number skills—within a broader context of basic reasoning and problem-solving skills. When adults introduce math concepts and skills within everyday play situations, children learn through experience that these skills and concepts can help them solve problems that are important to them. Second, because ours is a *developmental* approach, we introduce math concepts and skills only when the child is capable of understanding and using them. When traditional number skills are approached in this way, children not only learn basic math facts but also retain them and use them in the future.

—Sam Hannibal

At our preschool, children play outdoors for a half hour every day. Some of our teachers believe that children's physical skills will develop naturally during this outdoor play time. But others wonder if they shouldn't be "teaching" children the basic motor skills they need to master, like pumping themselves on the swings or catching balls.

—A preschool teacher

These kinds of basic motor skills develop from *experience*, not from direct training, but children do need our support to gain the maximum benefit from their spontaneous play experiences. We don't recommend the traditional approach of breaking down motor skills into small, limited objectives and then teaching to these objectives (for example, to teach skipping, "Now step, now hop, now step on the other foot, now hop on the other foot").

Teachers can't help children refine skills that the children haven't learned and experienced first in their own inventive ways; the adult's role is to provide opportunities and guidance as children develop these skills, not to teach them directly. For example, the child who has had a variety of beat experiences and who has been encouraged to explore different ways of moving from place to place—hopping, stepping, galloping, pretending to move like various animals or machines—will eventually start to skip. This may happen when the adult takes the child's hand and skips with him or her, but if it doesn't, the adult takes note of this but does not push the child to skip.

A nondirective approach does not mean that adults just stand around when children play outside. Instead, adults offer *active* support, for example, by offering a range of inviting play materials (bringing the music tapes and tape recorders outside on some days); by adding language to children's movements (chanting *out and back, out and back* while pushing a child on the swing); by asking questions that encourage movement exploration and awareness ("Can you throw it far?" "Can you find another way to go down the slide?"); and by joining in children's play
—*Phyllis S. Weikart*

Can we use the key experiences in our home-based program?

—A home visitor

Yes! The key experiences work wherever there are young children and things they can play with—at home, in the car, outside, in preschool, in day care centers, on a picnic, at grandma's house, on the bus, in the store. Since the key experiences describe the things young children are naturally inclined to do, they can guide adult interaction with children in virtually any setting. Here are some ways you might consider using the key experiences on home visits:

• **As you discuss things the child has done or is doing with parents, refer to the key experience(s)** most strongly suggested by the child's activity.

• **Plan the adult-child activity part of your home visit around something the child is particularly interested in.** Share observations with parents, noting the key experiences as they occur, so that the parent can encourage and support the key experiences in other home activities.

• **Watch the High/Scope filmstrip series** *Troubles and Triumphs at Home* (see list, page 297) for strategies parents have used in their homes to provide opportunities for active learning and experiences in language, sorting, matching, and sequencing.

—Mary Hohmann

The Daily Routine

HELP!! I have a child who refuses to make a plan. Does this ever happen to you?

—A Head Start teacher

It sure does. This is typical at the beginning of the year because children are unfamiliar with the classroom and the routine. This is one reason we recommend starting out with planning and recall strategies that are very simple and that help children become more familiar with the materials and the classroom. For example, if Tasha is having trouble planning, one of us may simply take her hand and walk around the room with her, looking at and exploring the materials available. If any interest is shown, we may then label her plan, saying, "I see you've made your plan to play at the water table, Tasha." We may also consider asking a child to point to where they would like to work, or to find an object in the room that they would like to play with.

Another way to look at this is to consider that *it's impossible not to make a plan*. One child we remember crawled under the table for all of work time for the entire first week of school. After talking with her mother, we found out that she was talking about the things she saw at school when she was at home. Her "plan" was to observe, and we tried to label it for her: "Your plan is to rest under the table and watch what is going on in the classroom." It was only after she became more familiar with the materials and the people in the room that she came out, slowly at first, but soon interacting with the other children. It's important not to force a child into planning something he or she isn't really interested in doing. This could interfere with the child's emerging ability to make and follow a plan.

—*Warren Buckleitner and Susan M. Terdan*

What if a child makes the same plan every day? Should I encourage the child to do something else?

—*A preschool teacher*

While a child's stated plan may not change for a number of days, careful observation usually reveals that, in fact, the child varies and builds on what he or she does from day to day. For example, Margo planned repeatedly to "be a doggie" with her friend Donna. While the two children did, in fact, pretend to be dogs many times, their role play expanded over time to include many variations on this theme: making dog dishes and dog food, reading stories before dog naps, making dog jewelry and dog toys, making dog houses from large boxes, decorating the dog house walls with pictures, and so forth.

For other children the variations on a repeated theme are less dramatic, but they are still there, if adults take the time to look for them. Michael, for example, often stated his plan in the same way: "Play in the sand-and-water area." Once there, however, he used a variety of containers and scoopers for filling and emptying and imitated other children who were playing there in many different ways. Some days he used sand to mold things, while on others he worked to keep the water inside holes he had dug. One day, he brought small plastic animals over from the toy area and used them to "play jungle farm."

Thus, when children verbalize their plans in the same way day after day, it is up to adults to look for and acknowledge the variety in their actual play. Rather than encourage Margo or Michael to do something other than their stated plans, the adult might make a comment to the child on a specific aspect of his or her play that she observed on a previous day. This, in turn might encourage the child to add more detail to his or her plan.

—*Mary Hohmann*

Sometimes my preschoolers only work on their plans for a minute and then move to another area. For example, a child may say he will paint, but when he gets to the easel, he puts only one stroke of color on the paper and then leaves. Should I wait until later in the year to introduce the idea of making plans and sticking to them?

—*A preschool teacher*

It's not unusual for children who are new to the idea of exploring a room and materials to get so excited that they quickly move from one activity to another. Some children need special help to stay on track, but it's impossible to be available to every one of the children as they begin or end their planning ideas. Therefore, observe children carefully to see which children have trouble getting started on their plans, which children have difficulty staying with their ideas, and which children independently carry through on their plans.

Don't give up on planning for the children who exhibit these types of behavior. Instead, get together as a teaching team to develop special strategies for dealing with them. For the child in the example above, you might decide to try the following:

Make it a point to help the child at the beginning of the work time period (members of the team can take turns sharing this responsibility). When you are finished planning with your group of children, look around the room to see where the child is working. Once there, the best strategy may simply be to work alongside him, imitating what he is doing: "Zachary, I see you made a plan to string beads. I'm going to string beads, too." Sitting close to a child and talking about what he is doing is sometimes enough to discourage flitting. You could also try to hold his interest in the activity by suggesting ways to continue it: "Zachary, you put one long red line in the middle of your paper. What are you going to paint on this side? How about at the top of the paper? There's purple paint here, also, if you like that color."

—*Michelle Graves*

Do you have any ideas on how I can use the High/Scope Curriculum when I am the only teacher with 25 children?

—*A kindergarten teacher*

The key is to establish groups that meet every day for planning, recall, and small-group time at tables in close enough proximity so that you can see what is going on at each table. Set up three groups of children—two groups with eight members, one with nine. During planning time, children at one table can write their plans, those at another can use planning boards to identify the sequence of their work, and the third group can dictate plans. You can concentrate on the verbal planners while the other groups can be relatively self-sufficient.

The same strategy can be used during small-group time. Plan three activities, such as exploring sinking and floating with a variety of objects, using magnets with objects that stick and don't stick, and vegetable printing. You can work with one small group each day and change activities every third day. During the rest of the daily routine, the children will be involved individually—

in work time and outside time—or will be in large-group activities, such as circle time.

Since you are working alone, your groups will engage in more self-sufficient planning, recall, and small-group experiences than if you had an assistant. The daily routine schedule, the focus on consistency in scheduling and group membership, the teacher's role, the key experiences, and planning and assessment remain the same.

We know of one kindergarten teacher who uses parent volunteers to help with both planning and small-group times. The teacher provides lists of key questions parents can use in these situations and provides some training for them at regularly scheduled parent meetings and during home visits.

—*Bettye McDonald and Mark Tompkins*

We've had a show-and-tell time for years in our preschool program, but I'm beginning to have mixed feelings about it. Do you think that show-and-tell can be a worthwhile recall experience for children?

—*A preschool program director*

Show-and-tell is a tradition in many preschool classrooms, but we recommend that you consider other alternatives. Children love to bring things to school, but this often causes problems in defining how and when the items they bring in can be used and shared. The "lecture-style" format of show-and-tell time can be a problem, too: for some children, standing up in front of the group and talking about their new toy is an uncomfortable experience. In addition, the other children often have a hard time listening quietly and waiting for their turn, and they are usually more interested in the toy the child has brought than in what the child has to say. Further, some children do not have many things to show off and may feel left out. In all, we feel that show-and-tell times can lead to management problems and can foster an individualistic "that's mine" philosophy.

As an alternative, we recommend that you emphasize active recall experiences throughout the daily routine. This eliminates the "mine" mentality, because all children are using and discussing the same materials—those found in the classroom. Another way to make recalling more of a "we-ours" experience is to allow all children to share actively in it by participating in the discussion of the reenactment of each child's work time experiences. When recalling is cooperative, active, and based on shared experiences, it has many of the same benefits as show-and-tell time, without the disadvantages.

—*Mark Tompkins*

Planning and Equipping the Setting

I recently attended a two-day workshop on the High/Scope Curriculum, in which the workshop presenter emphasized "open-ended" materials. I already have lots of materials in my center that don't seem to fit in this category—things like puzzles, sorting boxes, and Lotto games. Is it all right to use these materials?

—A preschool teacher

The materials you mention (all of which we've used, at one time or another, in our demonstration classroom) are often considered "one-use" or "non-open-ended" simply because their designers usually had one purpose in mind when they created them.

However, consider how four children of different ages, interests, and temperaments use a puzzle that has six knobbed pieces, each one a geometric shape. Brendan, who is 9 months old, picks up a puzzle piece with his thumb and forefinger, mouths it, bangs it on the floor, then discards it. Jessa, aged 2½, chooses a round piece, then pretends to feed this "cookie" to her doll. Caleb, aged 4, takes a hexagonal piece, tapes it to a unit block, and uses this structure as a stop sign for his racing car track. Kyle, aged 3½, puts the puzzle together, turning the pieces this way and that until he gets them to fit. Of the four children, only Kyle uses the puzzle as its designer intended. Nevertheless, all of the children use it to further their knowledge of the world, so it is a "useful" material for them.

The answer to your question, then, is that the kinds of materials you describe are appropriate, if children can use them in a variety of ways. The best way to decide if certain materials warrant space in your classroom is to watch how the children use them.

—*Ann Rogers*

I have a combination of preschoolers and school-age children in my family day care home. What kinds of materials do you recommend for the older children?

—*A home day care provider*

Since your school-age children will have spent all day in a structured elementary setting, you will want to provide an atmosphere that is more relaxed. One way to do this is to include equipment and materials children may not have access to in a regular school setting, for example, board games, construction materials, and sewing materials.

Here are some additional examples of suitable materials: Art area—warming tray and crayons, chisels, beginner's loom or hand loom; block area—rope, dowels, wooden or plastic boxes; math area—linear measurement tools, graph paper, geometric forms, area grids; bookmaking area—typewriters, blank books, picture file, cartoons, old magazines and catalogs, a model format for writing letters, etc., dictionaries. Other possible interest areas are: construction, cooking, drama, science, sewing, audiovisual media. Materials for these areas can be organized in "prop boxes" that can be stored in a special space reserved for school-age children. Booklets from the High/Scope Elementary Series, for example *Learning Through Sewing and Pattern Design* and *Learning Through Construction*, may be helpful in suggesting ways to work with children who are interested in using particular kinds of materials. (See resource list on page 297.)

—*Bonnie Lash Freeman and Ruby Brunson*

Most of High/Scope's training materials on room arrangement and materials focus on children in the 3–5 age group. Our day care center serves children ages 18 months to 7 years. Can you give me some suggestions for arranging and equipping our toddler room, in which children ages 18 months to 3 years are served?
—A day care center director

Toddlers, like preschoolers, thrive in a safe, supportive environment that allows them to initiate and carry out their ideas. Like a preschool room, a toddler room needs work areas—block, art, house, toy, sand and water, and climbing areas, for example. Toddlers are very mobile, but not yet as sensible as preschoolers. They enjoy exploring with their whole bodies, but need attentive adults to help them solve the physical problems they sometimes create for themselves (when they climb up something that they can't climb down from, for example). Toddlers need play equipment that can provide them with the physical challenges they enjoy, arranged so that adults can see them and assist them easily if necessary. For example, provide climbers; large boxes and bales; rocking boats; carpeted stairs; riding toys; beanbag chairs and other soft, low furniture, and offer opportunities for children to use them every day. Filling and emptying are other favorite activities for toddlers, so each work area needs containers—buckets, tubs, pails, baskets, and bags to fill, empty, and carry about. A toddler room also needs spaces and things for cuddling—blankets and stuffed animals, an easy chair, couch, or a rocking chair.

—Bonnie Lash Freeman, Mary Hohmann, and
Susan M. Terdan

My playground is all blacktop with a chain link fence around it. There is no equipment and whenever I leave anything outside, it is stolen by the next morning? Any ideas?

—A preschool teacher

A sandbox is one play structure you could consider, if the playground has adequate space. Because you have a hard surface, however, climbers, swings, or other stationary structures are probably out of the question, unless you have the resources to install another surfacing material, such as wood chips or rubber matting, over the blacktop. Because such materials are costly, resurfacing may have to be a long-term goal. For now, think about loose materials that could be stored just inside for easy access during outside time. Milk crates, cardboard boxes, sheets of plastic foam, and string or rope make excellent construction materials that young children love to play with. Another idea is to drill holes in the blacktop large enough for old broom handles or other poles. Children can stick the poles into the holes and use them as a frame to build collapsible tents and play houses out of old blankets or cardboard. Art activities are another possibility. Children could weave strips of cloth or yarn on the links of the fence, for example, or draw on the blacktop with colored chalk.

To lighten the burden of carrying things in and out everyday, make this job part of the children's routine. Note that everything doesn't have to go out every day. Varying the materials you take out will keep children interested in the materials, as well as ease the task of hauling things in and out. Store materials near the door or consider installing a lockable prefab storage shed outside.

—Vincent Harris

My principal would be more willing to introduce computers in our preschool and kindergarten classrooms if we can also demonstrate that teachers will use the machines for their paperwork. Any ideas?

—A preschool teacher

Here are just a few of the ways computers can lighten a teacher's workload:

• **Writing parent newsletters, reports, and plans** on the computer can be easier and less frustrating than writing at the typewriter. With a good word-processing program, errors are easy to correct, editing and revision are easy, and results can be saved, adapted, and reused at another time.

• **Making attractive, professional-looking signs, posters, and banners** for recruitment, fund-raising, etc., is a snap with poster-making computer programs that offer oversize letters and a selection of generic drawings to illustrate your message. The same programs can also often be used for making labels for classroom materials.

• **Preparing budgets** is also easier on the computer. Use a simple accounting or "spreadsheet" program to keep track of money budgeted and spent.

• **Keeping classroom records** is another natural for the computer, once you've cleared the initial hurdles of setting up your system. Use a "database" program to store class rosters, parent information, immunization records, etc. You can also keep anecdotal records, based on your daily classroom notes, on the computer. The resulting records are far easier to read than a handwritten version, and can easily be printed out for reports to parents and mid-year assessments. The computer's capacity to quickly retrieve and sort information for easy comparisons (for example, reviewing all the children's progress in a particular curriculum area) is another advantage of computerized record keeping.

To use the computer for any of the above tasks, be prepared to spend extra time at first learning the system and entering data. In the long run, though, computers will save you time and help you create better products.
—*Warren Buckleitner and Charles Hohmann*

Day Care

Does High/Scope have a day care curriculum?

—A day care provider

At High/Scope we do not have a specific "day care curriculum," just as we do not have a warm-weather curriculum, a special-needs curriculum, or a curriculum for inner-city children. Instead, our curriculum is designed as an "open framework" that guides adults in designing a unique program to meet the needs of their particular group of children and families. In this sense, every implementation of the curriculum is an "adaptation" and a particular day care program is just one of many possible forms the High/Scope approach can take.

High/Scope day care programs share with other High/Scope early childhood programs the same basic curriculum elements: a **developmental approach,** a carefully planned **daily routine,** and a **system for arranging the environment** that promotes **active learning.**

However, while the same general educational and management issues apply to all programs using the High/Scope Curriculum, particular issues do tend to arise more frequently when our approach is used in day care settings. In comparison to part-day preschool programs, day care programs usually perform many more routine caretaking tasks, deal with a wider range of ages, serve children for a longer day, and must meet more exacting licensing standards. All these necessities create special challenges for staff committed to a curriculum framework. Day care staff in a variety of home- and center-based settings have found creative ways to deal with these challenges within the framework of the High/Scope Curriculum.

—*Bonnie Lash Freeman, Mary Hohmann, and Susan M. Terdan*

As caregivers in an all-day program that serves 25 children ages 2–6 from 7:30 am to 5:30 pm, our days are filled with routine caregiving tasks: serving two meals and two snacks to children and cleaning up after them; making sure all children get the two-hour nap prescribed in licensing requirements; filling out health forms; administering children's medications; changing diapers; supervising toilet times; and talking with parents at the end of the day. After we do all this, there's hardly any time left to do the curriculum. What can we do?

—*A staff member in a center-based day care program*

Faced with so many routine tasks, teachers and caregivers may be tempted to get them out of the way as efficiently as possible, to allow more time for the "real" curriculum. Instead, we suggest that you **look for ways to incorporate the curriculum framework within your routine activities.**

Don't view "curriculum" as a series of structured, academic activities that adults plan and present to children, because you'll always feel that you are juggling "teaching" activities and "housekeeping" chores. Instead, look at the whole day as offering continual opportunities for active learning. In particular, you can look at toileting, eating, playing, and cleaning up in terms of the **ingredients of active learning:** materials, manipulation, choices, language from the children, and adult support.

Diapering, for example, can be a time for one-on-one conversations with children. Caregivers may want to involve children in singing or chanting about what is happening: "Sally put the diaper on, Sally put the diaper on, Sally put the diaper on, and She's all clean." Caregivers can also involve children as much as possible in the actual changing process—undressing and dressing, holding the clean diaper, fastening the tapes—so that children experience a problem-solving process and gain a sense of taking care of their own needs. Similarly, setting up or putting things away before and after meals, naps, and playtimes are tasks that children enjoy and should be involved in. Also, by actively participating in such "housekeeping" chores, children practice such skills as sorting, counting, and matching as well as play an important social role in the center community.

—*Bonnie Lash Freeman, Mary Hohmann, and Susan M. Terdan*

Afternoons are often a problem for the many preschoolers who are in our day care center. We find that the plan-do-review sequence as we do it in the morning doesn't work well in the afternoons because children are too tired. Can you give me some suggestions for afternoon activities for preschoolers? We have a similar problem with children in our after-school program who have been in a structured program all day. How can we provide some sort of focus for their activities while meeting their needs to "unwind" after school?

—*A day care center director*

Both for preschoolers and older children, it can be exhausting to spend the entire day in group settings. By afternoon, children may be tired and tense. Though you will want to keep basic curriculum elements in mind as you plan your afternoon program, you need not repeat your morning routine. Instead, plan a different program that takes into account children's changing needs throughout the day. We can't specify exactly what form your afternoon program should take, but we would recommend that it be more flexible and less structured than your morning program.

For example, for preschoolers who are in a center all day long every day, the period right after naptime can be problematic. A second plan-do-review may work for some children at this time, but many centers prefer to provide a long outside time to help children release tensions and recharge their energies. Other centers find that afternoons are a good time to plan special group projects: walking to the corner store to buy ingredients for cookies or tomorrow's snack; working on a group construction project outside; sledding; painting a large group mural together. Staff at some centers have found that it works well to offer a plan-do-review sequence at the very end of the day, with limited choices of materials and activities.

School-age children who have generally spent the day in fairly structured settings that allow limited physical movement and little personal adult attention have a similar need for afternoon care that is as supportive, and hassle-free as possible, and that offers plenty of choices. Some children relax best through strenuous physical activity; others by being inactive. We recommend that you greet children warmly when they arrive from school, then offer a snack and an opportunity to play outside for as long as possible. All children may not want to play outside; some may prefer to play by themselves in a cozy place or may already have plans to play cards or a board game with buddies. Others may want homework help. And some children may want to be involved in projects that span several days, such as sewing, gardening, or construction projects.

Planning and recalling should not be automatic rituals, but natural parts of all these activities that offer children the support they need to organize and think about their efforts. You may casually ask children for their afternoon plan while they are snacking, and then continue to plan and recall with children as an ongoing part of their afternoon activities. Children will appreciate these opportunities for planning and recalling when they are extended in this natural and supportive way.

Throughout the afternoon, be available to assist children with problems and to help them extend their play. At the same time, be sensitive to the older child's need for privacy and independence. While a child at home might choose, for example, to spend the time after school playing in a bedroom or in a backyard treehouse, children in day care rarely have the same opportunity to be even that distant from an adult's eyes. Thus it is important to provide support when needed but also to respect children's needs for private play.

—*Bonnie Lash Freeman, Mary Hohmann, and Susan M. Terdan*

Like many other day care centers, we have enrolled as many children as licensing standards permit; we have 24 preschoolers with 2 teachers in our class group. We feel that 1 adult cannot conduct an effective small-group time with 12 children. Any ideas?

—*A day care director*

We do not recommend exceeding an enrollment limit of 1 adult per 10 preschool children, though licensing standards in a number of states are more lenient than this. It would be best to hire more staff, but if you can't, don't give up on small-group time. Some centers we know of with groups of similar sizes have tried the following solutions: (1) Have one teacher do small-group time with a third of the class, while the other supervises two-thirds of the class outdoors; do this twice each day so that two-thirds of your group has small-group time every day. (2) Team up with staff from other rooms in the center; if you take turns supervising parts of each other's groups (on the playground, for example), then some staff members can be freed to work with smaller groups. (3) Train students or parent volunteers to help you in working with groups of 12.

—Bonnie Lash Freeman, Mary Hohmann, and Susan M. Terdan

Child Observation/Team Planning/Staff Development

High/Scope staff frequently recommend planning during naptime as the solution to the perennial problem of making time for team planning. Are you suggesting that we hire additional staff for naptime?

—A day care teacher

Not necessarily. Staff of an Oklahoma day care center report that they plan successfully in the same room with children who are sleeping. It's a large room, of course, and children sleep at one end while adults talk quietly at the other. This teaching team reports that regular practice has made them efficient planners—they do it in 30 minutes, leaving them plenty of time for staff breaks.

—Bonnie Lash Freeman, Mary Hohmann, and Susan M. Terdan

In our preschool we used to plan with the theme-based approach. But since receiving High/Scope training, we use the High/Scope key experiences as the focus of planning. Each month we choose a key experience category, like *number*, and then expect teaching staff to apply this focus to all aspects of their lesson plans. Is this method compatible with a philosophy of child-oriented planning?

—A Head Start teacher

While the High/Scope key experiences *are* a useful tool for planning, planning around the key experiences has drawbacks—*if* planning becomes exclusively focused on the key experience category for the day, week, or month. Just as teachers can be "theme-blinded"—so preoccupied with the theme of the week that they miss opportunities to build on children's interests and abilities—they can also be "key-experience-blinded." If adults are overly intent on fostering a particular group of key experiences, they may fail to see all the natural ways the other key experiences are occurring. And they may lose sight of the more important task of *becoming a partner* in children's play.

Instead of simply substituting the key experiences for traditional planning themes, we suggest using them *guides to child development*. The key experiences can guide you in interpreting and identifying the abilities that are currently developing in individual children, in anticipating what may happen next with a child, and sometimes, in planning to find something out about a child (e.g., "Today Katie counted 13 crayons. Let's see if she has one-to-one correspondence by having her pass out one napkin to each person at snack time tomorrow"). Rather than make one group of key experiences the sole focus of a lesson plan, try to blend many key experiences into it.

—*Mark Tompkins*

I am personally convinced that children in kindergarten should be active; they should have opportunities to play, explore, talk. . . but how do I convince my principal and some of the parents that the children are actually learning while they are playing?

—*A kindergarten teacher*

Observe . . . document . . . analyze!

• **Get in the habit of carefully watching how children approach, engage in, and complete their tasks.** Jot down quick notes or mark items on an inventory or checklist. Note the ways children organize their work, select and handle materials, and generalize information.

select and handle materials, and generalize information.

• **Get in the habit of encouraging children to save some samples of their work.** Children love to take things home that they've made in school, but also encourage them to save some things at school. Date the work so that there is chronological evidence of growth.

• **Be creative in documenting children's accomplishments.** Save paintings, examples of emergent writing, dictated experience stories. Compile writing folders, records of math activities, and computer printouts. Take photographs of children as they work; tape record storytelling and children's emergent storybook "reading"; videotape discussions, dramatic performances, play in the housekeeping area, or recall sessions.

• **Analyze the anecdotes and work samples.** Look for indicators of change, development, and growth. Look for patterns and evidence of children's increased understanding or special interests. Summarize, using the High/Scope K–3 key experiences as a guide.

The teacher who is prepared with such a collection of documents will have a strong case for demonstrating that learning is abundant in the active kindergarten!

—Jane Maehr

We have been using the High/Scope Curriculum for about a year now; yet, because we are not all together at the end of the day to evaluate and plan, we are having a hard time using the anecdotal notes we are taking on our observations of children. What can we do instead?

—A day care center director

Some day care centers that can't conduct planning at the beginning or end of the day

plan at nap time instead. But if this won't work
for you, try the following adaptation, which
was used successfully by a day care center we
worked with. This teaching team, who did
their planning on a weekly basis, posted a large
(2′ × 4′) sheet of easel paper to use in recording
daily observations. The sheet was divided into
nine key experience categories exactly like the
individual recording forms found in their assessment notebook. The staff recorded information
about children throughout the day using "Post-
it" notes that they stuck on to the large chart
under the appropriate category. At the end of the
week, one staff member took all the notes and
copied them in the assessment notebook on the
children's individual forms. They discussed this
record in weekly planning sessions.

—*Mark Tompkins*

**I recently went to a High/Scope workshop
and am very interested in using the High/Scope
Curriculum in my preschool classroom. However, my co-teacher and several of the other
staff at my center are very resistant to the idea
of changing their own (more directive) ways.
How can I encourage them to try new ideas?**

—*A head teacher*

First, we recommend that you be a model
for the others without seeming to push your
ideas on them. The notion of active learning is
really a very simple (though powerful) idea.
While putting into practice what you recently
learned about the curriculum is more difficult
in your situation, you can use the workshop information a little at a time. Gradually add more
materials in various areas of the classroom, for
example, and allow more opportunities for child-
initiated activities throughout the day. The successful and exciting changes you make will be
obvious to your colleagues, who will then be

more likely to use them as well. In most schools, good ideas travel fast!

Second, ask your director or principal to join forces with you. When the other adults see that your supervisor supports your change efforts, they may be more willing to give a child-oriented educational approach a try. Seek the administrator's active support in curriculum implementation. For example, you could involve the administrator in your training and team planning sessions. In these sessions avoid philosophical discussions and abstract arguments—focus on the children's behavior. Continually strive to bring the discussion around to what specific children are actually doing. Have the administrator substitute in the room so you and the others can observe children during specific segments of the daily routine. Encourage your team members to watch for when and how children learn best. Suggest that it might be helpful for you all to fill out some of the child study forms contained in the *Study Guide to Young Children in Action* (see resource list on page 297) during these observations.

—*Warren Buckleitner, Bonnie Freeman, and Ed Greene*

We have been using the High/Scope Curriculum for about a year now. Yet some of the teachers are still planning and leading activities that are quite teacher-directed and passive for children. What can I do to help the teachers realize that they are not involving the children in active learning?

—*A day care center director*

Sometimes teachers find it difficult to put active learning into practice. This is not so surprising since many teachers have received little or no training in an active learning approach. Training is the key to overcoming this problem.

The best way to understand active learning is to engage in it. So, why not design a training plan in which staff develop their own rationale for active learning and then devise teaching strategies that will encourage it?

Schedule active learning workshops that feature hands-on learning activities in which participants experience firsthand the ingredients of active learning: materials, manipulation, choices, language, adult support. The *Young Children in Action Study Guide* contains may such workshop ideas and suggestions for self study. Also, you could use High/Scope's, *Contrasting Teaching Styles* films to stimulate discussions on teaching methods. (For more information on High/Scope publications and audiovisuals, see list, page 297.) Videotaping can also be a powerful tool to help staff see if active learning is occurring in the classroom. As you watch your videotape, note systematically whether all the ingredients of active learning are present.

Another thing you can do is to plan a parent meeting around the topic. One High/Scope program we work with recently had a parent meeting in which the parents made modeling dough, then reviewed the experience according to the key experiences in active learning. At another site's parent meeting, the parents all experienced the plan-do-review process as they each made a plan and then completed it. At the end of the activity, the parents talked about all of the things they had learned during the plan-do-review sequence, using the key experiences and the ingredients of active learning as a guide. As with teachers, parents best understand "active learning" when they practice it!

—*Mark Tompkins*

When in this curriculum do we get to give teachers constructive criticism?
—A Head Start education coordinator

We've found that "criticism" generally involves judgments and evaluations, usually negative, which inhibit rather than enhance the feedback dialogue. Criticizing adults' teaching behaviors generally causes them to defend their actions rather than open up to new ways of interacting with children.

In our view, constructive feedback for teachers starts with the sharing of observed facts about children, which the teaching/observing team interprets in curricular terms. They then devise follow-up strategies for acting upon this knowledge so that they can support children at their particular developmental levels.

For example, one observer reported that Susie, a 3-year-old, had spent a considerable time during the morning lining things up and putting them back on the shelf—the big blocks, the small blocks, the rubber farm animals, the counting cubes, the stones. The observer/teaching team together interpreted these actions as Susie's way of exploring the classroom environment, sorting and matching, and ordering sets of materials new to her. They had also noticed that Susie tended to move around the classroom quite a bit. At first it had appeared that Susie was "flitting" from activity to activity, but closer observation had revealed that Susie was moving whenever other children intruded on her space— she would then continue her lining-up play in a new location. Together the team devised the following ways to support Susie's explorations:

• When other children intrude on Susie's space for lining things up, help her find alternative "safe" space for her play—under the table, next to the window, by the cubbies, on the couch.

• Play on the floor near Susie, imitating her actions.

• Use the materials Susie lines up as the basis for a small-group-time activity.

A constructive feedback dialogue is an effective way to build and encourage supportive teaching behaviors. Through dialogue and exchange, we build on collective observations to achieve a deeper understanding of each child, so that we can encourage each child's growth and development more effectively.

—*Mary Hohmann*

A·P·P·E·N·D·I·X

Related Books and Audiovisuals From High/Scope Press

Practical Guides for Early Childhood Program Staff

Books

An Administrator's Guide to Early Childhood Programs, L. J. Schweinhart, 1988

Child Observation Record (COR) Manual, 1991

Designing, Leading, and Evaluating Workshops for Teachers and Parents: A Manual for Trainers and Leadership Personnel in Early Childhood Education, J. Diamondstone, 1989

The Early Childhood Playground: An Outdoor Classroom, S. B. Esbensen, 1987

Head Start Program Manager's Guide, D. McClelland and B. McDonald, 1984

High/Scope Survey of Early Childhood Software 1991, W. Buckleitner

Movement in Steady Beat, P. S. Weikart, 1990

Movement Plus Music: Activities for Children Ages 3 to 7, P. S. Weikart, 1989

Movement Plus Rhymes, Songs, & Singing Games, P. S. Weikart, 1988

Round the Circle: Key Experiences in Movement for Children, P. S. Weikart, 1987

Study Guide to Young Children in Action, M. Hohmann, 1983

The Teacher's Idea Book: Daily Planning Around the Key Experiences, M. Graves, 1989

Teaching Movement & Dance: A Sequential Approach to Rhythmic Movement, 3rd edition, P. S. Weikart, 1989.

Young Children & Computers, C. Hohmann, 1990

Young Children in Action, M. Hohmann, B. Banet, and D. P. Weikart, 1979 (Spanish translation also available)

Audiovisuals

Bilingual Media for Teachers Series (filmstrips):
1. *Naturalistic Language Learning*
2. *Using the Community as a Classroom*
3. *Supporting Cultural Awareness in Young Children*

The Block Area Series (filmstrips):
1. *Setting Up a Block Area*
2. *A Place to Explore New Materials*
3. *A Place to Build All Kinds of Structures*
4. *A Place to Represent Things*
5. *Observing a Child in the Block Area*

Computer Learning for Young Children (videotape), 1989

Experiencing and Representing Series (16mm films):
1. *A Way Children Learn*
2. *Starting With Direct Experience*
3. *From Direct Experience to Representation*
4. *Strategies for Supporting Representational Activity*

Guidelines for Evaluating Activities Series (16mm films):
1. *Contrasting Teaching Styles: Small-Group Time*
2. *Contrasting Teaching Styles: Work Time, the Art Area*
3. *Contrasting Teaching Styles: Circle Time*

Helping Children Make Choices and Decisions Series (16mm films):
1. *A Good Classroom Is a Classroom Full of Choices*
2. *Questions That Help Children Develop Their Ideas*
3. *Exploring the Possibilities of the Room*
4. *Acknowledging Children's Choices and Decisions*
5. *Planning Activities That Include Choices*

The High/Scope Cognitively Oriented Preschool Curriculum (filmstrip)

The High/Scope Curriculum: Its Implementation in Family Childcare Homes (videotape), 1989

The High/Scope Curriculum: The Daily Routine (videotape), 1990

The High/Scope Curriculum: The Plan-Do-Review Process (videotape), 1989

Key Experiences for Intellectual Development During the Preschool Years (16mm film)

Learning About Time in the Preschool Years (16mm film)

Preschool Math Series (filmstrips):
1. *Understanding and Using the Concept of Number*
2. *Understanding and Using the Concept of Length*
3. *Understanding and Using the Concepts of Area, Volume, and Weight*

Small-Group Time Media Package (videotapes), 1988:
1. *Counting With Bears*
2. *Plan-Do-Review With Found Materials*
3. *Working With Staplers*
4. *Representing With Sticks & Balls*
5. *Exploring With Paint & Corks*

Spatial Learning in the Preschool Years (16mm film)

Supporting Children's Active Learning: Teaching Strategies for Diverse Settings (videotape), 1989

Supporting Communication Among Preschoolers Series (16mm films):
1. *An Important Opportunity*
2. *Opportunities in the Classroom*
3. *Encouraging Interaction and Cooperation*
4. *Referring One Child's Questions or Problems to Another*
5. *Interpreting or "Delivering" Messages*
6. *Encouraging Active Listening*
7. *Examples for Discussion*

Thinking and Reasoning in Preschool Children (16mm film)

K–3 Curriculum Guides

Books

K–3 Curriculum Guide Series, 1991:
• *Language and Literacy*, J. Maehr
• *Mathematics*, C. Hohmann
• *Science*, F. Blackwell and C. Hohmann

Supplementary K–3 Booklets:
• *Learning Through Sewing and Pattern Design*, S. Mainwaring, 1976
• *Learning Through Construction*, S. Mainwaring and C. Shouse, 1983
• *Children as Music Makers*, L. Ransom, 1979

Audiovisuals

K–3 Curriculum Video Series :
- *Active Learning*, 1991
- *Classroom Environment*, 1991
- *Language & Literacy*, 1990
- *Mathematics, 1990*

For and About Parents

Books

Activities for Parent-Child Interaction,
J. Evans, 1982

Getting Involved: Workshops for Parents,
E. Frede, 1984

*Good Beginnings: Parenting in the Early
Years*, J. Evans and E. Ilfeld, 1982

Audiovisuals

Bilingual Media for Parents Series
(filmstrips):
1. *Introduction for Parents*
2. *Parents as Classroom Volunteers*
3. *Observing in the Classroom*
4. *Your Child's Language and Culture*
5. *Staying Involved*

Troubles and Triumphs at Home Series
(filmstrips):
1. *When "I've Told You a Thousand
Times" Isn't Enough*
2. *Converting Conflict to Calm*
3. *Let Them Do It*
4. *Let Them Say It*

Public Policy & Research

Books and Papers

*A Better Start: New Choices for Early
Learning*, F. M. Hechinger, 1986

*Compensatory Education in the Pre-
school: A Canadian Approach*, M.
Wright, 1983

High/Scope Monograph Series:
- *Home Teaching with Mothers and In-
fants: The Ypsilanti-Carnegie Infant
Education Project, an Experiment*,
D. A. Lambie, J. T. Bond, and D. P.
Weikart, 1974
- *The Longitudinal Follow-Up of the Yp-
silanti-Carnegie Infant Education
Project*, A. S. Epstein and D. P.
Weikart, 1979
- *The Ypsilanti Preschool Curriculum
Demonstration Project: Preschool
Years and Longitudinal Results*, D.
P. Weikart, A. S. Epstein, L. J.
Schweinhart, and J. T. Bond, 1978
- *Consequences of Three Preschool Cur-
riculum Models Through Age 15*, L.
J. Schweinhart, D. P. Weikart, and
M. B. Larner, 1986
- *The Ypsilanti Perry Preschool Project:
Preschool Years and Longitudinal
Results Through Fourth Grade*, D. P.
Weikart, J. T. Bond, and J. T.
McNeil, 1978
- *An Economic Analysis of the Ypsilanti
Perry Preschool Project*, C. U.
Weber, P. W. Foster, and D. P.
Weikart, 1978
- *Young Children Grow Up: The Effects
of the Perry Preschool Program on
Youths Through Age 15*, L. J.
Schweinhart and D. P. Weikart,
1980
- *Changed Lives: The Effects of the
Perry Preschool Program on Youths
Through Age 19*, J. Berrueta-Clem-
ent, L. J. Schweinhart, W. S. Bar-
nett, A. S. Epstein, and D. P.
Weikart, 1984

High/Scope Policy Paper Series:
1. *Early Childhood Development Programs in the Eighties: The National
Picture*, L. J. Schweinhart, 1985
2. *The High/Scope Perry Preschool Program and Its Long-Term Effects: A
Benefit-Cost Analysis*, W. S. Bar-
nett, 1985
3. *Quality in Early Childhood Programs: Four Perspectives*, G. Mor-
gan, N. Curry, R. Endlsey, M.
Bradbard, H. Rashid, and A. Epstein, 1985

4. *The Preschool Challenge*, L. J. Schweinhart, 1985
5. *Policy Options for Preschool Programs*, L. J. Schweinhart and J. Koshel, 1986
6. *Prekindergarten Programs in Urban Schools*, L. J. Schweinhart and E. Mazur, 1987
7. *Shaping the Future for Early Childhood Programs*, L. J. Schweinhart and L. de Pietro (Eds.), 1988

Improving Life Chances for Young Children, R. Egbert (Ed.), 1989

Jerome Bruner Preschool Series, 1980:
1. *Under Five in Britain*, J. Bruner
2. *Childwatching at Playgroup and Nursery School*, K. Sylva, C. Roy, and M. Painter
3. *Children and Minders*, B. Bryant, M. Harris, and D. Newton
4. *Children and Day Nurseries*, C. Garland and S. White
5. *Working With Under Fives*, D. Wood, L. McMahon, and Y. Cranstoun

6. *Parents and Preschool*, T. Smith

When Churches Mind the Children, E. W. Lindner, M. C. Mattis, and J. R. Rogers, 1983

Audiovisuals

Lessons That Last (videotape)

Preschool: A Program That Works (filmstrip)

This Is the Way We Go to School (16mm film)

———

To order any of these High/Scope publications, please contact

High/Scope Press
600 North River Street
Ypsilanti, MI 48198
313/485-2000, ext. 74
FAX 313/485-0704

About the Authors

Ruby Brunson, a High/Scope endorsed trainer working in California's San Francisco Bay Area, is executive director of the Oakland Licensed Day Care Operators' Association. As an advocate for family child care home providers, she works at both local and state levels to promote improved working conditions for providers and high quality care for children.

Warren Buckleitner is a High/Scope educational consultant. A former elementary school teacher, he has conducted High/Scope training projects involving both preschool and elementary educators. He is the author of High/Scope's annual *Survey of Early Childhood Software*.

Bonnie Lash Freeman, formerly a High/Scope consultant, is the director of early childhood services for the National Center for Family Literacy, Louisville, Kentucky. Freeman currently trains early childhood staff throughout the U.S. who are implementing programs designed to break the intergenerational cycle of illiteracy, undereducation, and poverty. Freeman is using the High/Scope Curriculum as the basis for the preschool education component of the comprehensive family literacy programs she is helping to implement.

Michelle Graves, a former High/Scope educational consultant, currently directs the child care program for employees of Veterans and University of Michigan Hospitals, Ann Arbor. At High/Scope, Graves conducted a variety of training projects for early childhood educators, produced the *Small-Group Time* video series, and authored *The Teacher's Idea Book: Daily Planning Around the Key Experiences*. Graves also has been a classroom teacher in early childhood special education, preschool, and elementary programs.

Ed Greene is currently director of grants and programs for the Center for Educational Programs, a foundation based in New York City. His background and training is in child psychology and early education. Greene's work has focused primarily on staff development and training as well as human resources management. Formerly a High/Scope consultant, he conducted several long-term training projects for educators and consulted to early childhood advocacy organizations while at High/Scope.

Sam Hannibal is a High/Scope educational consultant who has worked with preschool and K–3 educators from throughout the U.S. He currently directs the High/Scope Visitor Program and coordinates the Annual Registry Conference.

Vincent Harris, a High/Scope educational consultant, conducts training workshops on playground safety and design for early childhood educators. Harris also directs High/Scope workshop programs for gifted disadvantaged teenagers.

Charles Hohmann, a High/Scope consultant, has directed the development of the High/Scope K–3 Curriculum since 1972. He has developed mathematics and science learning activities for High/Scope programs serving preschoolers, school-aged children, and teens. He is the author of *Young Children and Computers* and *High/Scope K–3 Curriculum*

Series: Mathematics and co-author of *High/Scope K–3 Currriculum Series: Science*.

Mary Hohmann, a High/Scope educational consultant, has conducted a variety of training projects for preschool educators throughout the U.S. and overseas. She is co-author of the High/Scope preschool manual *Young Children in Action* and the author of the *Study Guide to Young Children in Action*. She has also played a key role in the High/Scope Summer Workshop for Teenagers, directing the workshop's program activities for many years.

Marilyn Adams Jacobson is a director and education coordinator for state-funded Head Start preschool programs in Snohomish County, Washington. A former High/Scope consultant, she worked with educators from a variety of programs while serving in this role. She has been a teacher or director at various early childhood settings and has also taught adults at the college level and in English-language programs for immigrants. She has a special interest in supporting cultural diversity and anti-bias practices.

Jane Maehr, director of education at Bethlehem Church, Ann Arbor, Michigan, is a former High/Scope educational consultant. She conducts training activities for educators, develops curriculum materials, and teaches part-time at the college level. She is the author of *High/Scope K–3 Curriculum Series: Language and Literacy*.

Bettye McDonald is a communications specialist in the Information Services Department of the Ann Arbor, Michigan, Public Schools. A former High/Scope educational consultant, she has conducted training programs for educators through-

out the U.S., including many programs and workshops serving special educators. She has also developed training materials for educators and has extensive experience as a classroom teacher.

Patricia P. Olmsted is a High/Scope research associate. Prior to joining High/Scope, she directed the Parent Education Follow Through Program that was implemented in 11 school systems in 10 states. She is currently deputy international coordinator for the IEA Preprimary Project, a 12-nation study of the nature, quality, and effects of the experiences of children prior to former schooling.

Amy Powell directs High/Scope's Program for Infants and Toddlers With Special Needs, a training program for early childhood professionals who work with young special needs children and their families. The program is based on TRIP (Transactional Intervention Program), an early intervention model developed by Powell and Jerry Mahoney. Powell's experience in early childhood education includes teaching, research, curriculum development, and training.

Ann Rogers is a former High/Scope educational consultant and demonstration preschool teacher. She has worked with young children all her adult life in public schools, nursery schools, child care centers, and home day care settings.

Ruth Strubank is a High/Scope educational consultant and demonstration preschool teacher. She conducts training activities for trainers and caregivers throughout the United States and in Canada, and is currently developing a script for a video program on learning environments for children.

Susan M. Terdan is a High/Scope educational consultant who works with educators both nationally and internationally. Prior to joining the High/Scope staff, she used the High/Scope Curriculum for eight years in the Walker, Minnesota, school system in an early education classroom serving handicapped children aged 3–6 years.

Mark Tompkins, a High/Scope educational consultant for many years, conducts introductory curriculum awareness workshops and ToT (Training of Teacher-Trainers) Projects for educators in the U.S. and overseas. He has contributed articles on early childhood education to various High/Scope Press publications.

Phyllis S. Weikart is associate professor of physical education at the University of Michigan and is High/Scope's music and movement consultant. A longtime contributor to High/Scope Press publications, she has authored a number of titles on music and movement education and has produced the *Rhythmically Moving* record series and other curriculum materials on movement and dance. ∎